# Let the Good Times Roll

## The Michigan American Music Series

Richard Crawford, Series General Editor

The Michigan American Music Series focuses on leading figures of American jazz and popular music, assessing both the uniqueness of their work and its place in the context of American musical tradition.

*Jazz from the Beginning*
  By Garvin Bushell as Told to Mark Tucker

*Twenty Years on Wheels*
  By Andy Kirk as Told to Amy Lee

*The Song of the Hawk: The Life and Recordings of Coleman Hawkins*
  By John Chilton

*Boy Meets Horn*
  By Rex Stewart; edited by Claire P. Gordon

*Rhythm Man: Fifty Years in Jazz*
  By Steve Jordan with Tom Scanlan

*Sondheim's Broadway Musicals*
  By Stephen Banfield

*Let the Good Times Roll: The Story of Louis Jordan and His Music*
  By John Chilton

# Let the Good Times Roll

## THE STORY OF LOUIS JORDAN
## AND HIS MUSIC

## JOHN CHILTON

Ann Arbor

THE UNIVERSITY OF MICHIGAN PRESS

Published in the United States of America by
The University of Michigan Press 1994
First published by Quartet Books Limited 1992
Copyright © by John Chilton 1992
All rights reserved
ISBN 0-472-10529-9
Manufactured in the United States of America
♾ Printed on acid-free paper

1997   1996   1995   1994     4   3   2   1

For John and Liza Simmen

# *Acknowledgments*

Particular thanks to Martha Weaver Jordan, and special thanks to Carl Arnold, Jeff Atterton, Ira Berger, John Byrd, Dan Morgenstern, Brian Peerless, Arthur Pilkington, Howard Rye, John Simmen, Peter Vacher and John Whitehorn.

Grateful thanks for their assistance to: Berle Adams, Steve Allen, Arkansas Department of Health, Arkansas History Commission, Ed Attwater, Anna Bailey, Michelle Baney, Chris Barber, Bruce Bastin, Daisy Bates, Josephine Beaton, Jonas Bernholm, Harold Blanchard, Bob Burgess, Charles Campbell, Gary Carner, Mike Carr, Al Cobbs, Derek Coller, Chris Columbus, Gene Connors, Ralph Cooper, Ruth Coppage, John Cowley, Charlie Crump, Stanley Dance, William Davis, Bill Dayneswood, Iola Dickson, Mike Dine, Bill Doggett, James Doran, Teddy Edwards, Flora Jean Elledge, Franklin Elledge, Scott Ellsworth, Leonard Feather, Milton Gabler, Stanley Gaines, Danny Garçon, Callie Dill Gardner, Jesse Gardner, Virgil Gettis, Bob Glass, David Griffiths, Billy Hadnott, Pat Halcox, James Hale, Carita Harbert, Francis Harper, Nigel Haslewood, John Hayman, Jodie Hilliard, Chris Hollis, Sam Hollis, Hot Springs Visitors' Bureau, Camille Howard, Institute of Jazz Studies, Aaron Izenhall, Robert Jackson, Thurber Jay, Erefrett Jelks, Theodore Jelks, Eddie Johnson, Max Jones, Ingemar Jönsson, Charlie Mae Jordan, Harold Jovien, Louis Kabok, Dr Thomas W. Keaton, B.B. King, Johnny Kirkwood, Chester Lane, Norman Levy, Vic Lewis, Frank Liniger, Charles Linton, Tommy Löfgren, Doris McCarroll, Teddy McRae, Minnie Marshall, Wiley Marshall, Tony Middleton, Henry Miller, Hal Mitchell, Mick Moffatt, Katie Moore, Alan Newby, Stuart Nicholson, Konrad Nowakowski, Johnny Otis,

Jimmy Owens, Fred Mark Palmer, Ottilie Patterson, Bert Payne, Beverley Peer, Dave Penny, Ralph Porter, Charlie Rice, Norbert Ruecker, Trevor Salter, Bill Sayger, Phil Schaap, Theodore Seville, Marina Sheriff, Dorothy Smith, Valerie Roach Smith, Tom Stagg, Deems Taylor, George Whiteside, Courtney Williams, Val Wilmer, Laurie Wright, Les Zacheis.

# Contents

Prologue     1
1   Somewhere Deep in the Heart of the South     5
2   Small Town Boy     19
3   Helping Hand     35
4   Trouble Then Satisfaction     51
5   Keep A-Knockin'     63
6   Five Guys Named Moe     77
7   I Found a New Baby     89
8   Caldonia     105
9   Look Out!     121
10   It's a Low-down Dirty Shame     135
11   Work, Baby, Work     153
12   Slow Down     171
13   Time Marches On     187
14   It's Better to Wait for Love     201
15   Every Knock is a Boost     217
16   I've Found My Peace of Mind     233

References     247
Bibliography     259
Selected Discography     263
Index     279

# Let the Good
# Times Roll

*Prologue*

The short, broad-shouldered saxophone player stood almost motion-less in the deep shadows at the side of the stage. Out in front of the footlights, a line of dancers was going zestfully through a high-kicking routine, but the musician seemed oblivious of the movement. As usual, he had taken up his position in the wings five minutes before he was due on stage. He liked to stand there, silently preparing himself for the show; a stagehand, on duty nearby, knew better than to offer anything more than a nod.

One by one the other musicians in the group began assembling alongside their leader. There were still at least two minutes to go before the band would be required on stage, but each of them knew that the maestro equated punctuality with being early. No one spoke. The only discernible sound emerging from the small circle of men was a semi-muffled clacking, caused by the bandleader's fingers checking and rechecking that all the keys on his alto saxophone were working in smooth co-ordination. The sound of the saxophone pads opening and closing gradually took on a more insistent pattern; one musician hadn't yet appeared and the leader began directing a surge of vexation through his fingers.

He made no enquiry about the absentee, but as the seconds ticked away his face developed a definite frown. Just as one of the waiting musicians, made fidgety by the growing tension, was about to offer a comment on the latecomer, the missing man appeared. He was the youngest musician in the troupe, and had joined them only a few weeks earlier. There was nothing wrong with the way he played the tenor saxophone, but he was finding it difficult to settle in. He was by nature both carefree and careless; it seemed impossible for him to remember all of the bandleader's rules and he had already been reprimanded three or four times.

Tonight he felt that his excuse for being tardy was valid. Two of his cousins had travelled 150 miles to see him perform as part of this famous group, and he had waited for them to make sure that they got their complimentary tickets. He was about to explain this to the fuming bandleader, but as he opened his mouth he was kicked on the foot by the band's trumpeter. The youngster heeded the warning and remained silent, by now acutely aware that the bandleader was staring grimly at his crumpled shirt and wrinkled necktie.

The chorus line completed its part of the show and brushed past the waiting musicians, oozing a musky blend of sweat and strong perfume. The compere walked to the microphone, cracked a brief joke and then, raising his voice dramatically, announced, 'And now . . . the greatest little band in the world . . . LOUIS JORDAN AND HIS TYMPANY FIVE.'

The announcement caused an explosion of activity among the musicians, who began their superbly drilled routine by running at full speed across the stage. Within seconds the drummer was seated behind his kit, the bassist was ready to pluck his strings, the trumpeter's lips were already touching his mouthpiece and both sax players were in position. The pianist reached the keyboard and remained standing, his hands poised in the air, as if to underline the band's eagerness to begin playing for the people.

The bandleader counted the group in with two emphatic hand movements and the full-blooded blend of melody and rhythm immediately set the audience's feet tapping. There was no sign of a frown on Louis Jordan's face now; it was a picture of delight. Everyone on stage seemed to be projecting happiness, and this spirit radiated into the crowd.

After a rocking ensemble the leader stepped forward and began singing, his smooth voice offering a stream of good-humoured advice to his listeners, warning both sexes of the consequences of dalliance. The audience, like just about every crowd the band played for, was enraptured by the leader's personality: the young girls liked his devil-may-care attitude, the older women went for the experienced way he sang about the perils of love. The young men marvelled at his bold clothes and cheerful panache and the older males saw him as a figure of hope.

Louis Jordan's appeal cut through to every social stratum; his music was just as potent for white listeners as for black. Rich and poor, meek and bold, young and old, everyone warmed to his charms. Occasionally when he sensed that his wide-eyed presentation was worrying a young black listener he would offer a subtle 'I'm only kidding' wink and the doubter would be instantly converted. Louis knew exactly how far to go with his teasing of an audience and he could skilfully change the pace of his show by singing a beautiful ballad. To cap everything, he could play the alto saxophone in a way that delighted jazz fans and casual listeners alike.

At this Chicago theatre date the group was scheduled to be on stage for seventeen minutes. The time flashed by for the audience as the group bounced through one number after another before climaxing their presentation with the all-action version of their hit 'Caldonia', during which Louis had the crowd screaming with delight as he kicked one leg high above his head.

The only worried person in the entire theatre was the young tenor saxist. In trying to peer across the footlights to see if his cousins had taken their seats in the second row, he had missed a cue into the final number. Following his mistake by immediately glancing at the leader, he saw no reaction and assumed his error hadn't been noticed in the general excitement.

The fans shouted for more as the group took their bows and then waved goodbye. As soon as the musicians entered the dark recesses of the backstage area the leader's voice barked out an instruction: 'All of you come to my dressing room right now.' The perspiring group did as they were told and jammed themselves into the leader's changing quarters. 'There were too many goofs tonight. I want to have a rehearsal at midnight when the theatre's empty.'

Each of the sidemen had made his own plans to go out on the town as soon as he had showered and changed, but none of the veterans offered a word of protest about this irritating extra chore. The only voice of dissent came from the youngest member: 'Hey, Mister J. I've arranged to see my cousins after the show; they've come all the way from Milwaukee to be here tonight and . . .' He got no further with his protest. The bandleader stormed at him: 'You should have thought of that earlier. You kept us all waiting, you came on stage with dirty shoes, you wore a greasy tie and a funky shirt and you played a whole gang of wrong notes – and you missed your cue on 'Caldonia'. God damn it, you need to rehearse.'

With that, the bandleader kicked open his dressing-room door and gave all of the band an unequivocal 'leave now' gesture. The musicians trooped out silently, but as soon as they were out of earshot of the leader's room the young tenor saxist began complaining, 'That old-time dude, who's he think he is? Making us rehearse when everything sounds OK.' The trumpet player cut him short: 'Look, I've told you before, the guy is a perfectionist; everyone in the business knows that. He won't stand for any horseplay or sloppy musicianship'. The saxist bristled. 'Perfectionist? God damn it, I'll show him what wrong notes are.'

The trumpeter sighed. He knew then that the band and the young man would soon be parting company.

# Somewhere Deep in the Heart of the South

Louis Thomas Jordan's quest for perfection began during his adolescent years in Brinkley, Arkansas, where he was born on 8 July 1908. His mother Adell (who was originally from Mississippi) died in her twenties when Louis was little more than an infant and he was raised first by his grandmother (Maggie Jordan) and subsequently by his aunt, Lizzie Reid. She lived at 817 North Main, Brinkley, a small, wooden, one-storey house which stood close to an even smaller dwelling which was the home – or rather the home base – of Louis's father, musician James Aaron Jordan, who had been born in Dardanelle, Arkansas on 16 June 1876.

There were to be several inspirational figures in Louis Jordan's life, but none was more influential than his father, who made it abundantly clear to his only child that he wanted him to be a musician. Happily, the father's desire coincided with Louis's own main ambition and the two shared a long and happy relationship. Respect ran in the Jordan family: James, a great admirer of his own father, had named Louis after him.

James Jordan, a dapper man, five feet three inches tall, was a gifted multi-instrumentalist with the knack of teaching, and getting the best out of, young musicians. For a good part of each year he toured with various minstrel shows, but during his months at home he played an important part in organizing and coaching the Brinkley Brass Band. Known to most people in Brinkley as Jim, he was the band's original instructor on its formation in 1915. The band was the brainchild of a remarkable local African-American, Joackim Pelege Gettis. Its twenty charter members were all from Brinkley, and many were scholars at the all-black Consolidated White River Academy

(CWRA), where Professor Gettis taught maths and languages, but the band had no direct connection with the academy and its rehearsals were carried out at the Gettis family home on South New Orleans, Brinkley.

The local white population took little interest in the activities of the Brinkley Brass Band, and the young black musicians would have been surprised had they done so, since the two races lived in a rigidly segregated community. The town of Brinkley (founded in 1872) had a population of about 5,000 in 1915, divided roughly equally between the two races. The racial situation has slowly changed, but in Louis's childhood the accepted dictum was 'never the twain shall meet socially'. There was nothing especially sinister about white Brinkley's attitude; it simply followed and upheld the customs and prejudices of the Old South. Almost all of the town's black population performed menial tasks in the community and played no active part in local politics. White and black played separately, studied separately, worshipped separately and were buried in different cemeteries.

Today, Brinkley is a thriving town, situated in Monroe County, between the Arkansas state capital, Little Rock (to the west) and Memphis, Tennessee (to the east), sixty-nine miles from either on Inter State Route 40. In many ways it is like other pleasant-looking towns that skirt the nearby Mississippi river, but one tragic event set it apart from its neighbours. On a March evening in 1909 a terrible cyclone (the worst in Arkansas history) hit the town and virtually destroyed it. Only a handful of houses and one church stood undamaged; about sixty people were killed and over 600 injured.

Fortunately the Jordan family escaped without loss of life, but all five members of one black family were killed. In history a shared catastrophe has often brought two disparate races together, but it failed to do so in Brinkley. In a gesture that is still remembered by the black population of the town, the civic authorities failed to grant the bereaved blacks a chance to give their dead a dignified burial service, instead hurriedly depositing the black corpses in a mass grave. Many painful indignities have been forgotten by the black locals, but not this one.

Brinkley soon benefitted from outside relief and began rebuilding almost immediately, but social change was practically indiscernible at this time. It was in this atmosphere that the young Louis Jordan

6

first learnt the ways of the world. Yet despite the prejudice and discrimination surrounding his childhood, Louis always had a place in his heart for Arkansas and Brinkley in particular, frequently quoting a local saying or speaking about the town's customs. His attitude was not dissimilar to that of another great musical artist, Big Bill Broonzy, who despite often experiencing physical danger because of the colour of his skin, said without affectation, 'I still go down to visit my people in Mississippi and Arkansas, and I still love my home-town in the South.'[1] Even someone as unsentimental as Miles Davis acknowledged the mysterious, inspirational potency of the area; 'I also remember how the music used to sound down there in Arkansas when I was visiting my grandfather . . . that blues, church, back-road funk kind of thing . . . So when I started taking music lessons I might have already had some idea of what I wanted my music to sound like.'[2]

But James Jordan, who through his travels with various bands had seen a good deal of the outside world, was determined that his son would develop a talent that would carry him away from the restrictions of a small Southern town. Indeed his eagerness to start the boy's musical career was almost too intense. James preferred playing the brass bass to any instrument, but he was also adept on the cornet, clarinet and trombone. One of the Brinkley Brass Band's charter members, Dr J.E. Brooks, often had to miss band practice because of his teaching commitments at the CWRA and this meant that James Jordan regularly relinquished his position as conductor to play the missing trombone part. He conceived the idea that the vacancy could be partly filled by the young Louis, so he took home a trombone and proceeded to teach his small son the mechanics of blowing the instrument.

Almost immediately after giving his son these basic instructions, James left town to travel the summer months with a touring show. The young Louis was keen to become proficient and spent many hours doing his best to make music on the trombone, but he was only eight years old, and his little arms could not extend the slide out beyond the third position. He was therefore able to produce only a restricted number of notes on the instrument. The resultant limited permutations of notes, coupled with the rough tonal qualities of the beginner's efforts, almost drove his grandmother crazy.

Years later, Louis humorously recalled the situation:

I had a funny grandmother. She didn't like that blaring sound so I
had to drop it, she made me rehearse out in the backyard. My
father was on the road with a show so when he came back into
town he brought a thirteen-key Albert-system clarinet. She let me
practise that in the house providing I didn't play it in the high
register, so that's the beginning of me playing the reeds. After I
practised clarinet for about six months I got so that I could play up
high, then she wouldn't bother. I was doing pretty good then.[3]

Louis's progress on clarinet was so good that he was soon playing in
the Brinkley Brass Band. Several young men in the group had joined
the US Army in 1917, and since some of them chose not to return to
Brinkley after the war, there were vacancies in the reed section.
Louis was intensely proud to be part of the same musical organisation
as his father, but after he had settled in with the band he began to
indulge in a little horseplay with the younger members of the unit.

Part of the trouble was that Louis was, by now, good at reading
music. He soon learnt his part in the orchestration, but some of his
friends were much slower, which meant that Louis became bored
with rehearsing the same piece over and over again. At one rehearsal,
while waiting for the stragglers, he pretended that he was snoring
with the boredom of it all. It was an innocent enough piece of fun, but
James Jordan, who was in charge of the rehearsal, failed to see the
funny side of the incident and crept up on his son, cuffing him around
the head. Louis had never been physically chastized by his adored and
adoring father, so the shock of being struck by him, however lightly,
was a traumatic experience, made worse because it had taken place in
full view of close friends.

This incident played its part in shaping Louis's professional
attitude. Never again, no matter how indifferent the musical
company, did Louis treat a rehearsal in a light-hearted way. For the
rest of his life, Louis Jordan regarded rehearsals as seriously as the
most illustrious public performance. Latter-day colleagues sometimes
suggested that Louis's passion for rehearsing verged on mania, but
they were not aware of what had taken place years before in
Brinkley.

Although father and son soon re-established their previous closeness, another upheaval occurred in Louis's life when his grandmother died and he moved in with his aunt, Lizzie Reid. Her husband, Mack Reid, a tall, easy-going fellow in his thirties, did manual work at a local factory, and sometimes at a nearby hotel. Lizzie herself was a small, bustling woman of sharp intelligence and considerable musical ability, who played piano regularly for the local Mount Olive Baptist Church services and taught several local youngsters how to read music. Profiting from his father's expert tuition on the clarinet and learning about the theoretical side of music from his aunt, Louis soon became an outstanding young musician.

It was just as well that Louis was becoming a talented clarinet player, because his academic achievements were negligible. He had been enrolled at the CWRA by his father, but his progress in the classroom left a lot to be desired. A former schoolfriend commented: 'Louis was a slow learner. He was no trouble to the teacher, in fact he was very co-operative, but he was slow.'[4]

The only subject in which Louis eclipsed all of his fellow pupils was music, and at CWRA he had the benefit of receiving tuition from Mrs Naomi Gettis, a daughter-in-law of Professor J.P. Gettis. Although Lizzie Reid was eminently capable of writing short pieces for her students to play, Naomi Gettis had made a specialised study of composition and her explanations of musical form and harmonic progressions fascinated the young Louis Jordan. He was particularly impressed by the fact that Naomi had composed (in 1922) a song called 'Dear Old White Rose' for the newly organized black women's club in Brinkley; Mrs Gettis became a heroine for the youngster.

Louis's problems with the general subjects on the Academy's curriculum led James Jordan and Lizzie Reid to decide that it would be better for him to settle into a slower stream at the local Marion Anderson School. But twice a year this school interrupted its schedules so that the schoolchildren could take leave to plant and pick cotton. Most of the parents were happy with this arrangement, since it meant that their offspring were able to earn enough money in the cotton fields to buy the books needed for their studies, but this sort of activity had no part in Jim Jordan's great plans for his son. During one of these shut-down periods he therefore decided that Louis, by now a teenager, was old enough to come out with him on the road, not to participate in the travelling show's band, but to observe the routines and get used to the glamour and the hardships of a touring musician's life.

Louis had done some touring with the Brinkley Brass Band and had found it distinctly exciting. His close friend in the unit, Virgil Gettis, a son of Professor Gettis, played drums and brass horn. He recalled:

> We were like a band of brothers. We were all about fourteen and we loved it. We travelled by train all over Arkansas, Tennessee and Missouri. We liked meeting the girls. We wore nice uniforms and though we played for the people to listen it wasn't unusual for them to start dancing to the music. The Charleston was just coming in and we played that. Most of the musical arrangements were bought from Kansas City. We played a bit of everything. I think most of the time we played for expenses, but there would always be a fine spread for us to eat and various masonic lodges would pay something when we played for them. The band used to practise marching for its parade work. We played for our church, the Mount Zion Baptist Church, and for picnics, weddings and very occasionally for a funeral. Jim Jordan was a strict bandmaster, and he'd 'call you down' if you made mistakes or fooled around. He was competitive, too. I don't think he liked the idea of me getting as good on tuba as he was. Louis was featured on clarinet, but I think in his latter days with the band he also played saxophone. Music was in his system.[5]

The emergence of the Charleston played a part in shaping the way Louis projected his talents. In a 1971 interview he reminisced: 'At our church they were going around getting the kids together for some kind of a programme. I was the champion Charleston dancer in Brinkley but they wouldn't let me do the Charleston in church, so I had to sing, and I did "I'm My Mamma's Little Boy".' All of the Baptist church elders were well used to hearing fine singing, but they were greatly impressed by Louis's vocal clarity and his ability to pitch notes without being given a cue.

But these local successes were nothing compared with the prestige that Louis derived from being part, even an unpaid part, of a professional travelling show, and he said goodbye to all his local friends in a great state of excitement. Louis's father had worked with various minstrel shows from the age of twenty, and had had the opportunity of studying under the composer W.C. Handy. Handy's successes led him to be called 'The Father of the Blues', but a more accurate description might have been 'A Collector of the Blues' since many of the themes he 'composed' were current in the South long before Handy ever committed them to paper. Nevertheless, Handy's contribution to African-American music was substantial, since no one else, black or white, was ensuring that the early blues themes (which, had they been neglected, could well have disappeared altogether) were being written down.

Jim Jordan's view of the blues, like that of many schooled black musicians of the era, was somewhat ambivalent. He and his contemporaries had spent a good part of their lives practising orthodox European scales and intervals – their prowess was judged on the way they performed music that was almost exclusively written by white composers – so to re-create the deviations of pitch and timbre that are the essence of the blues was something they were reluctant to do. Yet every black musician in the South was as well acquainted with the sounds of the blues as he was with the harsh realities that had inspired their creation. Louis Jordan himself, like most of his young colleagues in the Brinkley Brass Band, knew the melody and lyric stanzas of dozens of blues, but was not encouraged to perform them. Church elders were happier to see their young flock copying the neat uniforms and manners of organized travelling bands than imitating the garb and habits of the itinerant blues singers whose random travels spanned the entire South. But according to Virgil Gettis the youngsters enjoyed surreptitiously playing the blues. Virgil's sister, who went to school with Louis and was a keen follower of the brass band, emphasized this point: 'Well, the blues was music with some meaning to our lives.'[6]

James Jordan would have had little difficulty relating to this sentiment. When his son was born, James temporarily abandoned his work in touring minstrel shows so as to help raise his infant son, continuing his local musical activities but earning his living in a local dry cleaners, where he pressed and repaired clothes. These activities brought in regular money but afforded Jim Jordan none of the

11

satisfaction that making music brought, so it was decided that he should resume his peripatetic life. He rejoined F.G. Huntington 's Mighty Minstrel Show, which used Belzoni, Mississippi as its base for touring throughout the Southern states.

Huntington's troupe was only one of many professional minstrel shows that toured the South in the 1920s. Among them were Bowens and Blonden's Dandy Dixie Minstrels (who travelled in a Pullman car that had once belonged to President Garfield), the Alabama Minstrels, Roscoe and Hockwald's Original Georgia Minstrels, F.S. Wolcott's Hi Brown Follies, Silas Green from New Orleans, Pat 'Fats' Chappelle's Rabbit Foot Minstrels, L.K. Holtkamp's Original Smart Set, the Georgia Smart Set, the Smarter Set and the Florida Orange Blossoms. Within these shows, many of the great names of black entertainment, including Bessie Smith, Ma Rainey and Ida Cox, gave their earliest professional performances.

The stigma that has grown over the very word 'minstrelsy' has obscured the eminent part that these shows played in the development of African-American entertainment. Much of the disgust associated with minstrelsy has been engendered by unsubtle white imitations of what was a noble tradition, presenting the talents of a variety of artists: singers, bands, dancers, comedians and acrobats. In the post-World War I period every black minstrel show was striving for (and in many cases achieving) a polished style of presentation in no way inferior to anything seen on the Pantages theatre circuit or at any of the halls run by the Theatre Owners' Bookers Association (TOBA). This last named (dubbed 'Tough On Black Asses' by performers) was a good deal harder to work for than a well-organized minstrel show, which usually travelled from booking to booking in comfort.

A 1924 advertisement in the black-owned *Arkansas Survey* for the Old Kentucky Minstrel Show (which pitched at 17th and Main in Little Rock) illustrates what was on offer: 'A cast of sixty excellent comedians, singers and dancers (ten lovely ladies) and a big Noonday parade by the Old Kentucky Brass Band. The band will give a concert for an hour from 7.15 p.m. until the curtains open at 8.15 p.m.' Veteran actress Artiebelle McGinty (who toured with Ma Rainey in a travelling show) recalled that the tent shows were often called minstrel shows, but were actually made up of elements of latter-day vaudeville forms, often working from a normal stage set-up but occasionally performing in the round – encircled by the audience.

One of the stars of Huntington's Minstrels was Mantan Moreland, an artist later to gain fame in Hollywood for his eye-rolling performances as Charlie Chan's valet. His performances appal and anger many of today's viewers, who see him as a racist stereotype, but Mantan was doing the same routine for black people in the 1920s and they were convulsed by his antics. No one laughed louder at Mantan than the young Louis Jordan, and some of his gestures later found their way into Louis's on-stage presentations. Jim Jordan conceded that Mantan was amusing, but for his money the greatest black comedian was Bert Williams (a view shared by many entertainers, including W.C. Fields, who described Williams as 'the funniest man I ever saw, and the saddest man I ever knew'). Williams suffered a deal of racial injustice but gradually achieved a national reputation, causing the black leader Booker T. Washington to observe: 'Bert Williams has done more for the race than I have. He has smiled his way into people's hearts.' Jim Jordan's admiration for Bert Williams rubbed off on Louis, who later learnt all he could about the comedian (who died in 1922), using the information he gleaned to benefit both his stagecraft and his repertoire.

As a result of his exposure to this rich and vibrant tradition, Louis was never quite the same after that first summer tour with his father, and any pretence of achieving success at school disappeared; he had set his heart on becoming a professional musician as soon as possible. He practised the clarinet for hours on end, then by way of contrast he spent a lot of time mastering a new instrument, as he recalled years later: 'Sidney Bechet was popular playing the soprano sax, so I bought one and learned to play it real good.'[7]

Louis's main relief from this self-imposed regime was baseball; in later years he sometimes told people that he had played semi-professional baseball in Louisiana (as a short-stop). This may well have been true, but one of his early team-mates in Brinkley, Jodie Hilliard, knew nothing about it, despite remembering Louis's efforts at the sport.

We used to play on the Marion Anderson School lot – but Louis wasn't a specialist then. He'd pitch, catch, do anything. I can remember him dashing around a lot; he was a likeable fellow, and he sure was active on the field. Another thing I remember about Louis; when he was a young man, he'd get dressed up in his best clothes for no reason at all – this was on any old day – he looked real sharp. It made him stand out, I guess.[8]

People who remember Louis in adolescence liked him. There were early signs of the mood swings that marked his later life, but in general he was cheerful, quite content to keep his own company yet happy to go off fishing with his friends, or in the winter months join them in hunting for rabbits and squirrels.

Less auspiciously, a health problem that was to affect Louis for many years also became apparent when he was a teenager. Due to a congenital weakness in his lower abdomen, Louis suffered from a persistent hernia. Dr Edward McKnight, a young white physician in Brinkley, did all he could to alleviate the condition but correctly forecast that the problem would be with Louis through adulthood. Since surgery was impractical, the only answer was to wear a truss. Embarrassed though he was, Louis accepted the advice and wore a cumbersome remedial truss, vowing that he would never let the problem affect his mobility. As if to prove himself, he made his on-stage performances as vigorous and mobile as possible, so that people who saw him doing high kicks in films twenty years later would never have guessed that he suffered from this chronic problem.

Louis's first big professional chance came through his father, who was by then working in the Rabbit Foot Minstrels. Jim came home with the news that the show's band was looking for a clarinettist who could double as a 'general utility entertainer'. Louis's versatility made him eminently qualified for the vacancy, he got the job, and for seventeen dollars a week he played, sang and danced his heart out. Over the years an untrue story has grown up that Louis ran away from home to play this job. Another legend, also apocryphal, has it that his first job was accompanying the famous blues singer Gertrude 'Ma' Rainey. Ma was indeed one of the stars of the Rabbit Foot Minstrels, but she was not in the show during Louis's initial season. Later, however, Louis did work in Mississippi with Ma Rainey's own show.

The black entertainer, Pat 'Fats' Chappelle, organized the Rabbit Foot Minstrels from his headquarters in Port Gibson, Mississippi. The group toured regularly but never aspired to win over Northern audiences. An old observer said: 'They were mostly around Texas, Louisiana and the South: they never got out of the cane breaks.'[10] Nevertheless, the troupe's musicians were always noted for their showmanship, particularly during the pre-concert advertising march, when the spectacular drummer Joe White led the parade. White was with the show for many years and was clearly remembered by saxophonist Teddy Edwards. 'Art Blakey's press rolls became famous, but years before, Joe White was even better at playing press rolls. He was fantastic during the ballyhoo march that took place to let everyone know that the Rabbit Foot Minstrels were in town.'[11]

Louis Jordan recalled his early travels with the troupe:

> The minstrels put up a tent, like a circus, and did the show from a platform. We had our own car in the train to carry the tent, and we had people to put it up. After they'd got the tent up we'd make a parade through the town. That night we'd put on the show then pack up the tent and get out to the next town. We travelled sometimes two or three hundred miles. All over the South – as far up as St Louis, and as far down as Florida. I got my food and a berth in the car, the seventeen dollars was clear. And at night the show was over about eleven o'clock, so we played dances in the town with eight or nine pieces from the twenty-three piece show band. We'd split 150 dollars a week from the dances.[12]

It was at one of these late night dances, in Woodville, Mississippi, that Louis experienced the keen rivalry that existed between various touring musicians. Louis, aged about fifteen, and still in short pants, crossed paths with another brilliant young reed player, Lester Young, then working in his father's travelling band. The trumpeter Leonard Phillips recalled the encounter:

> Louis put the clarinet down and started playing the soprano sax and it was on that he was battling with Lester. Lester was playing alto and Louis playing the soprano. They played 'Runnin' Wild', blues and so on. Louis got over his horn like he could at that time, but Lester ran away from him on his horn. Louis played all right, but he couldn't play the horn like that.[13]

15

Louis realized only too well that he had been outplayed, and that his opponent was close to mastering the art of improvisation. The fact that his vanquisher was a year younger than he was added to Louis's determination to devote even more time to practice. Accordingly, he made a point of setting aside a regular period in which he could grapple with the problems of learning how to improvise. When that particular minstrel season ended, Louis worked for a time in Helena, Arkansas, as part of the Dixie Melody Syncopators, whose job was to entertain the weekend customers at Jack Greenfield's Dixie Drug Store.

He soon returned to Brinkley and buckled down to an even stricter regime of practice, which he later estimated to have embraced at least six hours a day. In order to survive he had to take local, non-musical work. For a while he assisted in Tom Kelly's Drug Store, and he also worked in a grocery store close to his home on North Main. His black employer there suggested that Louis should consider following the trade, as he clearly had an aptitude for selling, but Louis just smiled and counted the weeks off until the start of a new minstrel season.

It was not uncommon for musicians to drift from one minstrel troupe to another and back again after they had completed their one-tour contract. In 1925 Louis did just that, accepting a place in the prestigious 'Silas Green from New Orleans' show. He had recently bought himself a C-melody saxophone, and he knew that the new band was eager to feature him on this more than on clarinet, so he would be getting paid for familiarizing himself with a new instrument.

When his long tour with the Silas Green Show ended, Louis again went back to Brinkley, but left to play in a Memphis, Tennessee dance band before again linking up with the Rabbit Foot Minstrels. Although he enjoyed the touring life, he was shrewd enough to realize that the years were slipping by and he was nowhere near achieving fame or fortune. He was, admittedly, only nineteen, but having been something of a prodigy he had expected swifter developments in his career. When the 1927 Rabbit Foot tour ended he decided not to go back to Brinkley but to try his luck in Little Rock, Arkansas.

He soon landed a semi-permanent job in one of the city's foremost black bands, Brady Bryant's Salt and Pepper Shakers, led by drummer James 'Brady' Bryant. The band usually functioned as an eight-piece, with Louis playing most of the jazz solos on his recently acquired alto saxophone – like many young players of his generation he had now come to regard the C-melody saxophone as obsolete.

Working alongside Louis, on tenor saxophone, was Hayes Pillars (later to become co-leader of the celebrated Jeter-Pillars Orchestra). As ever, Louis was watching points all the time, learning what he could from every musical situation. Brady's band was an all-purpose dance band, as Hayes Pillars recalled: 'We played jazz music, we played popular tunes, we played waltzes.'[14] This melange of various musical ingredients gave Louis the chance to admire Brady's skill in programming a repertoire, but he also noted that Brady didn't spend much time mixing socially with his sidemen (an attitude that later earned Brady the nickname of 'The Great Garbo'). Nevertheless, the leader seemed to get results from his musicians; Louis was impressed.

Louis had always nurtured an ambition to study music full-time and to this end he enrolled at the Arkansas Baptist College (established 1884) in Little Rock, but he never carried out his plan. In 1991, the Chief Executive Officer of the college, Dr W.T. Keaton, reported that there are no records of Louis Jordan regularly attending classes. Yet the saxophonist proudly claimed to be an alumnus of the college, and no one contradicted him (for reasons that will become clear later). The main reason for Louis not carrying out his academic plans was a shortage of cash. He had become heavily involved with Julia, a young woman from Arkadelphia, Arkansas, and was saving all his money for their forthcoming marriage. Not long after their wedding, Julia (usually known as Julie) gave birth to a daughter, Patty. A local friend recalled, 'That wasn't Louis's daughter. He thought it was and he married Julia, but as the time came it became clear, counting the days, that she wasn't his. He would have been the happiest man had she been.'[15]

Through the musicians' grapevine Louis heard that the oil-boom area of El Dorado, Arkansas, was crying out for musicians, and that the going rate there was ten dollars a gig (twice the amount he was being paid in Little Rock). After obtaining a contact name, Louis packed his bags and without further ado moved on to El Dorado.

# 2

## Small Town Boy

In 1920 the tiny sawmill town of Smackover in South Arkansas had a resident population of 139, but within two years, over 25,000 people had settled there. In the intervening time, on 10 January 1921, prospectors in the nearby El Dorado oil fields had struck a gusher, causing a boom. Thousands also flocked to El Dorado itself to seek their fortune in black gold, and throughout the 1920s in the whole locale there was money to burn.

Saloons and dance halls soon thrived in El Dorado, and the demand for good musicians exceeded the supply, both in the district where the black workers settled and in the larger, white section of town. Jimmy Pryor, an enterprising black pianist, moved to El Dorado in the 1920s and organized a band to play at the recently erected whites-only dance halls situated on the outskirts.

The atmosphere at this venue was wild and woolly, typical of any boom town's dance hall. Prohibition was ignored and violence easily ignited. The band, Jimmy Pryor's Imperial Serenaders, often had to play trite music for the hall's brash customers, but the performance of any request usually brought a hefty tip. Pryor paid his men ten dollars per engagement, and settled with them each night on a cash basis, just in case the local lawmen took a stand against bootlegging and closed the place down instantly. With salary and tips, most of the musicians – including Louis Jordan, who began work within hours of contacting Pryor in El Dorado – were earning more than they had ever done.

In 1929 the line-up of the band was Jimmy Pryor (pianist and manager), Leonard Parker (trumpet), Buster Bennett (banjo), Preston Killebrew (drums) and three saxophone players (all of whom doubled on clarinet): Richard Rambert, Jesse Steele and Louis Jordan. Buster

Bennett took most of the light-hearted, up-tempo vocals and Jordan sang the ballads. The band enjoyed a good deal of success and Richard Rambert reported in a letter that the band was 'knocking 'em cold at an ofay dance hall'.[1]

El Dorado was cocooned from the effects of the October 1929 Wall Street Crash, but by 1930 the peak of the oil boom had passed as the flow dwindled. The resultant disappointment and frustrations caused the town's atmosphere to become more violent, both inside and outside the white dance hall. Things also changed on the bandstand and Jimmy Pryor abdicated (or was deposed) from his position, taking several of his sidemen with him on his departure. Those left behind (including Louis Jordan) reorganized and found themselves a new leader, saxist Bob Alexander. This new outfit, Bob Alexander's Harmony Kings, agreed to Alexander's suggestion that he send for a brilliant young pianist, whom he had heard play in Hot Springs.

Chester Lane (born in Lexington, Mississippi in 1914) was down on his luck in a small Arkansas town when the cable offering him the job in El Dorado arrived.

I was only fifteen at the time, but I'd been playing professionally for over a year. Things had got a little slow and my landlady said to me, 'Your toes are just about ready to show through your boots. Why don't you go and make some money picking cotton?' Well, I didn't like the idea, I'd never done it before, but my landlady told me that people could make twenty-five dollars in real quick time. I guess my heart wasn't in it, because all I made was four dollars and eighty-five cents, and did my landlady laugh. Just as we were sharing the joke the telegram boy came to the door and said there was a cable for me. I pulled it open and saw it was from a guy named Wilson in Hot Springs who owed me some money from when I had worked for him. As I stood there reading this, the boy came back and said, 'I forgot, there were two cables for you.' When I opened the second I could hardly believe my eyes; it was an offer to join Bob Alexander's Harmony Kings in El Dorado at ten dollars a night – well, that beat picking cotton!

In El Dorado I met up with Bob Alexander who played all the saxes, James Finney (a fine player) on alto sax, Leonard Parker on trumpet, Killebrew on drums, Louis Jordan on alto sax, soprano sax and clarinet. Buster Bennett was on banjo, guitar and vocals and he was the showman of the group, with his singing and speciality numbers. During one feature he used to play the guitar behind his head. This was a seven-nights-a-week affair – so I was making seventy dollars a week. We played at a white roadhouse a bit out in the country and we had to get there in an old Jalopy. I got off on the wrong foot, literally, with Louis Jordan because I stepped into the car on my first night and accidentally trod on his toes. That was soon forgotten, but Louis was a little flighty and temperamental in those days. Later, we got on fine.

When the El Dorado job came to an end we took up an offer to play in Hot Springs at Wilson's Tell-'Em-'Bout-Me Café. We started there around 1 January just as the season was beginning and we played there for some months – I guess until the season ended in May – then the musicians went their own separate ways. I didn't work with Louis again until I joined his band twenty years later.[2]

Thus Louis Jordan found himself on the loose in Hot Springs, Arkansas at a time when it was regarded as the most wide-open city in the whole of the USA. Gangsters from many states visited it to negotiate in sybaritic conditions with fellow hoods. The local authorities proudly acclaimed Hot Springs the 'Baden Baden of America', but the lawless visitors gave the spa city the affectionate nickname of 'Bubbles'.

The early history of Hot Springs is chequered with violence, including a shootout between rival gamblers that left five dead on Central Avenue in 1898, and several subsequent fatal gun battles. Violence wasn't absent from the city during the 1920s and 1930s, but the main departure from the laws of other parts of the USA concerned gambling and bootlegging. For twenty years, from 1926 onwards, the city was held tightly in the grip of its legendary mayor, Leo Patrick McLaughlin who, when sarcastically asked by a visitor if there was any law in Hot Springs, roared: 'There certainly is. I AM THE LAW.'

Al Capone and his brother Ralph were frequent visitors to Hot Springs, and so too was Owney Madden, who found the atmosphere so sympathetic he eventually made his home there. In 1991 an old resident said, with some pride, 'In the 1930s there were 150 lamsters here at the same time' (a lamster, or someone on the lam, being a fugitive from the law).

But it wasn't only criminals who enjoyed taking the waters in Hot Springs. Movie stars relaxed there and so too did many professional baseball players, who benefited from the therapeutic qualities of the various spa outlets on Bath House Row. Today the city is a delightful tourist spot, one that welcomes thousands of visitors annually, many to attend the horse racing at nearby Oaklawn Park and take the health-giving water that flows continuously from sidewalk taps. The rows of elegant bath houses which so impressed Louis Jordan when he was a resident of the city are still intact.

It's said that the Ku Klux Klan had a powerful hold on local politics until 1927 but then lost a lot of influence when (on religious grounds) it refused to sanction any further gambling. A ban would have resulted in a drastic reduction in revenue for the city, so a conglomerate of various ethnic interests, known as the 'Little Combination', gradually asserted itself and established a system that tolerated (even encouraged) gambling and bootlegging, thus diminishing the KKK's power. Whatever the reason, by 1930 blacks in Hot Springs did not feel as threatened as some of their confrères in other parts of the South. This did not mean they enjoyed freedom from restrictions: if they were not employed there, blacks were discouraged from even walking on the same side of the street where the huge, luxurious Arlington Hotel stands. However, quite a few black-owned businesses thrived.

Louis Jordan liked the atmosphere of the city. Whereas El Dorado had been lively in an abandoned and hazardous way, Hot Springs was pulsating with a sense of controlled excitement. He sent for Julie and she joined him at a lodging house run by a Mrs Smith at the corner of Pleasant and Garden Street. He played some gigs at Wilson's Café, and also at the Woodmen of the Union Hall and at the Eastman Hotel. For a brief spell he seems to have returned to El Dorado to play at the Beverley Gardens Ballroom in a reconstituted version of the Harmony Kings. He kept reasonably busy, secure in the knowledge that when the new season started in January he could once again work full-time at Wilson's Tell-'Em-'Bout-Me Café.

Light-skinned Lucius Wilson had a flair for publicity and

showmanship. At least twice during each season, he organized a colourful 'cakewalk parade', with six waiters in top hats carrying large ornate cakes down the street. Behind them his resident band played aboard a flat-bed truck (with the piano pushed up against the driver's cabin), and the waiters strutted in time with the music, criss-crossing the street in a series of elegant dance steps. Louis's showman instincts found expression in being part of such a display, which travelled through the city before circling around the Hotel Majestic fountain and returning to the café, usually with dozens of new customers (black and white) in tow.

While Louis was working at Wilson's café he was heard by a bandleader employed at the swish Green Gables Club, on the Malvern Highway, about a mile south-east of Hot Springs. The bandleader was highly unusual for the time and place, being black and a woman. Her name was Ruby Williams and she played piano in the band, which also featured her husband, Selmer 'Tuna Boy' Williams on drums. Ruby was impressed not only by Louis Jordan's command of his instruments and his pleasant singing voice, but also by the fact that he seemed to know every popular song of the past decade.

He probably did, too, but this was not a casually gained gift. Typically of Louis, it was the result of hard work and planning: his routine was to stay up until nearly dawn listening to late-night radio shows to familiarize himself with every new tune broadcast. He had bought himself an Atwater-Kent radio set, and no matter how late he finished work he would tune the dial to find music. One of his favourite shows was broadcast from 9 p.m. until 3 a.m. on WGN Chicago and featured a white band co-led by drummer Carleton Coon and pianist Joe Sanders. Louis later admitted that in his innocence he thought the group was led by one man nicknamed 'Coon' Sanders, and realized this was not so only when Carleton Coon died in 1932.[3]

Louis joined Ruby Williams's band and began work at the Green Gables, impressed but not overawed by the plushness of the club, its immaculate white stucco walls and elegant green roof. Subsequently, Ruby (whose nickname was 'Junie Bug') was offered and accepted another even more prestigious residency at the Club Belvedere, on the old Little Rock Highway, about four and half miles north of the city limits. Louis Jordan moved with her into the new job, working with Selmer 'Tuna Boy' Williams on drums, Oscar 'O.B.' Brown on banjo and guitar, Ruby Williams on piano and trumpeter Eunice Brigham, a former member of the Jenkins Orphanage Band of Charleston, South Carolina and more recently with Alphonso Trent, one of the best black show bands of that era.

Playing in the de-luxe Club Belvedere, whose ornate interior of marble and cut-glass chandeliers stood within acres of landscaped ground, was a step up from working at Green Gables and a distinct promotion from the whoopee atmosphere of Wilson's Café. Just why the owners of the Belvedere chose to go against all local expectations and employ a black band to provide music for its exclusively white clientele has never been explained. It may have been an attempt to imitate an aspect of New York's Cotton Club, but one veteran employee thought it was because the management had previously experienced problems when white musicians had attempted to become too friendly with the fashionable customers. The bosses reasoned, not groundlessly, that in the early 1930s a black band employed in a segregated Arkansas niterie would not make any attempt to mingle with the clientele.

A local black girl, Callie Dill (now Mrs Gardner), who had just graduated from Howard University, Washington, DC sang at both the Green Gables Club and at the Belvedere with Ruby Williams, and she remembers her well:

> She was short and stocky but not fat, very pleasant. She drank and smoked, but not on the bandstand, and she cussed too. I remember she used to criticize her husband, a small man, for the way he played the drums – he used to drag the tempo – but she'd keep smiling on the bandstand. Ruby also sang with the band, but she was a good pianist, she could play, and she knew all the keys. She was a skilful accompanist and one of the features of the evening was when she backed Emma Prichard, a tallish white singer, well built, stately sort of woman (not local, maybe from Louisiana).
>
> I got the job at Green Gables through my father, who was a maître d' there; my job was to play piano and sing during the time Ruby's band took their breaks. It was an élite place, with good furniture and silver curtains. I was preparing to take up a secretarial job in Chicago at twenty-two dollars a week, but I was

24

offered twenty dollars for singing only a few hours a week, so I liked the idea, and Mr Ernest Evans who managed Green Gables soon put my wages up to thirty dollars a week. The musicians were getting more than that, of course. Later on I worked at the Belvedere with Ruby; like Green Gables, that was a six-night-a-week affair – nothing much opened in Hot Springs on a Sunday. I did three seasons there, and whereas Green Gables had a low stage, the Belvedere had a high one. The dining room and ballroom were very ornate; there was a huge mirror revolving constantly, all the women wore long dresses.

One night a party sent word to the manager asking if I would sing 'My Blue Heaven' at their table. Well, in those days coloured singers didn't 'hit the floor' in a place like that, they worked strictly from the bandstand. However, the manager said it would be OK. I had never done that sort of thing and I guess I looked doubtful, but he made it clear it was expected of me. So I crossed the floor a little apprehensively and moved close to the dimly-lit table. There were five men sitting around it. I sang the song, they smiled and clapped and I made my way back to the stage. At the next break the manager brought me round a fifty-dollar tip – from Al Capone, one of the men I sang to.[4]

Louis Jordan thrived in this ambience, and under Ruby's guidance worked up cabaret routines for certain feature numbers. He was still far from being an extrovert off-stage but he gradually became more open and joined in some of the band-room camaraderie, though he rarely touched alcohol and never smoked. In this way Louis developed the ability to tell jokes and anecdotes and to laugh at himself. Having time to spare during the day, he was determined to enjoy such of the local facilities as were available to him, and one of these was riding the mules that could be hired by the hour from Happy Valley at the foot of Reservation Mountain (one of the two peaks dominating the valley in which Hot Springs stands).

Louis decided on a two-hour stint. After an hour's leisurely ride to the top of the mountain he decided to dismount and relax, but as he did so the mule departed and trotted off down the slope, leaving Louis stranded. The man hiring out the mules had omitted to tell his customer that at noon they always hurried back to Happy Valley for their midday feed. Louis was more amused than angry, and told the story to his colleagues, his neighbours and to most of the black staff at the Belvedere. This led to one of the stable boys there offering Louis free horse rides, provided he arrived early in the morning. Louis took advantage of the offer but found out there was a snag: blacks were allowed to ride the horses but not to hire saddles. So although he got his ride for nothing it had to be bareback. Despite this, he persevered and learnt to ride well enough to take a horseback role in a film years later.

Of course all of the local facilities were available to the visiting hoodlums, and although they were positively not on any sort of desegregation crusade they sometimes amused themselves by causing consternation to the local diehards. On one occasion Al Capone decided to treat all of his entourage to new suits, and on a whim he decided to include a black pianist who happened to be playing in the bar where Capone made his decision to buy the outfits. Capone made sure that the pianist was at his side when he visited one of the town's leading white tailors, then gleefully watched as he asked for 'his friend' to be measured for a new suit. The tailor dutifully obliged.

One of Louis Jordan's friends, trumpeter Ralph Porter, then playing in a small roadhouse just outside Hot Springs, was startled to see Al Capone and his men come in one night. They didn't stay long, but asked the band to play 'After You've Gone'. Porter and his musicians were anxious to oblige and had played only a few bars when one of Capone's companions stepped forward and tossed a hundred-dollar bill at each member of the band. Porter recalls, 'We played the tune continuously for the next hour, just in case they popped their heads in the door again.'[5]

Louis Jordan observed the comings and goings of various hoods without passing comment. He too occasionally gained substantial gratuities from these visitors, some of whom he was to see again later in his career. He had become more outgoing with his companions, but he also knew that there were times to be silent and this side of his personality was bulwarked when he paid a return visit to Brinkley and was initiated into the local black masonic order at the behest of his father. The Providence Masonic Lodge No. 36 (founded in the 1870s) was typical of a whole chain of similar black institutions throughout the USA. As one veteran explained, 'It is especially useful

26

to be a mason if you're a travelling musician; you never know when you are going to need help on the road.' Louis tried whenever possible to spend Christmas with his father, allowing himself time to return to Hot Springs for a 2 January start to the season. He followed this procedure for two years, playing with Ruby Williams until the season ended in May, then freelancing wherever he could for the remainder of the year.

No one listening to Ruby Williams's Belvedere Orchestra could fail to notice Louis Jordan's talents. Compliments from customers came regularly and it became almost commonplace for visitors to say, 'You'd be a sensation back in my home town', without being any more specific. But during the course of Louis's second season at the Belvedere a particular diner spoke to Louis several times about bettering himself. Louis, observing the house rules, listened politely to the man's praise, but soon realized that this customer was offering him a genuine opportunity to better his musical prospects. The stranger said he was from Philadelphia and that he had contacts within the entertainment world there. He assured Louis that if he travelled North and called on a certain theatre owner he was sure the man would be able to find employment for his talents.

Louis thanked the man and said he would think it over. He then did his best to find out all he could about the stranger and was more encouraged than discouraged to hear a rumour that the man was 'on the lam' and probably did have powerful connections in Philadelphia. When Louis next met his benefactor he told him he was keen on the idea of working in the North, so the man gave Louis a letter of introduction to a theatre owner in Philadelphia, which Louis said he hoped to deliver during the coming months. But Louis was reluctant to take the bold step of moving so far by himself and simply tucked the letter away, out of sight.

When the Belvedere season ended in May 1932, Louis told Ruby and 'Tuna Boy' that he would be leaving Hot Springs shortly. They both wished him luck, but instead of developing a plan, Louis once more began playing local gigs, one of which involved him again taking part in Wilson's 'cakewalk parade'.

Visiting Hot Springs at that time was a singer and dancer, Ida Fields, who had recently been a member of the light-skinned Florida Orange Blossoms dancing troupe. She was on vacation with trombonist Walter Madison who, like Ida, was employed as an entertainer in Dr Sells's Travelling Medicine Show. Ida couldn't resist entering the dancing competition that climaxed the cakewalk parade. Her professional steps made her the clear winner and she was awarded the prize cake. Louis Jordan observed the display of talent with admiration and made it his business to congratulate the vivacious winner with a stream of compliments. Ida liked what she saw and heard and both she and Walter Madison were pleased to accept Louis's offer to drop into a local roadhouse to hear him play.

Dr Sells and his wife were also in Hot Springs on vacation, so they accompanied Ida and Walter to a 'fried chicken' roadhouse to hear the music. When they entered, Louis was singing 'Georgia on My Mind', on which he was featured playing clarinet. The visitors soon conceived the idea that Louis would make a useful addition to their travelling show. Ida recalled, 'We needed another instrument to play our concert in the Pennsylvania ball park where the medicine show always set up for two weeks. After we heard Louis, Walter said, "Maybe we could get him to go on the medicine show. On clarinet he'd be good for the parade." '[6]

Louis instantly realized that here was his chance to move North to Pennsylvania itself – he'd worry about finding Philadelphia later – so he accepted the offer. It was less than he'd earned at the Belvedere, but more than the seventeen dollars a week he was getting at the roadhouse. The more he talked with Ida the more he was impressed by her knowledge of show business. By this time Julia had left Hot Springs, and it wasn't long before Louis began making romantic overtures to Ida.

Ida, who was six years older than Louis, had had a desperately hard upbringing in rural Texas where she was born. She had no formal schooling at all and spent a good deal of her childhood working in the cotton fields, but she was intelligent and optimistic, with considerable business acumen. She was married orginally at the age of thirteen, and soon became a mother, but the child died in infancy. Ida left the cotton plantation and literally danced and sang her way out of poverty, eventually becoming one of the stars of the Florida Orange Blossoms. She was both realistic and debonnaire and showed her lively spirit by having a diamond inserted into one of her front teeth during a 1926 trip to Baltimore. She promised to help Louis all she could to further his career.

Ida took Louis to Brinkley in her old Essex car, so that he could say goodbye to his folks. She then began the long drive to the North while Louis travelled in a truck with the show's musicians. The troupe's destination was Huntingdon, Pennsylvania (some 180 miles west of Philadelphia), where they were contracted to a two-week booking in a ball park. The band's music caused a crowd to gather, and this was the signal for Ida to begin extolling Dr Sells's wonder medicine, which was claimed to be beneficial for countless ailments. Then the musicians put down their instruments to move among the crowd, offering them the chance to buy the brew, as Ida explained:

> I was the em-cee; they called it the interlocutor in them days. The doctor and I, and his wife, worked on this platform to sell medicine. We had a bottle of medicine; it was a dollar and we gave it to each of the men who worked in the show. They had to go through the crowd and sell it, and when they had sold it they'd shout, 'SOLD OUT.' But Louis's voice was too small, he had that little fine voice, and they couldn't hear him over the crowd – that ball park was big. So in two weeks the doctor said, 'I can't keep him because he don't fit in.' So I said, 'I'll quit with him.' You see, Louis had never been out of Arkansas.[7]

One is left with the impression that Louis probably didn't make any tremendous efforts to project his voice across the ball park and that he was not heartbroken to be given the opportunity to make his way to Philadelphia. Ida stuck by her decision and followed Louis there.

Louis did his best to make an assured entry into Philadelphia but his confidence was dented by the white theatre owner's reaction to the letter that Jordan had carried from Arkansas. He didn't go out of his way to discourage Louis and stressed that he was indeed a good friend of the signatory, but told him there were no vacancies in his resident band, and anyway he was about to follow his usual practice of closing down the theatre for the duration of the summer. The manager advised Louis to contact one of Philadelphia's leading black band-leaders, trumpeter Charlie Gaines. Louis knew without looking into his wallet that he could not afford to wait around, so he immediately made his way to Gaines's house at 1754 15th Street.

Charlie Gaines was then in his early thirties, married, with four children. He made Louis as welcome as if he had been a long-lost son. Although Gaines was only eight years older than Louis, he virtually became a second father to him over the next three years. If truth be known, Gaines (like the theatre owner) was well stocked with good musicians at the time Louis first appeared, but he promised to do what he could to help. Meanwhile Ida had arrived in the city: 'So I went to Philadelphia, and Louis was sitting on the fence in front of a restaurant. I saw a sign there saying they wanted someone to sell hot dogs, so I started selling hot dogs in the window of a restaurant on South 12th Street. Louis couldn't get no job nowhere.'[8]

The couple found an apartment at 705 South 15th Street, but Ida made it clear that she would not live permanently with Louis unless they were man-and-wife, so in 1932, on Ida's birthday, the couple married. Ida's childhood marriage had long been annulled, but Louis, by now so reliant on Ida, went through the matrimonial ceremony before he had obtained a divorce from Julia. Looking back, Ida said, 'He never said nothing about no wife.' An onlooker to the situation explained, 'Louis hadn't divorced Julia when he married Ida. So he gave Julia five hundred dollars – that was big money then – but Julia was a gambler and in no time the five hundred dollars was gone.'[9]

Charlie Gaines soon made contact with Louis and offered him some gigs, providing he was willing to join Local 274 of the American Federation of Musicians. Louis agreed to do this and began working regularly with his benefactor. Gaines, a native of Philadelphia, had worked in various cities during the 1920s, and had made a number of recordings, including some with Fats Waller. He returned to his birthplace in 1930 and subsequently led bands at various clubs, including the Gold Dawn, the Show Boat, the Show Time and the Dixie. He also played at several theatres in Philadelphia.

Gaines sometimes varied the size of his line-up to meet specific commitments, but most often he worked with a quintet consisting of himself on trumpet, Ellsworth Blake on tenor sax, Wesley Robinson on piano, James Winters on bass and Benny Hill on drums; with Louis Jordan's arrival the group became a sextet (Louis playing soprano and alto saxes and clarinet). Louis had consistently worked with good musicians for most of his professional career, but Gaines's group was a notch above Louis's earlier colleagues because it was capable of high-class jazz improvising – the leader's trumpet being a stand-out feature. Gaines was also a good businessman and a personable leader, adept at handling all sorts of audiences. Louis learnt many things from him that proved useful when he formed his own band.

Louis's sense of dedication was never more apparent than when Gaines's band played in a theatre. Whereas most of his colleagues left the building to relax elsewhere during their time off, Louis stayed and watched every act go through its entire routine, which meant he sometimes saw the same show four times during the course of a day. If a performer's casual (yet well-rehearsed) gestures earned a response from the audience Louis would pay that performer extra attention to find out why this was so. He always made a point of studying Fats Waller, Cab Calloway, Louis Armstrong and Bessie Smith.

Not long after Louis joined Charlie Gaines's band, the group had the singular honour of accompanying Louis Armstrong on a recording session in Camden, New Jersey. The recordings (a medley of Armstrong's previous hits) do not show Gaines's augmented band in a particularly favourable light, but doubtless it was an unforgettable experience for all of the accompanists, providing stolid support for the genius's voice and trumpet.

Louis Armstrong was scheduled to play a series of dates, beginning with a booking in Philadelphia, and Gaines's band had the opportunity of accompanying Armstrong on this brief tour. Gaines himself couldn't get leave of absence from his club commitments, so a unit was formed, consisting of the best young musicians from the Philadelphia area, and this included Louis Jordan. He recalled the tour:

We didn't need too much rehearsal. He had sent his music to Philly before he came and we had rehearsed it; all he had to do was give the downbeat and we were gone. The first place we played after he came to Philadelphia was Atlantic City, two nights in the City Auditorium, and then we went to Hartford, Connecticut; Worcester, Massachusetts; Buffalo, Syracuse and Schenectady before we came to New York to play the Savoy Ballroom and a couple of jobs around New York. It was fun because he was always

31

happy, he would never sit grumpy. In the East we had good accommodation. If you wanted to stay up and carouse, you could do that, and if you wanted to go to bed you could go to sleep. The dance generally started about 8.30 or 9.30 and lasted four hours; after that if I didn't feel like going out I went to sleep.[10]

One of the first things that Louis did after he had settled back into a working routine in Philadelphia was to resume his radio vigils, scanning the air waves to find music that he liked. His taste was broad, and Duke Ellington took no more of his time than did the more commercial sounds of Fred Waring's Pennsylvanians. One particular sound pleased his ears: the shuffle rhythm featured in most of the arrangements played by a band led by the former Paul Whiteman star, German-born trumpeter Henry Busse (1894–1955). It seems odd that a fine young black musician, raised with the sound of the blues and magnificent gospel music, should have been attracted to the output of one of the corniest bands in the world, but Louis appreciated diverse music, regarding every sound new to him as a possible ingredient to use in his performances. It's unlikely that he was impressed by the Busse band's stilted phrasing, but he enjoyed the emphatic bouncy rhythm that enlivened their music. He tried to hear as many of their radio shows as he could, and he also liked the shuffle rhythms created by another white band (popular in Philadelphia) led by Jan Savitt.

Louis got on well with Charlie Gaines and often spent time at his employer's house, where he made friends with Charlie's children, offering encouragement to Stanley who was learning the double bass and to Charlie Junior, who played the trumpet. Stanley remembers the visitor as being jovial and smartly dressed. Louis liked Philadelphia, but city life didn't change his ways and though he got on well with his colleagues he kept himself to himself and rarely discussed business with anyone. His attitude towards Ida gradually became sterner, and he reproached her by often saying, 'You should be seen and not heard.'[11] He had recently purchased a new baritone saxophone and was mastering it through long, intense hours of practice.

Louis relaxed enough to flirt with various female dancers with whom he worked. Ida, well used to dressing-room banter, didn't bother unduly about this, but one incident left a deep impression on her. In that era the Philadelphia club scene was noted for its legion of transvestite entertainers, including the incorrigible Mother Cushenbury. Many of them congregated at an after-hours club called Roscoe's, situated close to the Grand Theatre. Ida dropped in there one night unexpectedly and saw a sight that she vividly recollected fifty years later: 'Louis was doing a striptease on top of a table. I said, "What the hell is happening here?" He got off and said, "Let's go home." ' Louis tried to laugh off the incident, but Ida maintained, 'he was a little gay. I know so.'[12]

Bassist Jim Winters temporarily took over the reins of Charlie Gaines's band while the leader helped out a former boss, LeRoy Smith, by playing trumpet in his orchestra. Gaines soon returned and resumed his residences in local clubs and theatres, all the while using Louis Jordan in his line-ups. A solid routine was established, but an important development occurred early in 1934.

A song written by Gaines, that featured a Louis Jordan vocal, attracted the attention of the black bandleader and publisher Clarence Williams, who (on 19 March) sent a telegram to Gaines asking if the rights to the song were available.[13] Gaines confirmed that they were. Williams hastened to Philadelphia from New York, reaching the Club Dixie at 11 p.m. on 22 March. Gaines recalled the situation:

> I made some crazy words and set them to a simple tune: 'I Can't Dance I Got Ants in My Pants'. Clarence Williams got word of it and hopped down to see me. Waited for me to finish a job that night and I took him home. Next morning at breakfast he pulled a contract out of his pocket and said he wanted to record my song. I asked him how much money I would get out of it. Clarence said he didn't know.[14]

Gaines decided to sign the contract, which gave Williams the rights to the song. Things then began to move at a great pace, with Williams arranging for the piece to be recorded that day in New York by his own band, augmented by Gaines and Jordan. Gaines said, 'He gave me a hundred dollars and transportation for Jordan and myself to New York.'[15]

Louis Jordan took his baritone sax along and played in a band comprised mainly of Clarence Williams's regular sidemen. Louis wasn't allocated any solos and played a section role on the other tunes recorded that day, but his singing on 'I Can't Dance I Got Ants in My Pants' is superb, revealing the swing, clarity of diction, humour and control that eventually made him famous. Why these attributes weren't seized upon at the time by the recording industry remains a mystery.

The song's lyrics had a slightly risqué tinge and this caught the public's attention. Gaines said, 'The record sales jumped because the song was banned from the air due to the lyrics. A week later the Vocalion people made me do the tune over and that was the side they issued. Eventually I got 500 dollars out of the deal and I'm thankful to Williams since those Depression days were tough going.'[16]

Gaines was genuinely grateful to Clarence Williams, who must have been pleased with the deal since the song was also recorded by several well-known artists, and each of their versions would have brought him extra royalties. Williams himself probably earned 500 dollars from the song during a single week in 1935, and as it went on to be a steady seller for some years so his profits mounted.

Louis Jordan knew virtually nothing about royalties at this stage of his career, but he learned a lesson from the way that Charlie Gaines had signed his song away for only a tiny part of the money that accrued from its success. John Hammond, the writer and record producer, observed many similar follies, and not long after Gaines's session he gave advice in a *Down Beat* article in which he said: 'Leaders should be careful to have written in their contracts that composers of original tunes should receive full royalty ($1\frac{1}{3}$ cents on a 35 cent disc and 2 cents on 75 cent issues) on each side, lest the company or an official thereof pocket the lion's share of the royalty.'[17]

# *Helping Hand*

Louis Jordan never again met the 'lamster' who was initially responsible for his move to Philadelphia, but while he was working with Charlie Gaines another benefactor entered his life. This time it was someone who was experienced and influential in the top echelons of black show business; his name was Ralph Cooper. During the early 1930s Cooper was a bandleader, film star and ace compère, and in 1934 he began an association with Harlem's Apollo Theatre that was to last for well over fifty years. His guidance of 'Amateur Night at the Apollo' continued into the 1990s.

Cooper was not easily impressed by the various acts, dancers and musicians that he encountered during his travels, but as soon as he heard Louis Jordan in action he knew that he was listening to a potential star. In 1991 he recalled the experience:

> I first heard Louis playing in a five-piece band in a club in Philadelphia (I think it was called the Showtime or the Showboat; it was situated downstairs in a hotel). I thought he was outstanding, a good alto sax player and a wonderful ballad singer. I approached him and urged him to come to New York. I could tell that he knew he wasn't going to get any further in Philadelphia, and he was very interested in what I had to say to him. He nodded as I was talking and then said, 'OK. I'm on my way, just let me pack my bags.' So after he'd given in his notice he arrived in New York.[1]

Charlie Gaines wasn't surprised when Jordan told him that he was planning to move to New York: 'he was ambitious and asked me a couple of times if he could go to New York to try to get things started. He had a terrific personality and I was sure he'd make it sometime.'[2] But things did not go smoothly for Louis in New York. No sooner had Ralph Cooper settled Louis into the Apollo house band than it was pointed out by a delegate of the American Federation of Musicians that Louis was not a member of Local 802 and would therefore have to observe a waiting period before he obtained a valid transfer from the Philadelphia Local 274. Cooper immediately countered this by featuring Louis only as a vocalist, but this, according to Ida, was not successful because the choice of material was wrong: 'When Ralph Cooper brought us in, Louis sang "Love is Imagination". Everyone got so restless I thought they'd run Louis off the stage; that was a quartet song.'[3]

Louis had no option but to abide by the rules of the American Federation of Musicians, as he later explained: 'I went over and played a week at the Apollo with the band and then I went over to the union to join and they said I couldn't work on a steady job until the probationary period of six months was up, so I had to hang around and play some gigs.'[4]

Every musician, regardless of style, race or creed had to observe this rule, and in order to survive Louis worked as and when he could. It was a standing joke with Louis that both he and Dizzy Gillespie (during their respective waiting periods) had each undertaken engagements with someone who played the musical saw. Louis played a whole series of dates in New Jersey, at seedy clubs, often in poor musical company, occasionally suffering the additional woe of not being paid the previously agreed amount by shark bandleaders.

Noble Sissle, eager to find a replacement for Sidney Bechet, who had temporarily left the orchestra, auditioned Louis on soprano sax, but Jordan (who played in a gentler style than the great Sidney) failed to get the job. In desperation, Louis travelled back to Philadelphia, where Charlie Gaines (out of the goodness of his heart) added Louis to an already full line-up so that he could pay him some subsistence money. For a while Louis travelled from New York to Philadelphia at weekends so that he could earn enough money to cushion himself against the rigours of a barren week in the Big Apple.

Trombonist Clyde Bernhardt saw Jordan regularly during this period. He claimed that 'some of the black guys in Harlem wouldn't give Louis work because he was too dark'.[5] This bears out rumours that in the 1920s and 1930s certain good musicians lost opportunities because a few African-American bandleaders gave preference to players with lighter skins. Louis toyed with the idea of going home to Brinkley for a visit, but a sombre event had taken place there that dissuaded him from doing so. National coverage had been given to the death of Joe Porter, a local black, who was shot and killed in Brinkley jail by persons unknown while awaiting trial for assault and battery on his wife.

Eventually it was through Charlie Gaines that Louis found work in a band led by the ex-Fletcher Henderson drummer, Kaiser Marshall – Gaines and Marshall had worked together in LeRoy Smith's orchestra. Marshall's band never made the top league but Louis played a series of dates with them in New Jersey, Connecticut and Massachusetts, and also played gigs with them in New York at the Harlem Opera House, the Renaissance Ballroom, the Rockland Palace and the Ubangi Club. As the average wage in this band was about thirty dollars a week, the personnel shifted a good deal as people found better opportunities. For Louis the chance to move on came when he successfully auditioned (after being recommended by Marshall and Gaines) for a place in LeRoy Smith's orchestra.

All of Smith's musicians were members of the Local 802, but Jordan was allowed to join them because they were about to move en masse to play a season in Atlantic City – under the rules for a combined transfer Louis's Local 274 membership was as valid as his new colleagues' 802 cards. LeRoy Smith's orchestra was described by Charlie Gaines as playing 'symphonic jazz'; its pianist Lloyd Phillips called it 'a strictly society-style group.'[6] The leader, who played violin, encouraged people to call him 'the colored Paul Whiteman'[7] and, by design, most of the arrangements for his fifteen-piece line-up were styled on the sounds of that hugely successful white leader. As a result, Smith gained work in some exclusive surroundings, places where no jazz band had ever been invited before.

Louis was one of the youngest members of the aggregation. Most of Smith's veterans were masons, so it's entirely possible that Jordan's membership played a part in his recruitment. Several of these veterans had played in famous bands; musicians such as trombonist Wilbur De Paris, drummer Walter Johnson, pianist Lloyd Phillips and trumpeter Albert Snaer were well known in jazz circles, but their improvising skills were rarely called upon when working for Curtis LeRoy Smith (who had dropped his original first name when he began bandleading in 1917 in his native city of Detroit, Michigan). Smith's most prestigious booking had been to provide music for the successful show *Connie's Hot Chocolates*, but despite the lack of improvisation within Smith's staid, ornate orchestrations, the musicians were content and well paid. Reedman Geechie Harper called his colleagues 'the nicest group of people I ever worked with.'[8] Wilbur De Paris was a little more reticent in his assessment, but it does seem that everyone got along remarkably well. Louis did not toady to LeRoy Smith but he did pay careful attention to anything the leader said, particularly when he told anecdotes about one of Louis's heroes, Bert Williams; at such time Louis could have imagined himself back in Brinkley listening to his father extolling the virtues of the great black comedian.

After completing their Atlantic City booking, Smith's outfit temporarily disbanded, or 'took time off to rest' as Smith preferred to describe any period of inactivity. Louis Jordan returned to Philadelphia, where as Charlie Gaines recalled: 'He continued with me until April 1935, then he left for New York but returned to play until September that year waiting out his union card.' Stanley Gaines said that his father always kept a telegram from Louis which read: 'If I don't make it in New York can I come back?', so contrary to any outward appearances Louis was not oozing self-confidence at this stage of his career. But his hopes were raised by a call from LeRoy Smith, whose orchestra had the chance to take part in a theatrical production, *Hot Chocolates of 1936*, which played at the Apollo Theatre, New York for a week from Friday 27 September 1935 (in true show-business tradition it was three months early in acknowledging the New Year). High on the bill was the famous piano-moving comedy act of Radcliffe and Rodgers, singer Gladys Palmer and the Three Miller Brothers, but among the advertised artistes was Louis Jordan. It was a small start at a venue that was to play an important part in his rise to stardom.

Having been granted his provisional 802 union card (he became a full member of the Local in the spring of 1936) Louis felt distinctly happier, but unfortunately the *Hot Chocolates* idea soon melted away and LeRoy Smith's men were again 'resting'. Louis returned to

Philadelphia once more. It was there, on a gig with Charlie Gaines, that he first met up with guitarist and vocalist Slim Gaillard. Trumpeter Bobby Booker recalled the occasion:

> In the latter part of 1935 I had my own eight-piece band. Reese Dupree, who was a very popular Philadelphia promoter, presented a band contest between Charlie Gaines's band and my own band at the Strand Ballroom. Slim Gaillard, who was playing swinging guitar, was with me, while Charlie Gaines had Louis Jordan who, like Slim, was unknown at that time. My own band played first and the crowd really loved our group and went wild. Charlie Gaines's band would not play so we finished the gig alone; it was no contest. We were paid all of the money because they did not play.[9]

There were not many evenings like that in Louis's subsequent career.

In the late autumn of 1935, LeRoy Smith called all of his musicians back into formation to play for the opening of the new de-luxe Mayfair Casino in Cleveland, Ohio. During the next few months various white bands shared billing with Smith's orchestra (including groups led by George Duffy, Gene Baker, Johnny Lewis and Manuel Contreras) but Smith's unit was the star attraction and its monthly contract was renewed on four occasions.

Louis's previous experience at the Club Belvedere in Hot Springs had prepared him for the formal, non-fraternizing atmosphere that prevailed at the Mayfair Casino. He had established himself as a featured ballad singer and the orchestra's principal improviser; his reed-section colleague Geechie Harper said, 'LeRoy Smith only featured improvisation sparingly, but when he was a member of the band Louis Jordan played quite a few ad-lib solos.'[10] In recalling his time with the LeRoy Smith aggregation Louis said, 'It was real high-class music; in fact I was the only one allowed to play some jazz once in a while and to do a little singing. But it was valuable experience.[11]

Jordan listened to any advice that was offered. He had neither enemies nor any close buddies in the big line-up. When work was finished Louis usually went home to Ida, who had rented what she described as an 'unfurnished kitchenette', which allowed her to cook for Louis. As in the past, a degree of wariness existed in his social contacts with fellow musicians. An observer thought that Louis was a little overawed by the fact that the band contained a few college graduates, but LeRoy Smith did not encourage snobbery and welcomed tenor saxist Harold Blanchard (who had taught himself to play through a twenty-five-cents-a-lesson correspondence course) into the orchestra.

After leaving Cleveland the LeRoy Smith ensemble again appeared at the Apollo, New York – in March 1936 – this time as the top-of-the-bill attraction, and Louis Jordan was again given featured billing. On this occasion his choice of material delighted the Apollo audience. Ida recalled Louis saying, ' "I'm going into the Apollo next week and I'm going to sing 'I'm Living in a Great Big Way'." I said, "Do you know it?" and he said, "Yes, I think I know it," and I said, "Know it and *feel* it!" '[12]

Louis's vocal on the 1935 Fields–McHugh song impressed everyone, as did, Ida remembered, his impromptu dancing:

> When his turn came he jumped out of the band and he just broke it up. He had to go so far back to get the microphone he knew that the chorus would end before he could do so, so he said, 'You know folks what it's all about, so I guess I'll truck on out.' So he whirled around and started truckin'.[13]

LeRoy Smith continued to bill Louis Jordan prominently when the orchestra played at the Lincoln Theatre in Philadelphia for a week in April 1936. Louis was gratified because he knew that Charlie Gaines was coming along for a reunion; when Gaines saw the show he was apparently delighted to observe Louis's progress.

The orchestra moved back to New York in late April to take part in another attempt to revive the *Hot Chocolates* production at the nightclub, Connie's Inn. This time the revue was produced by Teddy Blackmon and included a big cast, but yet again the show enjoyed only a brief run and LeRoy Smith's men were faced with another 'rest' period. Louis was growing dissatisfied by the stop-start employment, and, urged on by Ida, decided to try again to find regular work in New York.

Just at this time a saxophone player in the Apollo house band fell sick and Ralph Cooper arranged for Louis to fill in temporarily.

During this brief engagement bandleader Chick Webb began looking for an alto sax player to take the place of Edgar Sampson. Sampson, who was the principal orchestrator and virtually the musical director of Webb's band, was leaving to become a freelance arranger. Chick Webb had checked on Louis Jordan's talent some while before, as Chick's vocalist Charles Linton recalls: 'Yes, Chick sent someone to hear Louis Jordan when he was playing a club in Philadelphia.'[14]

Chick had first become aware of Louis through conversations with his trumpeter Taft Jordan (no relation) and from Clarence Williams's recording of 'I Can't Dance I Got Ants in My Pants' (which Webb's band had copied and recorded, featuring a vocal by Taft Jordan). Taft's light-hearted vocals and showmanship played a featured part in Chick Webb's presentations, but for a brief period leader and sideman did not see eye-to-eye and a disgruntled Taft departed to work with Willie Bryant's band, leaving Chick a vocalist short. Chick sent someone to hear Louis Jordan but Taft soon returned to the fold, so there was no vacancy until Edgar Sampson decided to move out of the sax section. Chick Webb originally intended to replace Sampson with his former star saxophonist Hilton Jefferson, but 'Jeff', as he was known, decided to decline the offer. Meanwhile Edgar Sampson went ahead and officially handed in his notice on 21 July 1936.[15]

Chick Webb heard Louis at the Apollo and was impressed, and according to Louis made the first approach by asking: ' "Kid, do you want to play with my band?" I said, "Yeah" and Chick replied, "Be at rehearsal tomorrow." ' Full of excitement, Louis turned up at the Savoy Ballroom for the 1 p.m. rehearsal; he never forgot that day:

Chick had about 600 and some numbers in the book, so I said, 'No, I can't make it.' They told me how he worked. He didn't have a set pattern, he'd call out a tune, then skip over to the back of the book, and pick one you hadn't rehearsed in two months. Now, they had never let any musician take the book home to practise, but I said, 'Just let me have the book.' Chick said, 'You look like a nice kid,' and so I took the music. In about a week's time I was ready. I was nervous but I was ready.[16]*

*Some discographies list Louis Jordan in Chick Webb's 1929 band; this is incorrect.

In 1936 Chick Webb's orchestra was one of the leading black bands in America. To have attained such success was a remarkable achievement for Webb, a tiny hunchback who suffered from tuberculosis of the spine and other health problems. He had been born into a poor black family in Baltimore, Maryland around 1909. Due to ill health, he virtually went without any formal schooling and never became fully literate. Working as a newspaper boy in his native city, he saved enough to buy himself a set of drums, and from that moment on his destiny was shaped and it was only a matter of time before he was in New York making his reputation.

With all the hardships he suffered, it is no surprise that Chick Webb turned out to be a highly complex adult, but no one could fault his perseverance and his almost magical ability to spark a listless band into a swinging ensemble. He was outspoken to an alarming degree and early in his career fell foul of the Musicians' Union for his candour 'in belittling other orchestras to ballroom proprietors in an effort to get work'. At a 1928 union hearing Webb was alleged to have vigorously criticized the Alhambra Ballroom manager's choice of band by telling him: 'A good orchestra was on the street and a hamfat bunch was working in there.'17

Webb could be kind; he paid guitarist John Trueheart's wages long after it became obvious that he was too sick to rejoin the band, and he footed the bill for Trueheart's long stay at a Saranac Lake, New York convalescent home. But Webb could also be cruel. After listening to the early efforts of Art Blakey (then a teenager) he said, 'You're a drummer?' Blakey said, 'Yeah. Would you give me some some help?' Chick Webb asked Blakey to make a roll on his drums. 'So I made a roll and he walked to the door carrying a little chihuahua in his hands and he looked at me and said, "Shit", slammed the door and walked out. I started crying, but I learned to make a roll. I guess I was about eighteen.'18

Chick Webb was also notably slow in paying his musicians, yet he inspired a burning loyalty in nearly everyone who worked with him, and gained plaudits from almost every other top-flight drummer. Two white percussionists, Gene Krupa and George Wettling, always placed Chick Webb first in any listing of their favourite drummers and black ace Cozy Cole told Dan Morgenstern: 'We'd all come to the Savoy Ballroom and stand around Chick and it seemed the more drummers that were around the better he'd play. He could roll on his bass drum with the foot pedal. He had a beautiful conception and a great band. He inspired all of us.'[19] In 1936 writer George T. Simon enthused, 'There's more swing per cubic inch in little Chick Webb than in anybody else in the whole wide world.'[20] The public at the vast Savoy Ballroom on Lenox Avenue in Harlem revered Chick's ability and fervently supported his band. The Savoy became known to journalists as 'The Home of Happy Feet', but musicians gave it a more prosaic nickname: 'The Track'.

At the time Louis Jordan joined Chick Webb the Savoy Ballroom had been open ten years. It was owned by the Gale family (formerly called the Galewskis); Moe Gale was also the manager of Chick's band. The Savoy Ballroom's manager, Charlie Buchanan, was black, as was about 90 per cent of the venue's audience. During the mid-1930s the ballroom (which held 4,000) opened early in the evening, but it was not until about 11 p.m. that the atmosphere achieved its renowned liveliness, and then things remained constantly vibrant until the 3 a.m. closing. Admission was usually fifty cents, but on special nights this was raised to seventy-five. Two bands were employed to provide continuous music, each playing half-hour sets, alternating from different bandstands.

Chick Webb's orchestra played several residencies each year at the Savoy, and the rest of the year was spent touring or playing the theatre circuits, notably one the musicians called 'the around-the-world tour' which consisted of a linked series of bookings at the Apollo, New York, the Howard in Washington, DC and the Royal in Baltimore, Maryland. The band's annual summer tour usually involved travelling for thousands of miles over the Southern states, where conditions were often daunting but the money earnt usually high.

Chick's band had just finished a tour when Louis joined them, so he was able to ease into his new job. There was a happy spirit within the group, and no rivalry between its singers: Charlie Linton (usually billed as 'The Silver-toned Tenor'), the trumpeter Taft Jordan and a young woman, not yet twenty, who had joined the band in 1935. Her name was Ella Fitzgerald and it did not take Louis long to realize that she was, by far, the most accomplished vocalist with whom he had ever worked. She was also the most consistently popular aspect of the band's presentations. Ella and Louis soon began what a Chick Webb sideman called 'a little love affair'.[21]

Louis, like Taft Jordan, had a double role in that he was an instrumentalist who was also a featured singer, but unlike Ella, Charlie Linton and Taft, Louis was never given billing by Chick Webb on the band's theatre dates. So when he returned to the Apollo (in October 1936) as a member of Chick's band, there was almost a sense of demotion because his name had always featured on the posters, and in the press advertisements when he had worked there with LeRoy Smith. It would be fair to say that Chick Webb never really took to Louis Jordan. Chick was an irrational man who often turned against people for no obvious reason, and something about Louis Jordan's personality jarred on Webb. It may have been nothing more than the emphatic way that Louis smiled, or it might have been that Jordan's mobile ebullience on stage irked the handicapped drummer. The reason might also, of course, have been simply that he did not particularly like the way that Louis played the alto saxophone and was unwilling to admit that it had been a mistake bringing him into the band.

Tenor saxist Teddy McRae, a long-time member of Chick's band, recalls the leader saying to him: 'What am I going to do with the guy? Got any ideas about a feature for him?' McRae replied, 'Let him sing that thing I used to do: "Vote for Me – the Mayor of Alabam'''. (This was a Frank Trumbauer number that McRae had done some time before.) 'So Louis did that and he worked hard at it. He was a barrel of fun – but you never knew anything about what he was thinking, or anything about his personal life. '[22]

Chick Webb soon became reluctant to feature Louis playing jazz on the alto sax. It had become obvious that, in this league of music, Louis did not quite have the *élan* and brilliance to lead the saxophone section. As Teddy McRae commented, 'Louis was a good alto player but he wasn't a first man. '[23] It was therefore decided that Louis's main instrumental work with Chick's band was to be as a baritone saxist in the section, his solos to be taken on clarinet and on soprano saxophone. The strategy worked, as Helen Oakley reported in the March 1937 issue of *Jazz Hot*: 'Louis Jordan plays fine clarinet and soprano saxophone.'

Louis was disappointed with the change of roles, but he accepted the situation. At this stage of his career he was a smooth-toned alto saxophonist. A good deal of his earlier roughness had been honed away during his stay in the refined surroundings of LeRoy Smith's orchestra, but the process had begun from the moment that Louis first heard Benny Carter play the alto. For a while Louis had copied Carter slavishly, but not too convincingly, which may not have pleased Chick Webb, who was a close friend of Benny's. In summarizing Louis's work with Chick Webb, critic Barry Ulanov wrote, 'Jordan was a good hot man, somewhat stereotyped in his ideas but contagiously enthusiastic and always driving.'[24]

While working in New York at the Savoy, Louis found another potent musical inspiration at the nearby Brittwood Club. There a lively trio was led by the rotund alto saxophonist Pete Brown, whose playing fascinated Louis. Brown created a wheezy, hoarse-toned style that was decidedly unacademic but tremendously rhythmic. His playing swung prodigiously and he seemed able spontaneously to create thousands of short, jumpy phrases that were exciting enough to get a Trappist monk yelling. Louis became an ardent fan of Pete Brown's playing, and so too, in later years, did many other eminent jazz saxophonists, including Flip Phillips and Paul Desmond.

One of the factors in Chick Webb's success was the large amount of air time his band received by means of their regular broadcasts (often as many as eight a week). Some were direct NBC 'wires' relayed from the Savoy Ballroom; others, such as 'Good Time Society', were regular weekly shows, as was 'Gems of Color', which was relayed (short wave) via Schenectady, New York to reach European listeners. This exposure was useful to Louis Jordan, who diligently learned as much as he could about microphone technique by asking more experienced performers such as Charlie Linton for advice.

Webb's band also had a recording contract with Decca, which meant they entered the studio approximately every eight weeks to produce new 78 r.p.m. discs that were usually on the market within weeks of being originally committed to the wax masters. In addition, Ella Fitzgerald had her own contract with Decca, and it was with Ella that Louis made his first records as a Chick Webb sideman. The role he played on Ella's recordings was usually as an unobtrusive sideman, and his part in the instrumental numbers that Chick Webb's orchestra recorded was scarcely more prominent.

Louis's first discernible appearance is as a singer on a January 1937 session where he, Ella and Charlie Linton form a bright-sounding vocal trio for a recording of 'There's Frost on the Moon'. Linton recalls: 'I think the arrangement of that number was by Edgar Sampson, but we were left to work out the vocal harmonies ourselves, the three of us, and we did so without any problems.'[25] On the other tune recorded that day, 'Gee but You're Swell', Louis takes the solo vocal. The tune is undistinguished, but so too is Louis's performance, being stilted (perhaps through his being over-careful); it has none of the charm and zest that were to become his forte.

What is apparent from most of these early Chick Webb sides is how sloppily the band often performed. They could be dynamic and exciting on fast numbers, but on the commercial offerings the playing within the sections is sometimes near woeful, with intonation being one of the principal weak points. Charlie Linton, as a vocalist, observed this from the sidelines; interestingly, he feels that the surfeit of radio work the band undertook meant that they spent more time preparing for their radio shows than their recordings, and suffered accordingly.

Chick Webb, because of his physical deformity, invariably remained behind the drums on stage, entrusting the job of presenting (and announcing) the band to the man he hired to be master of ceremonies, Bardu Ali (Bhadru Mohhamad Ali). Ali, who was born in the South of part-Egyptian parentage, was not a musician; he danced a bit, and told jokes passably well, but he was a good compère who also fulfilled the role of go-between when the musicians had a complaint to make. Bardu and Louis got on well together and Louis let it be known that he felt he was not being featured enough. Chick Webb heeded the complaint and on the next recording session (in March 1937) Louis sang on the first three numbers. His performance on 'Rusty Hinge' is bright and appealing, with clear glimpses of his personality shining through; on 'Wake Up and Live' he is part of a vocal trio (with Ella and Taft Jordan); and on 'It's Swell of You' he is again the featured vocalist, here defeated by the poor quality of the song.

Ella Fitzgerald took the three remaining vocals on the session, but

Louis's baritone sax playing is prominent on both the instrumental sides recorded that day: 'That Naughty Waltz' and 'Clap Hands Here Comes Charley' (where he is given a brief chance to display his skills as an improviser during a robust eight-bar solo).

Louis Jordan did not have a vastly inflated opinion of his own musical talents, but he was disappointed that he was granted only instrumental vignettes within Chick Webb's set-up. He was proud to be part of a 'name band' which recorded and broadcast regularly but he craved more features and came to the conclusion that the only way to improve the situation was to form his own band. Years later, Louis liked to give the impression that the idea of becoming a bandleader came to him suddenly, like an apocalyptic vision, but one senses that he had been storing away useful pointers for years.

Louis's ambition took definite shape through an incident that occurred at a Chick Webb rehearsal, as he later explained: 'We used to have rehearsals every Wednesday at one o'clock, so one day in between rehearsing we were playing records and I heard the Ambrose band and he used the timpanis to change keys. So I saved my money for about a year before I got them.'[26]

That a saxophone player in Harlem should have got an inspirational idea from a British band (led by Bert Ambrose) seems remarkable, but during the 1930s that band enjoyed a certain popularity in the States, and its records were often favourably reviewed in the American music magazines. In using the timpanis, Ambrose's arrangers (and his timpanist Jack Simpson) were only carrying forward ideas created by American percussionists such as Vic Berton and Chauncey Morehouse, who had recorded on timps (Carleton Coon – one of Louis's early favourites – had also played them).

Nevertheless, it was Ambrose's particular use of the large tunable drums (whose pitch can be altered by foot pedals) that inspired Louis to formulate long-term plans. He did not mention his aspirations to anyone except Ida, who immediately offered to put down a deposit on a set of timpani. This was done and they were gradually paid for by instalments. Louis meanwhile decided to bide his time in Chick Webb's band so that he could save enough capital to launch his own small group.

After a bout of work that saw them featured at the Apollo Theatre on three separate occasions during the first four months of 1937,

Chick Webb's band prepared themselves for an extraordinary engagement to be held at the Savoy Ballroom. The 'Swing Era' had begun in earnest, and one facet of that period was 'band battles', where two famous swing orchestras attempted to outplay each other in front of a ballroom audience. Contests between bands and rival soloists had been part of early jazz history, but often those battles were chance encounters where marching bands' routes clashed or where a belligerent soloist suddenly appeared at a rival's workplace. But the Swing Era battles were invariably pre-planned and well-publicized events, with promoters delightedly stimulating rivalry between the protagonists before upping the admission prices and dusting off the 'House Full' signs.

Chick Webb's band was fearsomely competitive when playing on its home ground, so when Benny Goodman, the white bandleader who had been dubbed 'The King of Swing', made it known through his agent that he was willing to do combat with Webb at the Savoy, the news attracted an immense amount of interest.

The contest took place on 12 May 1937. Four thousand lucky patrons got into the Savoy, but another five thousand disappointed people milled outside the ballroom in such a state of excitement that mounted policemen were called to control them, while another five officers were stationed on each bandstand to stop the exuberant audience from mobbing the musicians (a pre-taste – by some thirty years – of events at big rock concerts).

Chick Webb played the theme 'Jam Session' after Goodman had just completed his version of the piece, and Goodman countered by blasting into 'Big John's Special' to follow Webb's arrangement of the same tune. As usual, Chick inspired his men to raise their game, and as the evening wore on the Goodman band buckled under the musical onslaught emanating from the right-hand-side platform. The crowd, in doubt about the result for a long while, suddenly felt the Goodman outfit waver a little and knew that Chick Webb had triumphed again. Goodman's ace drummer, Gene Krupa said, 'I was never carved by a better player than tonight. He just cut me to ribbons.'[27]

For Louis Jordan it was a baptism by fire. He had been aware since an early age that playing jazz could be a competitive endeavour, but to be part of a big musical team locked in combat with another big ensemble was a new and exciting experience. He loved the atmosphere the battle engendered, but he, like all of the Webb sidemen, was disappointed that so little of the $4,550 taken at the Savoy's box office that evening reached him. As usual Moe Gale was the real winner. Chick Webb took a fair slice of the band's earnings, but the biggest percentage went in management and agency fees.

The band worked on a sliding scale which meant that star performers and long-serving members were paid most, but rarely did anyone earn more than a hundred dollars a week, and Louis's share was often nearer seventy-five. Of course, in this era, a cheap breakfast cost only a dime, and a lunch fifty cents; the average wage for a Post Office worker was $15 a week.[28] Because Moe Gale was making so much, the situation rankled, but Webb's men were slightly consoled by the knowledge that when other bands played residencies at the Savoy they were usually paid $37.50 per week, basic scale. However, in May 1937 the Chick Webb band were soon to embark on a long summer tour of the Southern states, where despite the hazards they were able to earn a lot more money. For Louis Jordan it was to be his first trip below the Mason-Dixon line for a long time.

# *Trouble Then Satisfaction*

Louis Jordan's feelings about the South were decidedly ambivalent. He had experienced indignities during his life there through segregation and racial injustice, yet there was always a bitter-sweet quality about his memories, and he frequently spoke of the good times he had had in his home state of Arkansas. Throughout his stay in Chick Webb's orchestra, Louis was in the habit of either remaining silent for long periods or being talkative; during the loquacious spells his colleagues could be fairly sure that some reference to Arkansas would seep into the conversation. Louis was, it seemed, a walking encyclopaedia on the subject of Arkansas folklore and often spoke of local remedies, omens, rhymes and superstitions. This attitude seemed out of place in someone as sharp as Louis and the incongruity led some of his fellow musicians to mock him for his absorption in early customs, but Louis had the strength of character to shrug off the derision with a smile. He was proud that he could make 'hot water corn bread' (an art his father had learnt in Mississippi and passed on to his son), and was always delighted to meet any black people from Arkansas, addressing them affectionately as 'home folks'. He was also happy to talk about his former days in the minstrel shows.

Most of the members of Chick Webb's band, in common with many of the black dwellers in the Northern states, were anxious not to adopt any attitudes that could be mistaken for an 'Uncle Tom' glorification of the bad old days, but one of Jordan's sayings was 'You must take the good with the bad' and he regarded his on-stage movements and gestures as simply being part of the tradition of black American theatricality. However, his fellow musicians in Webb's band were troubled by Louis's antics, and some called him 'Stepin

Fetchit' behind his back: a reference to the subservient roles that black actor Lincoln Perry played. Louis always countered any criticism of his stage mannerisms by pointing out that it was black audiences who laughed loudest at him, and so it was on the Webb band's 1937 Southern tour, but 'on the road' laughter was sometimes in short supply as the entourage hit a sequence of racial problems during their summer tour of the South.

One particular aspect of Webb's travelling party seemed to ignite resentment among certain white Southerners and this was the presence of Webb's white road manager, Frank Herz (Moe Gale's assistant). In 1937, a bus full of fashionably dressed black men would not have gone unnoticed in the South, but when one white face was visible on the same vehicle it signalled integration to people who were spoiling for trouble. The bus was stopped by a policeman in Houston, Texas for a minor traffic violation and Herz was asked what he was doing so far from home. When he gave the officers the reason for his visit he was told: 'You ought to be lynched for travelling with that bunch.'[1]

To avoid the discomfort of travelling long distances in the hired band bus, Bardu Ali drove his luxurious three-thousand-dollar car throughout the tour. In one town he was refused permission to park it next door to the hall where the band was working, being told: 'Niggers are not allowed to park here unless they are driving for a white man.'[2]

In his book *Listen to the Lambs*, Johnny Otis recounts Bardu Ali's anecdote about driving Chick Webb into a little town in Georgia. No service seemed forthcoming when Ali pulled up at a service station, though other customers were being attended to. Ali finally got mad enough to say: 'Well, I guess if white people had kept driving in here all day you would have kept me waiting all day?' 'That's right,' the assistant said. Ali was so frustrated he shouted, 'You act like you don't know who I am. DO YOU KNOW WHO I AM?' The man drawled. 'No, by God, I don't, who are you?' Ali bawled, 'I'm Duke Ellington, that's who.' The cracker thought for a minute and said, 'Shit, nigger, never heard of ya!' Chick Webb had been dozing under a blanket, and Ali admitted: 'I was praying that Chick was asleep and hadn't heard this. I'd never hear the end of it if he did.' Suddenly

Chick Webb's little voice said, 'Say man, for all the good it did you, you might as well have said Chick Webb.'

Chick Webb usually rode with Bardu Ali but sometimes travelled in the band bus, and on one of these occasions an incident occurred at another service station, involving the band's magnificent jazz trombonist Sandy Williams, who recounted the story to Stanley Dance:

> Chick would laugh at anything. He made me as hot as hell one time when we were in Texas. There you just ride, ride and ride. We had one of those big Greyhound buses and we stopped for about seventy-five gallons of gas and seven or eight quarts of oil. The bus had one of those big water coolers and everybody in the band was supposed to take his turn to fill it up with ice before we left town. That particular day, somebody had forgotten, and it was hot, hot. We all bought sandwiches and soda, but when you're thirsty after drinking you want water. A little old funny-looking woman had charge of this gas station. 'Madam,' I said to her, 'would you mind giving me a glass of water, please?' 'We don't give your kind no water down here,' she said. 'There's the river over there. Go help yourself.' Chick laughed like hell. That was funny to him, and then the guys started laughing too. It burnt me up. 'I'm going to quit the first big town we come to,' I told Chick. 'I'm going back home.'[3]

Fortunately Sandy Williams cooled down and remained for the rest of the tour. Most of the dances (held in ballrooms or in converted warehouses) were attended mainly by black patrons, but sometimes, where the audience was mixed (black and white), a rope across the middle of the dance floor ensured there was no racial mingling. At the City Auditorium in Galveston, Texas, this precaution was taken, but proved unnecessary – not a single white person turned up to hear the band.[4]

This was in stark contrast to some of the other engagements in Texas during the same tour. In Dallas the band gave a free concert in the 6,000-seater Amphi-Theater then played for a dance in the Exposition Ground's Agricultural Hall; this was billed as a 'Negro Dance', but hundreds of white swing fans went along. Another dance at a black ballroom in Fort Worth drew white followers, including several members of Paul Whiteman's orchestra (who were also working in Texas).

After leaving Texas, the Webb band zig-zagged through an itinerary that took it to Oklahoma (Muskogee, Oklahoma City and Tulsa), on to Greenville, Mississippi, then back to the North, where it played at Kimball's Ballroom in Boston, Massachusetts, before returning to New York City to fulfil a prestigious week-long booking (in September 1937) at Loew's State Theatre on Broadway. They were so successful that they were rebooked for the following month. Things were really looking up for the band, but the material progress did not please critic John Hammond, who had championed Chick Webb in earlier days. In November 1937 he wrote in *Down Beat*:

> At least partly because of Ella Fitzgerald the band is extremely popular these days, but I'm afraid its musicianship is far below the standard Chick ought to set for himself. Instead of giving the public the Swing it desires and the kind of stuff he can do best he bores them with the sweet genteel work of a saccharine male vocalist, elaborate badly scored 'white' arrangements, a 'comedian' saxophonist and an athletic director who jumps around but contributes not a whit to the musical proceedings.

The cast that John Hammond did not name was Charlie Linton (singer), Louis Jordan (comedian), and Bardu Ali (athletic director). The arrangements were by Al Feldman, a young white musician then in his early twenties, who was later to gain fame as composer and bandleader Van Alexander. Feldman scored many of Ella Fitzgerald's recorded arrangements, and he and Ella collaborated on the 1938 hit 'A Tisket a Tasket'.

Ella's close friendship with Louis Jordan was proving irksome to Chick Webb. Chick, who was happily married to Sally, had no romantic designs on Ella, but he felt that any romances within his band would eventually bring heartaches and affect work. He had expressly asked his musicians to bear this in mind when Ella joined the band; most of the sidemen tolerated Ella off-stage but none of them envisaged her as a partner. When Louis joined he soon became openly flirtatious with Ella and she responded to a degree that caused onlookers to realize that a love affair was on the cards. One sideman later commented: 'We couldn't understand this at all. Louis was a sharp, good-looking cat and he was making up to Ella. In those days she was quite a gawky girl, who, it must be said, was real plain.'

Chick Webb's health was deteriorating, and he was often too ill to play the drums for an entire evening. Various deputy drummers played the first set of the evening, which allowed time for Chick to rest and brood. He became angry about the Ella–Louis relationship, but instead of talking the issue over with the couple he projected his annoyance into criticizing Louis on musical issues. The lack of alto sax solos within the band continued, and was commented on by reviewers. Throughout the latter part of 1937 Louis's only brief moment of glory on record is a bustling eight-bar clarinet solo on 'Harlem Congo'. Looking back, Louis commented, 'I still got a chance to sing, I did "I've Got You under My Skin", and played soprano in "The Mayor of Alabam", and did a tune called "Rusty Hinge".'[5]

But despite this aura of animosity there were still exciting times to be had on the bandstand when Chick's musicians moved into top gear. Chick Webb knew better than anyone if the group was on form, and said, 'When I'm at the drums and I feel the band thick and strong around me, we're swinging.'[6] After playing in Chicago at the RKO-Palace Theatre and touring through Tennessee and Ohio the band began another stint at the Savoy Ballroom. On 16 January 1938 they were involved in another celebrated 'battle of the bands', this time vying with Count Basie's orchestra, whose reputation had been growing since their arrival in New York (from Kansas City) in late 1936. Publicists stoked the fans' interest in the coming battle, and one writer suggested that there was a feud between Webb and Basie caused by Webb innocently offering Basie a job in his band when the Count's own orchestra was already well established.

The combat took place on the same night as Benny Goodman's historic concert at New York's Carnegie Hall, and many of the participants in that show made their way up to the Savoy to enjoy an exciting but even contest. One of these visitors was Duke Ellington, who was lifted on to the stage by excited well-wishers and responded by playing a number with Basie's band, performing, according to one reviewer, 'some down-to-earth, gut-bucket keyboard thumping'.[7]

Fortunately Duke Ellington did not bring his band, which was the one unit that Chick Webb feared musically. On an earlier encounter at the Savoy (in March 1937) Chick forlornly admitted defeat as the Ellington crew romped through their unique arrangements, and on that occasion he said, 'I can't take it. This is the first time we've ever been washed out.'[8]

Ella Fitzgerald played only a subsidiary part in these band battles, contributing a few vocal numbers that allowed the band a chance to catch their breath and prepare for the next musical onslaught, but Ella's singing was, by early 1938, the main factor in the marketing of Chick Webb's orchestra. With both the public and booking agents becoming increasingly aware of her extraordinary vocal talents, Moe Gale began receiving offers for the band to play sophisticated venues that had previously shown no interest in booking Chick Webb. One of these, in Boston, was a nightclub owned by Jack Levaggi. Levaggi was used to booking solid commercial successes such as Guy Lombardo's orchestra to play for his club's audiences, which usually contained a fair sprinkling of students from Harvard University. This policy gradually caused business to diminish as more and more young people became interested in the music of the swing bands.

Jack Levaggi therefore decided to take a chance on Chick Webb's orchestra, and signed them for a month from 7 February 1938, with an option that allowed him to renew the booking month by month. He also agreed that Webb's band could be absent from the club for two nights during the first month to allow it to play for a previously contracted Spring Dance at Yale University (Teddy Hill's orchestra filled in at Levaggi's during this brief hiatus).

Ella Fitzgerald, in particular, registered an enormous success with the patrons of Levaggi's Flamingo Room and, mostly by word of mouth, the venue temporarily became one of Boston's most popular nightspots; Levaggi renewed his option and extended the booking until 2 May. Unfortunately Chick Webb's health worsened and early in April it became necessary for him to enter hospital for surgery. An able deputy, Arnold 'Scrippy' Boling (who had frequently substituted for Chick) took over the drum duties, and, as Bardu Ali was not available, the task of fronting the band was generally shared by Taft and Louis Jordan.

It was not a case of 'when the cat's away the mice will play'; rather it was that the band, determined not to let Chick Webb down, redoubled their efforts to entertain the crowd, and this enthusiasm immediately reached the audience. Scrippy Boling (who was one of Chick's greatest fans) was also an extrovert and at Levaggi's he projected his skills by boldly leaving the bandstand to beat his drumsticks on the table tops; the crowd loved it. Louis Jordan went down on to the dance floor to do a cabaret spot, re-creating the Deacon Jones preaching act that he had seen performed on the minstrel circuits; he was so funny the audience went wild with delight. Beverly Peer recalls, 'I've got a clear picture of us playing "Alexander's Ragtime Band" at that club, with "Scrippy" tapping his drumsticks on the wall, then we'd finish up by marching all around the club. Louis Jordan playing soprano sax and me playing my King double B-flat tuba.'[9] Levaggi's became increasingly crowded as people flocked to the Flamingo Room. George Frazier, a noted local critic with a reputation for being extremely candid, wrote, 'The informal floor show that the band stages nightly should convince Tim and Moe Gale that the band packs a world of showmanship.'[10]

Chick Webb, out of hospital but feeling far from well, made his way to Boston to resume his place in the orchestra. He noticed that his musicians and Ella were more pleased to see him back than Jack Levaggi was, and he had no sooner taken his coat off than Levaggi told him that he was not going to pay a full salary for the period of Webb's absence.[11] This annoyed Chick, but he controlled his anger. However, he shook with fury when he learned the news (from an informer) that Louis was intent on starting his own band, and had already made tentative offers to trumpeter Taft Jordan, bassist Beverly Peer and to Ella Fitzgerald. Louis's wooing overtures to Ella now made complete sense to all of Chick's sidemen. Chick also heard that Ella and Louis had been involved in a violent altercation after Ella had rejected a manicure set that Louis had bought for her. Louis's wife, Ida, also became aware of the squabble, and subsequently gave the details: 'Louis was messing around with Ella. He bought her some fingernail scissors. It wasn't what she wanted so she threw them on the floor and he hit her and she hit him right back.'[12]

Chick surmised that the three who had been approached by Louis would remain loyal to him. His forecast proved correct, but this did not diminish the anger he felt towards Louis Jordan. Nevertheless, he decided to bottle his feelings until the booking at Levaggi's ended, in case he gave the club owner further leeway to reduce the overall salary. Saxophonist Garvin Bushell recalled the dismissal scene between Webb and Jordan: 'In the summer of 1938 we were at the RKO in Boston when Chick decided to get rid of Louis without giving notice. Louis was always hollering, "If you don't like what I do, fire me!" I heard this down the hall, after the show. I remember Chick said, "Well, that's exactly what I'm going to do."'13

Louis's pride was severely bruised by the manner of his dismissal from Chick Webb's orchestra, and for the rest of his career he told interviewers that he had remained in the band until Webb's death. Sadly, the diminutive drummer did not have long to live after he and Louis parted company, dying in June 1939, just over a year after he dismissed Louis. At the time of their parting, Louis could not bring himself to take into account Chick Webb's enormous pride and his unpredictable character (one sideman called Chick 'a Jekyll and Hyde personality'). Chick was genuinely wounded to discover that one of his musicians actually felt that he would be happier leading his own band than being a Webb sideman, and he was furious that the same person had attempted to take away the main reason for his growing success: Ella Fitzgerald.

In truth there was something a little madcap about Louis Jordan's initial plans to form a band; he had no definite offers of work and insufficient money to buy uniforms, arrangements and band photographs, yet he seriously proposed that Ella Fitzgerald, then a rising star and earning enough to begin indulging in various luxuries, should abandon the prospects that she had worked so hard to achieve. He genuinely imagined that Taft Jordan, a well paid and featured soloist, was going to leave a lucrative job to join someone with virtually no experience of leading a band. The third of Louis's selections, bassist Beverly Peer, renowned for his honesty, recalled the whole busines in detail:

> When Louis was planning to form his own band he may have thought it was a secret but to everyone else it was obvious. He began collecting suitable tunes, and sounding out guys in the band, asking if they would go with him. He and Ella were pretty close at the time and he was definitely trying to corral her in his great plans

for a band. But Louis was always for Louis, he was aggressive and always scheming. I can remember lending him money when he lost it gambling. So when he asked me if I was interested in joining his band I said, 'There's no way I'm going to leave Chick to go with you.' I don't think he ever forgave me.[14]

Chick Webb relented sufficiently to allow Louis to work out his two weeks' notice, which meant that he left the band when they returned to New York in May 1938. Eventually Louis was able to say of Webb, 'Chick was the greatest drummer who ever lived, and the band was an inspiration,' but for some while after his dismissal he did not harbour many kind thoughts about his former bandleader, especially when he discovered that Chick had released the news to journalists that saxophonist Hilton Jefferson would be rejoining the band *before* he got around to telling Louis that he was fired.

Two people in New York City were anxiously waiting to see Louis to ascertain what his immediate plans were. One was his erstwhile drummer, Walter Martin, who had been taking lessons on the timpani from Saul Goodman of the New York Philharmonic Orchestra, so that he could be ready to fulfil the role of percussionist in Louis's new band. The other was Ida Jordan, who had paid a deposit to secure the timpani (and had kept up the instalment payments while Louis had been in Boston). Louis spoke of the expense years later: 'They cost eleven hundred dollars* for two of them. In the meantime I had my drummer take lessons to learn how to use them. So by the time I had paid for them he had learned to use them.'[15]

Louis assured Walter Martin and Ida that he had no intention of abandoning his plans despite the early setback over his choice of personnel. But Ida could see that Louis was wavering so she took command of the situation:

I was the one that rushed him all the time. I already knew how to get around because I had been working in theatres. I found the musicians for Louis; they had played for me when I was dancing.

*Ida said that she purchased them from Manny's on 48th Street, New York, for 150 dollars.

We could only rehearse in the Amsterdam Club, around 30th Street, but there was no piano, so I bought a piano from Powell's for seventy-five dollars (at a dollar a week), and uniforms and stands. I spent all my money on Louis, I bought him a blue serge suit for thirty-five dollars. I had a telephone put in Louis's name, ten deposit and three dollars fifty cents for installation. I was making twenty dollars a night as a dancer. I went up and told an agent I had an expensive band and he said, 'You're either crazy or you've got something.'[16]

At the Jordans' apartment (2135 7th Avenue in Harlem), Louis kept up his solitary practice routine. Ida recalled,

He would go in the room and fasten the door. When I knocked on the door he'd have a fit. If he was rehearsing his saxophone he'd holler, 'Honey come in and let the window down.' He wouldn't even reach over and let the window down. I got tired of him slapping me around, and I said, 'I'm going to leave you.' He said, 'Don't leave me. I can't make it without you.' He liked to gamble. He used to play tonk, and I think he lost most of his money like that. Louis was very sick. He was ruptured real bad. If I'd known he was that sick I wouldn't have married him. He had to wear that truss all the time. He wasn't much service to no one. When he went to the doctor he made me wait outside. I was very unhappy, but I wouldn't leave nobody when they need you.[17]

The three founder members of Louis's first group were the drummer Walter Martin, the Texan trumpeter Chester Boone (who had arrived in New York in 1937 after working in various territory bands) and pianist Clarence Johnson (originally from Massachusetts). Louis and Ida did their best to rustle up work for the band but nothing positive emerged. At this time, Louis's publicity billing was a trifle quaint; it read 'LOUIS JORDAN, HIS SILVER SAXOPHONE AND HIS GOLDEN VOICE', and for a time (until he was dissuaded from doing so) he described himself as 'THE MODERN BERT WILLIAMS'. He still retained an affection for Williams's work. His comic titles for songs such as 'Eve Cost Adam Just One Bone',

'Lonesome Alimony Blues' and 'Moon Shines on the Moon Shine' appealed to Louis's sense of humour.

To keep the wolf from the door Louis took a job playing lead alto sax in a band led by pianist Edgar Hayes. He rehearsed with Hayes's group at the Renaissance Ballroom and played various engagements with them in and around New York City. His final dates with the band were at the Apollo Theatre, for a week commencing 15 July 1938. There, Louis was featured singing 'Flat Foot Floogie' (a recent hit by Slim Gaillard and Slam Stewart).

While at the Apollo, Louis had a chance to talk with Ralph Cooper (who was topping the bill that week). Cooper, who also had a hand in fixing entertainment for various clubs in Harlem, advised Louis that the Elks Rendezvous on Lenox Avenue was auditioning for a new resident band. Louis called in to see the club's owner, John Barone, then rounded up his musicians, and passed the audition with flying colours. The vacancy was only for a quartet, so Louis's first regular group was launched as Louis Jordan's Tympany* Four.[18] It began work at the Elks Rendezvous (close to the Savoy Ballroom) on 4 August 1938.

---

*The correct spelling should have been 'Timpani'; the error was perpetuated in most of Louis Jordan's subsequent publicity.

# 5
## Keep A-Knockin'

The Elks Rendezvous (464 Lenox Avenue at 133rd Street) was one of many small clubs that flourished in Harlem during the late 1930s. The repeal of Prohibition in 1933 and the economic improvements of the post-Depression years meant that visits to such places became a regular part of ordinary people's lives. They went to such clubs to drink and eat, to dance, and to enjoy a cabaret. There was nothing highbrow about most of these nightspots, but customers made a point of looking as fashionably smart as they could, and few audiences, anywhere, were as cheerfully determined to enjoy themselves. Usually the music was provided by a small rhythmic group (featuring a trumpet and a saxophone); these outfits were originally called 'jump' bands, because their music made the customers want to jump and dance.

At the Elks Rendezvous the first of three nightly shows began at 10 p.m. First, Louis Jordan's Tympany Four played for dancing, then Louis did his own cabaret feature (which often included impersonations of other singers); a compère (such as Danny Henry or Allen Drew) announced the individual acts. Some of these, like singer Rodney Sturgis, were local favourites and appeared there often, but most of the six available slots in the show were changed regularly. Louis's band accompanied these various cabaret acts, and again played for dancing (about fifteen couples could squeeze on to the tiny dance space) until the club closed somewhere around 4 a.m. (3 a.m. on Saturdays because of a law relating to the sale of liquor on Sundays).

The clientele, black and white, from all walks of life, took to Louis Jordan, and so too did Dan Burley (1907–62), a black journalist who was also a pianist and a composer. Burley was in the habit of calling into the Elks on his late-night news-gathering rounds. Through his own experiences as a musician he recognized Louis's talent on saxophone and vocals and liked the neat way the band phrased together. The timps were something of a gimmick, but overall it seemed to Dan Burley that there were many worse groups on record, so he recommended them to J. Mayo Williams, a black talent scout and recording manager for Decca. Burley's favourable mention was endorsed by two recording artists, Coot Grant and Sox Wilson.

Williams went to the Elks Rendezvous and he too was impressed, but felt that a string bass and a tenor saxophone needed to be added to the group before any recordings could be made. Decca had already recorded the Elks' vocalist, Rodney Sturgis, who was due for another studio session, so Williams decided it would be advantageous to use Jordan's group to back the singer, enabling him to hear how they sounded in the studio before he formulated any long-term plans. Somewhat prematurely, the *New York Amsterdam News* announced, in its issue of 15 October 1938: 'JUMP BAND WILL RECORD. Described as one of Harlem's hottest small combinations, Louis Jordan's orchestra is due for a recording date with Decca soon: Chester Boone (trumpet), Clarence Johnson (piano), Louis Jordan (leader and saxophone) and Walter Martin (drums). The band plays at the Elks.'

But Louis Jordan, showing the acumen that was to make him into such a successful bandleader, had no wish to be rushed into making the all-important debut recordings – he wanted his band rehearsed to perfection first. Louis was already in the habit of calling frequent rehearsals, and these were in addition to the regular weekly run-throughs at which the band familiarized themselves with the music parts provided by the various cabaret artistes. Louis even spent time organizing routines that would increase the band's showmanship. Trumpeter Chester Boone, feeling that the band was over-rehearsed and under-paid, decided to move on to new pastures.

Boone's replacement on trumpet was a twenty-two-year-old from New Jersey, Courtney Williams, already an accomplished arranger. By the time the changeover of trumpeters occurred, Louis had persuaded the club's owner, John Barone, to increase the money so that he could also hire bassist Charlie Drayton. Courtney Williams recalled the period:

I had come off the road after a tour with Fats Waller's big band and I heard that Louis Jordan was looking for a trumpet player to take the place of Chester Boone. I think it was common knowledge that Louis really wanted Taft Jordan, but Taft wouldn't leave Chick Webb. So I went along and talked things over with Louis, did an audition and joined as trumpeter and arranger. The owner was an Italian, John Barone; he looked something like Edward G. Robinson, but he was a very pleasant man and friendly towards the musicians. My lasting memory of him is seeing him eating a giant bowl of salad while he listened to us rehearse. He definitely liked the music and he sat there contentedly eating the salad. It was Louis Jordan's first residency with the band and he was very anxious to succeed. He was nice to me; off-stage he was rather quiet, not at all rowdy. He wasn't highly educated, but he was gentlemanly, and he was a good musician. He could read any music that was put in front of him, and was a fine player on alto sax, clarinet and baritone.[1]

Few bandleaders could have been keener than Louis Jordan. He continued to rehearse endlessly, and was always searching for new songs and new ways of getting them across to his public. Looking back, Louis said, 'See, before I got a band I knew what I wanted to do with it. I wanted to give my whole life to making people enjoy my music. Make them laugh and smile. So I didn't stick to what you'd call jazz. I have always stuck to entertainment.'[2]

Louis's wife was also determined that Louis was going to succeed, as Courtney Williams emphasized:

Ida was ambitious for Louis. She had been a singer and dancer and understood the business. The band worked well together; the drummer Walter Martin was an intelligent man – a bachelor who kept to himself socially – but once in a while he'd drink too many boiler-makers (consisting of a gin short and a beer chaser) then he'd stand up behind his drums and make a statement about the world, giving out unsolicited advice to the customers. Louis would have to turn around sharply and say, 'Sit down and shut up,' but things soon got smoothed over. The pianist Clarence Johnson (from Boston) also liked a drink and sometimes I'd sort of act as a chaperone to make sure he didn't have too many.

When Louis felt that the band was nearing the standard he wanted to present on record, he contacted J. Mayo Williams and acquiesced to the suggestion about adding tenor saxophonist Lem Johnson to the group (just for the recording). As a compromise to John Barone, Jordan agreed to the group being described on the record label as 'The Louie Jordan Elks Rendezvous Band'. The spelling 'Louie' was stipulated by Jordan himself; he had grown weary of people pronouncing his name as 'Lewis', and for a time in the 1930s he always signed his name (even on contracts) as 'Louie'.[4]

Finally, on 29 December 1938, over two months after the initial press announcement, Louis Jordan took his band into the recording studio. The first task of the day was to record 'Toodle-Loo on Down' – a tune by Rodney Sturgis in which the session organizer J. Mayo Williams, had a half share. One suspects that Sturgis had arrived at the studio owning a hundred per cent of the composition but thought it advantageous to give half of the rights to Williams. He may even have had no option about making such a donation; the prospect of gaining money from royalties still induced many entrepreneurial figures in the record industry to get their names on songs that had already been completed.

Sturgis kept all of the rights on two of his other compositions recorded that day, 'So Good' and 'Away from You'. All of his vocals reveal him as a competent club singer, with no great originality. The band perform their accompaniment neatly, and on 'So Good' Louis takes a well-executed alto solo, which opens with a phrase that later turned up as the theme of a Frankie Newton tune, 'Parallel Fifths'. The rhythmic placement of Louis's notes is highly effective and the general shaping of his phrases excellent.

The final two tracks of the day featured the band without Sturgis. 'Honey in the Bee Ball' was, for a time, the band's theme song, written by Louis Jordan and based on a children's game popular in Arkansas. The band's painstaking rehearsals had melded it into an impressive unit, with close attention paid to phrasing and to dynamics. Interesting tone colours are created by Lem Johnson doubling on clarinet and Louis doubling on baritone sax. The main inspiration for the band is the John Kirby Sextet, a small group led by bassist John Kirby then enjoying great popularity in New York. Jordan's group make use of certain effects featured by Kirby, including the muted trumpet lead, the close scoring for the front line, similar bridge passages and a tendency for the drummer to utilize brushes instead of sticks. Jordan does not copy Kirby's alto sax player, Russell Procope, but plays a markedly similar role. Louis sings the thirty-two-bar vocal pleasantly, and Lem Johnson creates a well-devised tenor sax solo, but nothing about the record augurs immortality.

The best moments from the entire session are provided by the bold phrases that Louis, on baritone sax, blows on the introduction of a comedy offering, 'Barnacle Bill the Sailor'. After a cheerful vocal from Louis, complete with high-pitched answers from the musicians, the band again drifts into John Kirby waters. Louis's alto again fulfils a Procope role, and he also adds a dash of Pete Brown and a shade of Benny Carter, showing that he was drawing on various influences in developing his own originality.

So a new band-leading name was added to the record catalogues, but along with most releases by contemporary black artistes Louis Jordan's discs were issued in the 'Race Record' series. In the 78 r.p.m. era, the break-even figure for a double-sided recording by a small band was low. Sales of a few thousand usually meant that the company had paid for the pressings of the disc, the printing of the labels, the advertising, the recording manager's services (often a staff man) and allocated the thirty dollars apiece union-agreed musicians' fees (double for the leader). Decca easily covered their outlay on Louis Jordan's original recordings and J. Mayo Williams was given permission by the recording company's supremo, Jack Kapp, to go ahead and book them for another session in March 1939, this time without Rodney Sturgis.

Exactly the same personnel (but this time billed as Louis Jordan and His Tympany Five) assembled on 29 March and cut six sides, which serve to show how versatile the band was. The numbers include an evocative instrumental blues, on which the timpani are used as a sparing, and not totally appropriate, tone colour, and here Louis plays two intensely effective alto choruses. On 'Keep A-Knockin' (a close cousin of the old favourite 'My Bucket's Got a Hole in It') Louis gives early indications of his appealing vocal personality. The happy-sounding 'Sam Jones Done Snagged His Britches' is followed by 'Swinging in a Cocoanut Tree' with its hints of Caribbean rhythms and some heavy-handed piano playing. The best number from the date, 'Doug the Jitterbug', is a bouncy song dynamically sung by Louis. Here the timps are genuinely effective, and Louis's fine alto solo is a model of swing and spirit. The remaining number, a swift 'At the Swing Cat's Ball', is a compendium of the stock 'licks' that figured on dozens of small-band recordings of this period, but its saving grace is a fine Jordan vocal, the first of many in which he was to extol the goings-on at an ultra-lively party.

Decca found the sales figures from this batch of recordings positively encouraging, with 'Keep A-Knockin'' becoming a localized minor hit (much to the joy of its composer, veteran Perry Bradford); it even attracted a cover version by the successful white bandleader Jimmy Dorsey. 'Flat Face' was issued in Britain and was picked by the Number One Rhythm Club as its top disc of November 1939.[5] 'Doug the Jitterbug', also issued in Britain, made jazz fans there fully aware of Louis Jordan's prowess both on alto sax and as a vocalist.

A radio line had been installed at the Elks Rendezvous, which meant that Louis Jordan's band could broadcast live on Station WNEW, Mondays and Fridays at 11.30 p.m. Most of these transmissions were beamed only to the immediate locale, but as the radius of the station included all of Manhattan, the effect on record sales was considerable. Various disc jockeys, including Martin Block on WNEW, began including an occasional Louis Jordan record in their programmes, and this also helped establish the name.

Popular though Jordan's band was at the Elks, neither John Barone nor Louis wanted the group to wear out its welcome, so by mutual consent Louis and the group temporarily moved further along Lenox Avenue to number 115 (at 116th Street) to work at Barone's other club, the New Capitol Cabaret, from where they continued to broadcast on WNEW (but on Thursdays from 11.30 until midnight). At the New Capitol, inspired one suspects by the similar billing previously given to John Kirby's band, the group was billed as 'The World's Biggest Little Band'.[6] Frankie Newton's band moved in to fill the vacancy at the Elks Rendezvous. Louis's line-up remained the same as he had used at the Elks, but a new freelance tenor saxophonist, Stafford 'Pazuza' Simon, was brought into the group for its next recording session in November 1939.

'Pazuza' was no jazz almighty, but he was a good, straight-down-the-line tenor saxist with a buxom tone, who (like Johnson before him) was called on to double on clarinet. He and Louis share a brief clarinet duet on "Fore Day Blues', a vocal twelve-bar theme sung somewhat unconvincingly by Louis, who sounds as though he was unable to make up his mind whether to be jocular or 'ethnic'. Courtney Williams solos well, as he does throughout the whole series of Jordan's recordings; nothing spectacular emerges from his horn, but there is a nice flow of pertinent ideas and (as might be expected from an arranger) an impressive sense of form in his improvisations.

Louis Jordan does not solo on the brisk 'Jake, What a Snake', which is again very Kirbyish, or on 'Honeysuckle Rose', where he takes an almost 'camp' vocal, redeemed by the skilful emphasising of various nuances within the lyric. As usual his diction and sense of pitch are exemplary – one feels this was one of his 'visual' productions. Jordan's vocal flexibility is also apparent during his own up-tempo composition 'But I'll be Back'; the half-chorus solo on alto sax is a gem. Louis's vocal on 'You Ain't Nowhere' (which he co-composed with bandleader Don Redman) is smooth and convincingly sardonic, and as a bonus he plays a baritone sax solo. The final track of the day, 'You're My Meat' (by another bandleader, Skeets Tolbert) contains a vocal message that was often featured in Louis's future repertoire. Here it takes the form of a lyrical assurance to those ladies who are no longer young ('fat and forty' he sings) yet still remain desirable. On stage this sort of number gave Louis the chance to project the sassy gestures that bowled women over, whatever their age and dimensions.

During the late 1930s, a sizeable proportion of the fans who had gone wild over the powerhouse music of the big swing bands became keener to listen to small jazz-orientated groups. An extrovert sextet led by violinist 'Stuff' Smith (featuring the irrepressible trumpet playing of Jonah Jones) won many fans with its blend of hot jazz and impromptu showmanship. Fats Waller, backed by a small group, picked up enormous record sales, and in so doing inspired other vocalists, such as Bob Howard and Putney Dandridge, to copy his example. Other small bands like Muggsy Spanier's Ragtimers catered for those listeners who wanted a return to the old values of Dixieland, but the most unexpected success of the period was achieved by John Kirby's sextet, playing ingenious arrangements, and commanding attention by frequently playing at the level of a musical whisper. After a two-year stay at New York's Onyx Club, the Kirby band began playing lucrative and exclusive venues such as the New York Waldorf-Astoria, gaining engagements where no black groups had ever been booked before. They also did similar trailblazing by being one of the first black groups to get its own sponsored radio series. Vocal numbers (usually sung by the drummer O'Neil Spencer) formed only a tiny part of a huge repertoire.

Observing this success had led Louis Jordan to develop an ambition to base his band sound on Kirby's but also to develop a more general appeal by featuring a whole range of songs and to present the music with unashamedly overt showmanship. By 1940, Louis was quietly confident that his method was gradually succeeding. It was not that he ever aped Kirby's band musically, or sartorially – the Kirby band wore white tie and tails and Louis's group light tuxedos and black pants – but he often asked Kirby for advice. John Kirby was one of the few new friends that Louis made during this period, and the two musicians would often meet after they had finished work to eat soul food at a ribs restaurant opened at 110 West 52nd Street by Benny Goodman's brother, Harry.

One subject bound to come up at these dawn meetings was Chick Webb (who had died in Baltimore on 16 June 1939). John Kirby had been one of the cornerstones of Chick Webb's band in the early 1930s, and he had worked with the drummer through thick and thin until 1936, when Chick turned against him on the grounds (Kirby later discovered) that a new member of the outfit had convinced him that a hex (or evil spell) was on the band because of Kirby's presence. The two ex-Chick Webb sidemen got on well. Kirby, who had experienced a tough upbringing in Baltimore, had suffered a series of disasters before finding success as a bass player. He was likeable and, never having enjoyed much formal schooling, made no attempt to lord it over Louis, who was thus able to relax in Kirby's company.

But Louis Jordan had gleaned musical ideas from many sources before he ever formed the Tympany Five, and the inspiration he got from Kirby's band only helped him to conceive an overall sound for his group. Another Arkansas musician, trombonist Leo 'Snub' Mosley (from Little Rock), firmly believed that Louis gained a lot by listening to the band that he, Snub, led in New York. He openly said:

I was Louis Jordan's inspiration. My idea was to have this small band with arrangements like Alphonso Trent's, on the idea of entertainment, singing and playing – like Jimmie Lunceford. We got going in the latter part of 1937, at a downtown club called the Club Afrique, 43rd and 8th Avenue. We were downstairs. Louis Jordan was still with Chick Webb but he came down there and listened. I was entertaining – then he started that stuff, but he got famous on it.[7]

Snub Mosley may have indeed provided Louis Jordan with twigs for his musical nest, but Snub must have realized that Louis was familiar with Alphonso Trent's presentations, having seen that band often in Arkansas (Trent was from Fort Smith), and having worked with several ex-Trent sidemen. Looking back years later, Louis cited his own reasons for his success: 'Generally a black artist at that time would either stick to the blues or do pop. I did everything.'[8]

Decca, increasingly delighted with the sales figures Jordan was achieving, stepped up the frequency of the Tympany Five sessions; during the first part of 1940 they recorded in January, March and April. For Louis the task of finding new material, getting it arranged (usually by Courtney Williams), then rehearsing it endlessly before entering the recording studio was very time-consuming. He was also, of course, busily occupied with his club work and with an increasing number of outside engagements, which the band played on their nights off from the Elks or the New Capitol. One such booking in January 1940 was at the Speedway Gardens (at the uptown end of the Harlem River); the band also worked as the relief group at the Café Society nightclub on Monday nights.

On their January 1940 recordings, Stafford 'Pazuza' Simon augmented the group as before. The opening piece, 'June Teenth Jamboree' was written by Texan pianist Sammy Price in honour of the annual 19 June celebrations that take place in his state (and in Arkansas) to commemorate President Lincoln's Emancipation Proclamation. Louis sings the song with real enthusiasm and plays a supple alto sax solo, punching out brief, highly rhythmic figures and boldly spicing his phrases with telling blue notes. The cleverly scored ending has an attractive boogie-ish feel.

Next, Louis recorded a song written by Lillian Hardin Armstrong,

'You Run Your Mouth and I'll Run My Business' (subsequently Louis
Armstrong showed there was no ill feeling towards his ex-wife by
also recording the piece). Jordan's version is full of effective
vocalized acting, and complete with a spoken tag 'Do You Dig Me
Jack?', *à la* Fats Waller. 'I'm Alabama Bound', shows how
marvellously relaxed Jordan's vocals were at a fast tempo – a skill
born of his super-fine sense of rhythm. The song (not to be confused
with the 1920s hit 'Alabamy Bound' by De Sylva, Green and
Henderson) was an ancient one that Jelly Roll Morton claimed as his
composition,[9] though it was copyrighted by another New Orleans
composer, Robert Hoffman, in 1909. Something made Morton
change his mind about claiming it as his work, but he took a section
from the piece and recorded it in 1939 as 'Don't You Leave Me Here'.
On Jordan's record Walter Martin's drumming is a model of vigour
and swing and he cleverly negotiates the final move into half-tempo.
The arrangement is effective, particularly the crisp trumpet and
tenor sax answers, but the piano is practically inaudible.

The oddity of the date was the final title, 'Hard Lovin' Blues',
which features the voice of Yack Taylor, an authentic-sounding
female blues singer, whose five choruses form the bulk of the record,
the only other section being a four-bar introduction (and coda)
played by trumpet and two clarinets. But each of the absorbing vocal
choruses is enriched by Jordan's superbly apt clarinet phrases, most
delivered in the warm-sounding chalumeau register of the instrument. The majority are softly played but (in the manner of an
exemplary accompanist) Louis changes register to follow the nuances
of the vocalist's line. The stark qualities of the track are highlighted
by the absence of piano, which places an effective emphasis on
Charlie Drayton's accurate, pulsating bass notes.

Undoubtedly this blues vocal had been incorporated into Louis
Jordan's session at the behest of J. Mayo Williams. Almost as a
backwash of the Harlem Renaissance (which had stimulated
widespread interest in black literature and art), there developed a
Blues Renaissance in the 1930s, and the key figure in this movement
was J. Mayo Williams, who was recording dozens of blues artists for
Decca.

Williams, the first black executive to work for a white recording
company, was a controversial character whose business ethics

enraged some of the people he recorded. Alberta Hunter was vehement about him; 'He was swiping my money,' she said. Alberta had recorded for Williams when he was the manager of the Paramount 'Race Series' (from 1923 until 1927), and she felt certain that he had collected royalties due to her without passing them on.[10] To balance this there is Sammy Price's view that Williams was a genius, the man who changed the world's conception of blues music. Williams assessed himself by saying. 'I've been better than 50 per cent honest, which in this business is pretty good.'[11] Williams certainly played a big part in the selection of material that Louis Jordan recorded and told Clyde Bernhardt; 'I'll fix it with Louis Jordan to record your songs. They fit him good.'[12] According to one black musician, Williams 'played the horses and drank a lot'.[13]

Born in Monmouth, Illinois in 1894, Williams (known as 'Ink') attended Brown University, Rhode Island, and played professionally for a Hammond, Indiana black team in the National Football League before becoming recording director of Paramount Records. He operated his own Black Patti label in 1927 prior to working for Decca and Vocalion, where he was responsible for organizing recording sessions for many black artists who later became famous. His base through most of the 1930s was Chicago, but he spent long periods in New York, organizing sessions, talent scouting and listening out for new songs. Some of the material he heard was raw indeed, but his feel for melody and lyrics often enabled him to make the alterations to a song that brought success. Occasionally he took a half-share in a song when he had not performed any other duty than that of approving it, but this was common practice by managers, and by bandleaders, many of whom claimed part-ownership of any song written by musicians in their employ.

It was early days for Louis Jordan to adopt such a practice, but he was rapidly getting wise to the royalties that could be earnt by composers and co-composers, and from this period onwards he made sure that he was listed whenever he collaborated on a song that he recorded, even if his role was minimal. Louis came to regard the royalties that accrued as fair payment for detecting and developing a song-writing idea into a potential hit.

On the band's next recording session, a new freelance tenor saxist, Kenneth Hollon (a player with more urgency in his style than his predecessors) worked with them. The band also had a new regular member, Arnold 'Tommy' Thomas, who had recently been playing solo piano at the New Capitol and at the Famous Door. Thomas's technique was more impressive than Clarence Johnson's, and his touch much lighter. Johnson's sudden departure from the band's previous recording session was probably caused by his unwillingness to change a long-established style.

As before, the band was allocated a guest singer (by J. Mayo Williams). This was Daisy Winchester, who turned in a competent performance on the minor-keyed 'You Got to Go when the Wagon Comes' (a truly flimsy tune). A second woman, Mabel Robinson, was called in to sing a Jordan and Cook composition, 'Lovie Joe', because the lyrics were intended for female interpretation. The main musical satisfaction here comes from the restrained alto sax solo, with Jordan showing that he could skilfully inflect his tone by using different fingerings while reiterating the same note (much as Lester Young did).

Louis was employing a wide choice of material in his recordings in the hope that one of the attempts would prove to be the hit that changed the band's fortunes. One of his more obscure attempts to reach the Hit Parade was 'Someone Done Hoodooed the Hoodoo Man', a joky song in which Louis delivers a light-hearted jibe at primitive mysticism well enough. The commercial appeal of his vocal, however, is almost cancelled by a round of solos from tenor sax, trumpet and alto. The improvisations are all well conceived, but seem incongruous in the context of the opening and concluding vocals. 'Bounce the Ball' introduces a band vocal chorus and some conundrums and rhetorical questions that could well have been part of one of the less successful tent-show routines; happily, there is a fine alto sax solo.

'Penthouse in the Basement' is an early effort by the Jamaican-born composer Walter Bishop, then working as a porter at the Movietone company's New York office; he was later to write several songs for Louis. Competition for new songs was intense among bandleaders, and this sometimes led them to suspend their critical judgement in order to record a composition that had not been covered by anyone else. The rivalry between the lesser maestros was exacerbated by music publishers usually giving first option on their best songs to established recording stars. Walter Bishop went on to write many fine compositions, but 'Penthouse in the Basement' is an apprentice piece. Some graceful, flowing piano playing enhances the recording, but a less attractive feature is the return of the timpani, whose role here clashes grievously with Charlie Drayton's bass notes.

During this period radio programmes by disc jockey Symphony Sid (Sidney Torin) were highly popular with teenagers, who switched on the show (on the Bronx radio station WBNX) as soon as they arrived home from school. Songwriter Buddy Feyne (then in his twenties), who knew Louis Jordan through their mutual association with Radio WNEW hit upon the idea of writing a song beamed at these teenagers. He took 'After School Swing Session' to Jordan, who worked on it and had it arranged. As its obvious target was not the WNEW listeners who caught Louis's late-night transmissions, the piece was subtitled 'Swinging with Symphony Sid'. Torin responded by plugging the disc and many young listeners bought the record. It was not an ideal introduction to Louis Jordan's art, since neither the song nor the vocal is first-rate, and Louis's baritone sax solo (during which he sounds a little rusty) would not have made many young hearts leap (the dreaded timps are also in action again). Louis himself was not pleased with his baritone sax playing here, and never again soloed on the instrument for a commercial recording; nevertheless, the record sold well and brought him new followers.

# Five Guys Named Moe

Just before Louis Jordan and his Tympany Five returned to play another residency at the Elks Rendezvous they completed a further session for Decca (on 29 April 1940). But whereas each preceding visit to the studio had produced at least one excellent track, this session is (by Tympany Five standards) positively ordinary. 'Oh Boy, I'm in the Groove' is another song aimed at young fans, but without the cheeky appeal of 'After School Swing'. Louis introduces a brief scat-singing interlude and the positive drumming of Walter Martin creates a rocking off-beat, but the medium-paced song hardly created a ripple of interest among reviewers despite the fact that it was an early composition by Ella Jane Fitzgerald (one that she had written while Louis was still with Chick Webb). 'Never Let Your Left Hand Know what Your Right Hand's Doin'' is a bouncy sermon delivered with panache by Jordan, but the storyline is not quite clever enough, and 'Don't Come Cryin' on My Shoulder' is simply an indifferent song. The most subtle arrangement of the four is of an old favourite (from 1912), 'Waiting for the Robert E. Lee'. Louis sings this enthusiastically, but his alto playing sounds uncomfortably jerky. The cosy lyrics, picturing the Old South, were an unusual choice, but the number was popular on gigs so it seemed sensible to record it.

The message that emerges from this session is that Louis Jordan had lost his way in the endeavour to establish his band via recordings, and his progress in live bookings also seemed to be at a standstill. When Louis returned to the Elks in May 1940 the crowd there was just as vociferously enthusiastic as before, but the dimensions of the club meant that it needed only 200 customers to pack the place. The only way that John Barone could have made more money to pay the band an increase was to introduce a cover charge for the week-night shows, but as competition was so stiff he was reluctant to do so. The club had a 'minimum fifty cents per person at the weekends' policy, compared with the Village Vanguard, which had a one-dollar minimum (a dollar and a half on weekends), and Café Society's one dollar fifty cents on weekdays and two dollars on Sundays.

Louis felt frustrated that he could not gain an increase, because his present earnings left him little with which to promote the band. Ida (who was doing some singing gigs herself) did all she could to supplement band overheads, but there was no question of launching a big promotional campaign. When he was not working for John Barone, Louis played engagements with his group at the newly opened Golden Gate Ballroom, at the Harlem Opera House and for various private associations, but often these dates called for big line-ups, and Louis had to take out an augmented Tympany Five which was restricted to playing stock, printed arrangements. The headaches involved, however, strengthened his resolve to achieve success with a small group, and at Ida's instigation he again trailed round to various band agencies seeking work. But all they had to offer were trial bookings in boroughs over the bridges, or in various towns in upstate New York, or in New Jersey.

Jordan was in something of a dilemma. Already his fine bassist, Charlie Drayton, had begun to put in deputies while he went off to play better-paid gigs; the leader did not want to lose key sidemen at this crucial stage, but he decided to remain at John Barone's clubs and continue to search for the right formula on record. Fortunately, Decca eased up in their requests for more Jordan sessions, and there was a five-month gap before Louis entered the studios again (in September 1940), which allowed him time to improve on his previous session. As a result, he took on the new date with stronger, more varied material.

'A Chicken ain't Nothing but a Bird' is a definite landmark in Louis's recording career. He makes the most of the light-hearted lyrics and the three front-line instrumentalists each take solos. In these aspects, there is nothing drastically different here from several previous Jordan discs. The important change occurs in the rhythm section, which has been drilled into producing an attractive shuffle rhythm. The shuffle effect is a four-in-the-bar rhythm in which each of the four beats is divided into two notes, one being two-thirds of a beat long, the other third being lightly accented. A legato feeling is maintained and this produces a smooth bounciness. Shuffle is a cousin of the eight-in-a-bar boogie-woogie feel, but differs in being a subsidiary 'carpet' effect rather than being flamboyantly obvious. This swing-evoking effect and the title (which had an appeal of its own) combined to get Louis a lot of air plays.

'Pompton Turnpike' was made to cover an already established instrumental hit by Charlie Barnet; Jordan's version was the initial release in Decca's new Sepia Series (thought to be better name for what had been the 'Race Record' section of the catalogue). Decca reasoned that a vocal version of a successful instrumental was a good bet for launching the new marketing ploy, but as sometimes happened, the public preferred the 'B' side, 'Do You Call That a Buddy?' – a sombre tale of infidelity, well sung by Louis and movingly played by him on alto saxophone. This effective performance did not achieve any chart success, but Decca were soon able to announce that the coupling had sold 62,000 copies. 'I Know You', a jumpy theme composed by Jordan, was issued on the back of 'A Chicken ain't Nothing but a Bird' and this also picked up encouraging sales.

For Louis Jordan's sidemen, the session fees earned from these recordings helped provide them with much-needed cash. John Barone again said he could not pay Louis any more; Charlie Drayton again took leave of absence to earn more money playing a New York hotel residency with the up-and-coming vocalist Lena Horne, so bassist Henry Prather temporarily came into Louis's band.[1] Jordan decided to take anything that offered more money than the Elks Rendezvous job and gained some bookings in New Jersey in upstate New York and at various university dances.

Trumpeter Courtney Williams was positive that he did not want to leave New York City just as he was beginning to build his reputation as a freelance arranger. Charlie Drayton also declined the chance to do Jordan's out-of-town residencies. 'We were young and ambitious,' explained Williams. 'There was no quarrel with Louis but we just didn't want to leave town, and he appreciated our position.'[2] Later, Williams and former Jordan pianist Clarence Johnson worked at the Elks Rendezvous in Herman Flintall's band.

Louis used various trumpeters for his gigs, including the widely experienced Freddie Webster (from Cleveland, Ohio), and Edward Francis 'Eddie' Roane (who had previously worked with Hot Lips Page and Eddie Durham). Jordan tried several bassists before settling on Henry Turner. Walter Martin remained (on drums and timpani), as did pianist Arnold Thomas, who was granted a brief feature on the band's next recording session in January 1941. This was a 'Pinetop's Boogie Woogie', but consistent as Thomas was, his boogie-woogie playing is not in the top class, devoid of the powerful intensity that marks the work of the giants of the genre. Here Louis takes two satisfactory choruses on alto and (more unusually) two choruses on clarinet, putting down on wax a clarinet routine that he incorporated into future renditions of this number. Louis also plays a clarinet solo, spiky-sounding and rather unrelaxed, on 'Pan-Pan', his alto sax solo also sounds curious, the later stages consisting of a half-hearted attempt to imitate the 'laughing saxophone' effect popular in the 1920s.

The slow 'T-Bone Blues' (written by bandleader Les Hite and guitarist T-Bone Walker) has an attractive ostinato bass figure from the pianist, and two vivid choruses by Louis on alto sax, but his three vocal choruses have a slightly contrived air, as though he were paying undue attention to achieving a smooth delivery – the absorbing moments are provided by the cup-muted trumpet obbligato. Excessive frivolity marks 'Two Little Squirrels', a twee novelty written by veteran composer Mack David, which ends with the band shouting in unison, 'Nuts, nuts to you'. In between the two vocal bouts there is an instrumental chase between alto sax and trumpet, marred by the brass player's fidgetiness.

Louis's quest for work secured the band a part in a new show called *On Striver's Row* (written by James P. Johnson, Dan Burley, Jesse Stone and Abram Hill), which played at the Apollo Theatre for a week beginning 7 March 1941. The cast included the fine singer/actress Amanda Randolph, but despite hopes that a wide-ranging tour would follow the New York première, nothing developed.

Dan Burley and Louis had attempted to collaborate on writing songs, but nothing spectacular emerged. However, Burley kept in touch with Jordan and continually encouraged him to include authentic black material in his repertoire. By this time Burley was one of the editors of the *New York Amsterdam News*, and he was also a competent pianist whose proud knowledge of the differences in black regional music allowed him to demonstrate piano styles from various locales, including Tennessee, Texas, Florida and Arkansas.[3] He advised Louis to think more about the vast treasure-trove of folk melodies and vernacular couplets that had played a part in both of their childhoods. Burley, born in Kentucky in 1907, had spent part of his childhood in Texas before being raised in Chicago. His appetite for seeking out and learning the music he heard from pianists who had drifted into Chicago from various Southern states meant he was a regular at any local rent parties (also known in Chicago as 'skiffle', 'shake' or 'percolator' parties). Burley later relayed the informal music he heard at these gatherings via his own recordings.

Jordan's April 1941 recordings show that he was beginning to feature a shuffle rhythm on a large percentage of his up-tempo tunes, and he was also regularly recording twelve-bar blues, both fast and slow. His main problem, as ever, was finding well-written catchy material. 'St Vitus Dance' is good and lively, with a raffish sixteen-bar muted trumpet solo and thirty-two bars on alto from Louis, incorporating a clever harmonic twist in the twenty-third and twenty-fourth bars, but the composition itself is not very appealing. 'Brotherly Love' written by journalist and pianist Leonard Feather, who had not long arrived in New York from his native England, is a straightforward twelve-bar blues. Feather, who shared composer credits with Louis Jordan and J. Mayo Williams, contributed the neat lyrics that begin and end the record, and in between Louis created his first recorded tenor saxophone solo, which sounds inspired by Lester Young's work. Although Louis had not the technique on tenor sax that he had on alto, it's a pleasing diversion.

Louis was still an avid radio listener, but now he also spent a good deal of time enjoying and analysing current 78 r.p.m. record releases. He bought most of the Duke Ellington small-band sides, and recent recordings by Benny Carter, Jimmie Lunceford and Pete Brown. He paid special attention to the work of his fellow altoists and on the way picked up ideas for arrangements, sometimes by osmosis. This meant that, occasionally, snippets of something released a few months earlier surface on a Louis Jordan record.

One such example is 'Sax-A-Woogie', in which Louis makes a

direct quote from a Benny Carter solo; the piece itself is lively throughout, with two spry alto sax choruses, an enthusiastic band vocal and effective use of a shuffle rhythm. 'Boogie Woogie Came to Town' also benefits from a shuffle beat, but here pianist Arnold Thomas sounds hampered by a truly poor instrument. This is another number by Walter Bishop (which he shared with Louis and J. Mayo Williams). Bishop was at the time anxious to reach the landmark of having ten compositions published so that he could apply for active membership of the American Society of Composers, Authors and Publishers (ASCAP).

Looking back to this period, Bishop recalled spending every available moment with other black songwriters, congregating at the Gaiety Theatre Building situated at 46th Street and Broadway. This was one of Louis Jordan's regular ports of call during his continuous search for new material, and he also continued to visit various band agents to remind them he was still leading a band, perhaps stirred on by a December 1940 trade-paper item which said: 'Negro bands are in a temporary lull which will break up as soon as some bright Negro leader comes up with something new.'[4] One of the leading band agents at the time was the General Amusement Corporation (headed by Tommy Rockwell). Louis's persistence caused one of the bookers at GAC to send through the band's details and background to Berle Adams, twenty-three-year-old assistant in the company's Chicago office.

Berle Adams decided to try to get Louis Jordan's Tympany Five a residency at the Capitol Lounge on Chicago's South Side but, as he readily admits, he was outwitted by one of the wiliest agents of the period, Joe Glaser (Louis Armstrong's long-time manager). Glaser told the club's owners, Al Greenfield and Milton Schwarz, that Louis Jordan had only a part-time band and strongly advised them to book one of the bands handled by his agency: trumpeter Roy Eldridge's quintet. This they did, and Eldridge began a season there on 1 December 1940.

Roy Eldridge (who was a particular favourite in Chicago, having played a long residency at the Three Deuces in 1936 and 1937) did good business at the Capitol Lounge and had his contract renewed, but eventually it was time for him to move on. There was still no opening for Louis Jordan, however; instead the Capitol management signed violinist Stuff Smith, who brought in an eight-piece band, most recruited locally, and when Stuff fell ill with pneumonia, a band led by local drummer Red Saunders filled in until Stuff had recovered. Despite Berle Adams's continued efforts, the Capitol Lounge's bosses showed no interest in booking Louis Jordan, but in the spring of 1941 Tommy Rockwell, head of GAC visited Chicago to secure a residency for one of his top acts, the Mills Brothers. He successfully negotiated with Greenfield and Schwarz by promising them that he could get Station WGN to broadcast regularly from the Capitol Lounge.

As a speciality vocal act, the Mills Brothers' sets were briefer than those played by the bands that had preceded them at the Capitol Lounge; the venue's other resident entertainer was pianist Maurice Rocco, who worked as a solo attraction. Berle Adams quickly realized that the combined duration of performances by the Mills Brothers and Rocco were not going to be long enough to fill the time the club was open – from 9 p.m. to 4 a.m. He immediately offered the services of Louis Jordan's Tympany Five, at union scale (thirty-five dollars a week for the sidemen, with extra for the leader). The Lounge owners accepted these terms and, as Adams recalled, 'When they agreed to pay Jordan's transportation from New York I closed the deal.'[5]

But Jordan was less than delighted when he heard the news, as he told Arnold Shaw:

So they came and asked me if I could play with the Mills Brothers in Chicago. The Capitol Lounge was for white folks. It was across the alley from the Chicago Theatre. Not many Negroes came because they felt they weren't welcome. They wanted me to play intermission for the Mills Brothers. I started not to go – that was a big mistake.[6]

Louis soon realized that he had no other options if he wanted to keep his band together, so he accepted the terms and the group travelled to Chicago. 'At first I was doing ten minutes, then they raised me to fifteen, then I got half an hour. The Mills Brothers went over big, and Maurice Rocco – he was the third act – they had their following and he had his. And after a while I had my following.'[7]

By offering such an entertaining bill, the Capitol Lounge soon became one of Chicago's busiest nightspots, regularly admitting more than its comfortable quota of 280 customers. Things were also crowded on the bandstand (situated at the back of the bar); so much so that there was no room for the timpani and they were dispensed with. Despite the loss of the big drums, Louis continued to bill his group as the Tympany Five. There was not even room for a small piano stool on the bandstand, so Arnold Thomas had to play standing up, as did the resident pianist, Maurice Rocco. Louis Jordan later claimed that Rocco had copied Thomas's space-saving strategy, but publicity photographs of Rocco, published before Louis's arrival at the Lounge, prove this was not so.

After Louis had been in Chicago for two weeks, he telephoned Ida and asked her to visit him. She recalled, 'He bought me a ticket. I was there two weeks, then he sent me home.' Ida returned to New York half realizing that Louis was not going to return to their apartment. There was no question of him wanting to collect his possessions from the Seventh Avenue home. All he left there, according to Ida, was 'a silk scarf and some tails'.[8] Forty years later, she reflected, 'It wasn't a good marriage. But when you get your hand in the lion's mouth you have to take it out easy. He didn't allow me to question him. He was never pleasant, and never came in and told jokes.'[9]

Louis Jordan and Berle Adams got to know each other during the Capitol Lounge residency, and cemented a friendly relationship that was to last for some years. Speaking of those Chicago days, Berle Adams said:

> You see although Louis was a sparkling fellow, in those early days he didn't want to make a fool of himself in front of musicians who dropped into the Capitol Lounge. Louis wanted to be thought of primarily as a fine musician. He knew all of the show tunes and could play them well, but I said to him, 'Look, you're never going to be a Johnny Hodges or a Willie Smith – be a showman. I was always on his tail to be a comic. I could see he excelled at that. So one day he did a Deacon Jones thing he'd learnt way back, he put on a stove-pipe hat and he was wonderful.[10]

Despite enjoying warm receptions from the clientele, Louis Jordan was encountering a serious problem at the Capitol Lounge: he was desperately short of money. Berle Adams explained:

> Louis asked to see me one day, and caught me by surprise by saying he would have to quit the Capitol Lounge and return to New York. He said he just couldn't live on the money. I didn't know quite what he meant, but he explained that he could only get the members of his band to come to Chicago if he guaranteed them forty dollars a week. As he was only being paid thirty-five dollars for each musician he had to find the other five dollars from his own salary and this meant he was permanently broke. I was angry at the musicians and went to the club owners and asked them to fire the whole band, so that Louis could re-form and use local guys. So the Tympany Five got their notice, but then one of their number, the bassist (Henry Turner) went to the Chicago Local and reported Louis Jordan for working below union scale – despite the fact that the reason that Louis himself was receiving under scale was that he was paying his musicians the extra. But I had an eye for contracts and I saw that in order for this sort of charge to be valid the complaint had to come originally from the musician who had been underpaid – and Louis certainly wasn't going to go to the union to report himself. So the matter was forgotten and Henry Turner departed for New York, but the rest of the band decided to remain with Louis and accepted the local scale.[11]

The band's new bassist was Dallas Bartley, who had been leading his own group in Chicago. He was an important addition, a good player who was also a fine showman. In the past, Louis had had to provide most of the light relief and fun himself, but the group's showmanship was considerably augmented by the arrival of Bartley. Berle Adams commented: 'Dallas Bartley was a great asset, and played a part in shaping the band. He knew a lot of novelty songs and comedy routines, including "Five Guys Named Moe" – he had featured that song himself.' Part of the bassist's professional experience had been gained playing at one of Chicago's transvestite bars and there he had deliberately 'camped up' 'Five Guys Named Moe'. Jordan saw how effective this interpretation was, even for the straight clientele at the Capitol Lounge, and made a point of broadening some of his own gestures on various songs.

The owners of the Capitol Lounge were delighted to continue renewing Louis's contract and the booking stretched on for months, but Berle Adams did not want the band to be permanently associated with one venue, so he booked them first into the 115 Club in Grand Forks, North Dakota and then into Lakota's Cocktail Lounge in Milwaukee, Wisconsin. These engagements gave Louis and his musicians ample spare time to rehearse the new numbers that they were due to record at an impending session at Decca's Chicago studios. After completing a late-night session at Lakota's, the band gathered at the Schroeder Hotel in Milwaukee for a 5 a.m. call and made their way to Chicago for the first of two November 1941 recording dates.

By the time these sessions took place, Berle Adams had successfully negotiated a new contract with Decca, via one of the company's vice presidents, David Kapp. The deal stipulated that Louis was to receive royalties for further recordings he made for Decca, as opposed to the straight 'buy-out' fee that had applied to his previous recordings. GAC were pleased with Berle Adams's growing acumen but were reluctant to give him a raise, so they compromised by telling him he could retain the agency commission due on the Decca recording payments. This gave Adams the confidence to plan a long-term strategy: instead of accepting Decca's offer of one cent on each issued side, he said he would be content with half a cent. His reasoning was that if Jordan's sales were no better than other artists on one-cent deals, he might well soon be dropped from their list of contracted artists. Adams also believed that Decca were more likely to present good songs to artists to whom they had to pay only a half-cent royalty. With better material, Louis Jordan would stand an improved chance of getting his discs on the ever-growing number of jukeboxes (there were about 400,000 operating in the USA at this time). Adams said: 'I saw records as a means of exploitation: to build audiences for personal appearances and to help us increase our fees, rather than as a money-maker.'[12] Things worked out perfectly. The records soon hit the jukeboxes, and Decca's boss, Jack Kapp, decided to increase Jordan's percentage rate.

J. Mayo Williams, paying one of his periodic return visits to Chicago, was in charge of the two November 1941 sessions. He brought with him various songs for the band to rehearse in the studio and these, combined with the items that the band had recently polished, formed the basis of two productive sessions. It was originally planned to record all that was needed at one date, but because the band had had to travel from Milwaukee that morning, the procedure had to be repeated on the following Saturday.

The band's recently honed panache lifts 'How 'Bout That', a quite ordinary song by Louis Jordan, into an attractive, swinging issue, with a pleasing cup-muted trumpet solo from Eddie Roane. Louis's vocal ending has a slight nuance of Trummy Young's 'Margie' vocal (with Jimmie Lunceford) but overall it is a rocking, lilting performance. 'Mama Mama Blues', a slow twelve-bar blues written by J. Mayo Williams (mostly from stanzas that had been part of the blues from yesteryear), has Louis singing his lines with a sense of dedication and involvement. He reserved his light-heartedness for 'Knock Me a Kiss', a clever song from the Louisville-born pianist and composer, Mike Jackson (who had previously written 'Bounce the Ball', which Louis recorded). The song deservedly became an evergreen, and Louis Jordan's version played a big part in establishing its longevity. The song also brought royalties to the veteran writer Andy Razaf, who had contributed some of the lyrics.

A week later Louis's band took up their task again and began by recording 'The Green Grass Grows All Around', a song on which J. Mayo Williams had collaborated with 'Stovepipe' Johnson. The record features an enthusiastic band vocal (almost in the glee-club tradition) complete with rounds and a canon – the jazz content is nil but the performance itself is jubilant. 'Small Town Boy', a song by Dallas Bartley (with assistance from Louis Jordan), is enhanced by some sweet-toned, almost tender trumpet playing from Roane. Jordan imparts a lot of vocal feeling to the slow thirty-two-bar ballad and unusually, does not play at all on the track.

The final number of the session, 'I'm Gonna Move to the Outskirts of Town', is a twelve-bar blues structured firmly on tradition, with none of the harmonic frills or substitute chords that were finding their way into many contemporary recordings of the blues. But the song's lyrics sounded bang up to date, with slyly humorous references to the problems of modern urban living. It was a few years old, having been first recorded in 1936 by its composer William Weldon (often known as Casey Bill Weldon). Weldon was also sometimes referred to as K.C. Weldon, giving people the idea that he was from Kansas City, but this was not so; his place of birth might not seem to be a major issue, yet it was, for he was born in Arkansas, in the town of Pine Bluff. His style of singing was therefore probably not dissimilar to the vocal sounds with which Louis had grown up in Brinkley.

Louis found no difficulty in interpreting Weldon's song, and delivered the lines with the sort of relaxation that comes only when an artist is totally sure of the direction of his performance. Louis pays homage to Weldon's style by hinting at a sudden octave descent as he begins singing some of the stanzas, but the refined mellowness of Louis's own vocal expertise is always apparent. Louis precedes his vocal by playing a perfectly apt, soulful alto sax solo.

It was the telling blend of vocal and instrumental feeling on 'I'm Gonna Move . . .' that really launched Louis Jordan as a major recording star. None of the ingredients of the recording was totally new; he had sung in a loosely similar way before, and he had played saxophone effectively on countless occasions, but everything gelled on the day, and fortunately this magic was captured on record. The results were originally issued as the 'B' side to 'Knock Me a Kiss', but this time, the public were evenly divided in their enthusiasm, with the result that the record became a double 'A' side. This meant that both sides were plugged by the music publishers. In no time both titles were being played on thousands of jukeboxes and hundreds of radio shows.

As soon as 'I'm Gonna Move . . .' became a hit, several people claimed the credit for bringing it to Louis Jordan's attention. J. Mayo Williams felt he should be given credit, so too did Lester Melrose (a one-time partner of Williams) who, together with his brother Walter, ran a publishing company in Chicago. Melrose, then a forty-six-year-old veteran of the music business, told *Music & Rythm* that he had taken Weldon's recording to Jordan. Weldon did not enter the debate, being doubtless delighted to receive royalties on a scale he had never dreamed of; Jordan himself simply said (without explanation) that he had first heard the song years before 'on the tracks in Dallas, Texas'.[13]

# I Found a New Baby

Louis Jordan's Tympany Five completed their residency at Lakota's in Milwaukee well satisfied with their Chicago recordings and ready to move on to their next engagement, at the Fox Head Tavern in Cedar Rapids, Iowa. The band had quite enjoyed their stay in Milwaukee, happily sampling some of the nightlife in the black quarter of the city. Even Louis, who rarely sat in with other bands, played tenor sax with drummer Vernon Brown's band during a late-night jam session at the Elite Club. There was no opportunity for such activity in Cedar Rapids, a quiet town in corn-growing country with a population that was predominantly white, and most of whom loved to listen to polkas. The locale would not have been selected by any black musicians out to enjoy themselves, yet the Cedar Rapids booking proved to be one of the most important engagements that Louis's band ever played. Jordan certainly thought so; as he put it, 'The Fox Head in Cedar Rapids was a great turning point in my career.'[1]

The Fox Head Tavern stood almost in the shadow of Cedar Rapids's vast Federal Building. The Tavern itself was a long narrow room with no cover charge, and no space for dancing; most of the customers sat in small booths or at a bar that ran the length of the hall. The club owner observed the state law of Iowa that forbade the sale of hard liquor, so his customers could buy only beer or soft drinks. Louis Jordan remembered the place well: 'It was a beer joint. It ran from a street to an alley. Beer was fifteen cents. The owner was a ham radio operator. He insisted that I stay at his house. He was a wonderful man.'[2]

The owner, Rod Kenyon, was not a dedicated jazz fan, but he liked the music and decided to experiment by booking, via Chicago agencies, various small jazz groups. The move was a success and later led to jazz giants Coleman Hawkins and Jimmie Noone working at the club. Perhaps because of their mutual love of scanning the late-night air waves, Kenyon and Jordan got on well and the club owner said that the band could use the Fox Tavern as often as they wanted for day time rehearsals. This was welcome news for the musicians, because they had nothing else to do during the day and were only too willing to rehearse as a way of defeating boredom. Louis capitalized on this by calling them together each day, not only to polish up the arrangements but also to learn comedy routines. Informal fun and natural showmanship formed part of the band's performances, but from now on well-rehearsed comedy routines, amusing asides and 'stage business' were worked on almost as conscientiously as the musical presentations.

The Fox Head Tavern was the ideal place for trying out these newly-established comedy routines. Berle Adams explained: 'They were not known and could make fools of themselves. That was where they developed all the novelty songs that later made Jordan.'[3] Louis reasoned, quite sensibly, that if Iowa audiences liked his material then so too would Mr Average American.

When the USA entered World War II in December 1941, Louis Jordan was among the first of many bandleaders who offered to play for the troops via the USO (United Services Organization). None of Louis's personnel was due for immediate call-up so the same line-up that had worked in Iowa returned to play a brief but highly successful season at the Capitol Lounge, Chicago early in 1942. Berle Adams recalled: 'When they came back to the Capitol Lounge Louis had a wealth of material and became a smash overnight.'[4] The band's comedy routines and polished showmanship delighted the Chicago crowd, but at the same time, via the nation's jukeboxes, Louis was winning fans among people who had never seen him perform. A July 1942 survey of the most popular items on Harlem's jukeboxes showed that Louis Jordan was in the 'top ten'. This was mainly for 'Knock Me a Kiss', ironically the number-two spot was taken by Jimmie Lunceford's double-sided cover version of 'I'm Gonna Move to the Outskirts of Town' – first place was taken by Glenn Miller's 'Moonlight Cocktail'.[5]

Louis's successes led GAC to take a series of advertisements boosting him and, claiming that Louis Jordan was playing 'Music for the Morale of a Fighting America', they listed the group's appealing facets: 'They Swing. They Sing. They Clown'. GAC also proudly claimed sales figures of 300,000 for the 'Knock Me a Kiss' coupling and 200,000 for 'Mama Mama Blues' b/w 'Small Town Boy'. The band's ecstatic receptions in Chicago were repeated when they went out on tour. Ballroom operators, club owners and various band bookers heard the rumblings of what was to prove a musical earthquake and began showering the GAC office in New York with offers of work. These were passed on to Berle Adams in Chicago, who continued to plan Louis's future with a mixture of strategy and daring. He was encouraged both by the Decca sales and by the enthusiastic tone of important record reviewers like Mike Levin, who said of the 'Small Town Boy' coupling: 'One of the best vocals in recent months. Jordan takes a good tune with fair lyrics and makes a terrific performance out of them. Helping plenty is the bassman on the session, cut when Jordan was in Chicago.'[6]

The bassman was of course Dallas Bartley, whose example had persuaded the rest of the band that showmanship did not negate musicianship; Bartley also played a significant musical part in the band's next recording session, which took place in New York City on 21 July 1942. The first tune waxed, 'What's the Use of Getting Sober', became a standard part of Louis's repertoire for many years. Eddie Roane's broad-toned trumpet deliberately introduces a comic effect during the opening bars, then Jordan and Bartley begin a quasi-preaching routine before Louis glides into the chorus, swinging effortlessly as he imparts the message of the lyrics. The late stages offer a lesson in smooth phrasing, with Roane, a much-improved trumpeter, creating a good effect by rising effortlessly to a high C.

'The Chicks I Pick are Slender, Tender and Tall' is a medium bounce number whose introduction, with its deliberately exaggerated even eight-note feel, anticipates countless rock and roll performances. Louis's vocal is smooth and yet rhythmic and the trumpet solo keeps up the momentum, helped by being effectively nudged along by Louis's backing phrases. In turn, Roane creates a similar effect under the leader's alto sax solo. Demonstrating his super-fine breath control, Louis ceases his emphatic blowing and resumes singing immediately, without seeming to take in any extra air. This skill, learnt over the years, was envied by countless instrumentalist-singers, who usually had to pause briefly for an intake of breath.

The success of 'I'm Gonna Move to the Outskirts of Town' meant that Decca were willing to go along with Louis's idea of creating a joky follow-up entitled 'I'm Gonna Leave You on the Outskirts of Town', the droll lyrics of which continue the saga of the jealous husband. After moving out to the suburbs, he discovers that the change of air has done nothing to diminish his wife's ability to attract other men. Louis tagged his lyrics on to Bill Weldon's previously recorded tune (and shared the royalties with him). The format is deliberately similar to Louis's previous release, but this time there is no introduction. Louis, on alto sax, immediately launched into a well-constructed blues chorus, then sings a warning to his erring partner (emphasising the falsetto octave jumps even more than hitherto). Like most follow-ups, it achieved less impact than the original, but it was another personality-filled performance from Louis, one that gave lay listeners a further chance to enjoy Jordan's alto sax playing.

If a jazz almighty like Sidney Bechet or Charlie Parker had created the opening solo on 'I'm Gonna Move ...' (or 'I'm Gonna Leave ...'), the intensity of their playing would probably have proved too startling for the general public, preventing them from feeling involved enough to enjoy the next section of the record. But Louis Jordan's controlled passion and his ability to balance the emotional content of his instrumental and vocal work intrigued and attracted every sort of listener. It was not by accident that Louis reached the multitude, because he deliberately aimed straight at them, summing up his attitude by saying, 'Jazzmen play mostly for themselves. I want to play for the people.'[7]

This did not mean that Louis Jordan ever coasted, or that he played down to his listeners. On 'That'll Just 'bout Knock Me Out' he obviously tries his hardest to raise a trite tune, full of poorly-rhymed lyrics, up to a level it did not deserve – his alto playing here is full of effort. The song, a joint creation by Wesley 'Sox' Wilson and Louis's previous A & R man J. Mayo Williams, is a hangover from past obligations.

This July 1942 session was under the control of Milton Gabler, long regarded by musicians as a man who not only understood their feelings and intentions, but was also capable of encouraging them to produce their best work in the recording studio. Louis Jordan developed a long-lasting regard for Gabler's sympathetic skills and said in 1973, 'Milt Gabler of Decca, he's one of the main fellows in my life. If we were recording a tune and I said, "I would like to do it this way" he never said, "No, don't do it that way."'[8] Gabler, born in 1911 (American mother, Austrian father) spent years learning the record business, first working in his father's store, then (with his brother) opening the Commodore Music Shop in New York.

Milt Gabler went along with Louis's idea of recording another of Bill Weldon's Arkansas blues, 'Somebody Done Changed the Lock on My Door', but the version the band recorded did not please either of them, so the group moved on to a song that Dallas Bartley had introduced into Louis's repertoire, 'Five Guys Named Moe' (written by Chicago pianist and composer Jerome Bresler and lyricist Larry Wynn). The song's comic qualities encouraged a flamboyantly visual routine (which fifty years later inspired a highly successful musical). The music on the original recording is extremely well performed, with Louis Jordan playing an exciting tenor saxophone solo that can be regarded as the prototype for the whole school of rhythm and blues saxophonists. Countless examples of dynamic and ingenious tenor saxophone playing – by Coleman Hawkins, Bud Freeman, Ben Webster, Illinois Jacquet, etc – had been recorded before Jordan's performance on 'Five Guys Named Moe', but no one had conceived a tenor sax solo that linked brief, highly rhythmic phrases in a way that moved simply but inexorably towards a climax.

The July session ended with a blues written by pianist-singer Ollie Shepard, 'It's a Low-down Dirty Shame', which the composer had recorded for Decca in 1937. Jordan revamped the song, added a shuffle rhythm and introduced call-and-answer patterns between the alto sax and trumpet (an effect that was often to recur on Louis's recordings). His vocal is urbanely but effectively phrased, showing that he was establishing his own way of relaxedly singing the blues, without sounding mannered (as he had sometimes done in the past).

All in all, it was probably the band's most important recording session of this early period, with the introduction (and consolidation) of several musical features that were to remain a stock-in-trade of the

Tympany Five for as long as it existed. The moguls of the entertainment industry were aware of Louis Jordan before the results of this session were issued, but when the recordings were released their content backed up everything that Berle Adams had been saying about the sensational musical attraction he managed.

The release of the new Jordan discs took place just as a nation-wide recording ban came into effect. The ban was instigated by the American Federation of Musicians as a protest against the failure of record companies to pay royalties to its members for jukebox plays of their work. The timing of the ban actually enhanced Louis's progress. He had been able to record several excellent items before the drawbridge went up, which meant that in the coming months the disc jockeys, unable to get their hands on newly-recorded material, were delighted to play good recent discs (made just before the ban) over and over again.

Louis's growing success meant that Rod Kenyon, the owner of the Fox Head Tavern in Cedar Rapids, was eager to take up the option to rebook him, which had been part of their original contract. So the band returned to Iowa for three weeks in August 1942, before playing at the Club Riviera in Columbus, Ohio and at the Beachcomber, in Omaha, Nebraska. During this Nebraska booking, a pattern emerged concerning the ethnic mix of the audiences who went to see Louis Jordan's Tympany Five. Looking back, Louis said: 'The Beachcomber in Omaha was basically a Negro place. When I played there I had white audiences. Many nights we had more white than colored because my records were geared to the white as well as the colored, and they came to hear me do my records.'⁹ Interestingly, of the six numbers recorded at Louis's 1942 recording session, three were by black writers and three by white.

Louis Jordan's music cut right across existing racial barriers, a fact that greatly pleased him and Berle Adams, since it meant that the band was as likely to gain big attendances at venues that were predominantly black as they were when the engagement was at a hall usually frequented by whites. Louis had achieved an ambition by 'straddling the fence', playing to blacks and whites with equal success. A test came during the summer of 1942 when the band played dates in the South. They encountered segregation, but black and white listeners were full of enthusiasm for the music. Berle Adams commented: 'Louis wasn't political but people might not have realized that he was very aware of discrimination and the problems of ordinary black people. He was sometimes misunderstood, but he felt if he absented himself from the South he would not only be harming himself financially, he would also be depriving many of his record buyers the chance to see him.'[10]

Perhaps only Fats Waller and Louis Armstrong had previously been able consistently to appeal to both black and white mass audiences. Waller had been trailblazing for years. Like Louis Jordan, he was a fine musical performer, a great showman and an ebullient vocalist whose clear, smooth voice won over audiences who would have been baffled by the timbre and dialect of an authentic black rural singer. Clarity was also a big factor in the appeal of blues singer Josh White, whose vocals succeeded while other no less gifted but rougher-sounding artists failed.

Louis continued to triumph in clubs and theatres, but the band had yet to be tested in the big ballrooms. An unplanned series of events soon provided that challenge. The group was due to play another season at the Capitol Lounge, but due to vigilant wartime surveillance several clubs in Chicago were closed for serving liquor to under-age service personnel. The Capitol Lounge was not directly involved but, because its owners also controlled other clubs that were affected by Mayor Kelly's closure order, the place was padlocked.

As a fill-in date the band played a Sunday dance at Chicago's Savoy Ballroom (sharing billing with Floyd Campbell's band) and achieved an enormous success. *Down Beat* reported the event: 'With the usual sum total of five men, Louis Jordan knocked out a crowd of several thousand zoot-suited characters there.'[11] The success was positive proof that Louis's appeal crossed racial divides and transcended the gap between old and new tastes: zoot-suited trendy 'cats' were just as likely to be bowled over by a new Tympany Five record as were stolid executives or uninhibited factory hands.

Louis continued to use the Tympany Five billing, but in August 1942 he dispensed with drummer (and former timpanist) Walter Martin and brought in a new percussionist, Eddie Byrd (from Springfield, Ohio), who had recently worked in Floyd Ray's band. Besides changing his band personnel, Louis was also altering his private life. The domestic readjustment occurred soon after Louis met up with a former girlfriend from Arkansas, Fleecie Ernestine Moore. Fleecie was born in Brasfield, a small town twelve miles from Louis's birthplace, Brinkley. She and Louis were about the same age, and had first become acquainted when Fleecie had been a schoolgirl in Pine Bluff, Arkansas. Looking back, she said:

> I won't say he was my first boyfriend, but we were girlfriend and boyfriend since were about fourteen. He was working at the Capitol Lounge and we finally got together. I was always in love with Louis, but my mother did not want me to go with him, no, no. They did not want their daughters to marry musicians. I was living in Chicago, but he was there seventeen weeks before I saw him. I heard him on the radio but I didn't see him. Louis never did talk about Ida. She and Louis separated, we were together, wasn't a lot she could do about it. She didn't know me. I remember seeing her three times. Louis was never a person to talk like the average person about things.[12]

Fleecie was not a striking beauty, in face or figure, but she was a good businesswoman. But whereas Ida, who was also shrewd and organized, had gained her acumen by trial and error, Fleecie had been born into a semi-prosperous farming family who also owned a restaurant. By her own enterprise she bought herself a two-storey apartment block in Chicago.

On 25 September 1942, Louis's group opened at the Regal Theatre on Chicago's South Side, where the mainly black audiences gave Louis a tremendous welcome. Louis wanted everything to go well because he was working opposite one of his idols, Benny Carter, but after the opening night, Jordan went down with a throat infection (diagnosed as streptococcus) and was forced to rest for three days. T-Bone Walker, who was appearing locally at the Rhumboogie Club, was brought in to deputize. Jordan suffered the throat infection as a result of overwork; he was not only playing and singing throughout long sets in clubs and at dances, but he was also following his usual practice of rehearsing the group for several hours each week. However, there were no lasting ill effects from the illness, though he was often to encounter the same malady in the future.

Much to the consternation of the booking agents at GAC, Louis received a 1A draft classification as a preliminary to his appearing before a draft board to register for military service. Draft notices were decimating the personnels of several famous big bands, and to add to the bandleaders' worries the rationing of petrol was making touring a perpetual headache. Once again Louis's luck held; instead of having to find gas for two buses to ship his men and equipment around (as most big-band leaders had to do), Louis was able to squeeze most of the band into one car, with one musician travelling with the driver of the equipment and instrument truck.

Until Louis Jordan arrived on the scene it was thought impossible for small bands to work successfully in huge ballrooms (this was long before the days of sophisticated amplification), but Louis's all-action presentations and the swing that his group generated made them favourites with dancers, and with the people who liked to group around the bandstand. Try as they might, no big band could convincingly present Louis's hits, and even those leaders who brought musicians out from the main ensemble to form a band-within-a-band could not catch the nuances of the Tympany Five's sound and beat, nor could any of their vocalists successfully imitate Louis's singing.

But it was not only Louis's successes in ballrooms which provided him (and Berle Adams) with satisfaction in the latter part of 1942. They were delighted to play a lucrative circuit of big theatres, visiting Baltimore and Washington in November, then doing a split week, half in Hartford, Connecticut and half in Worcester, Massachusetts, before concluding the mini-tour with a week at the Apollo, New York, where the audience went wild with delight from the moment Louis appeared on stage. In some ways the Apollo was the perfect venue for Louis's music; audiences were rarely less than ecstatic about his bookings there, and continued to be so over a twenty-year period.

In late 1942 the Chicago draft board granted Louis Jordan a ninety-day deferment to allow him to settle his affairs, and this meant that he was able to start (on 25 December) a lucrative booking at the Garrick Stagebar in Chicago's Loop district. Berle Adams negotiated a guarantee plus percentage (of the take) deal, which over a holiday season brought in a lot of money – it was the first time that the club's feisty manager, Joe Sherman, had ever agreed to such a deal. To swell the coffers even more, the band repeated its previous success at the

Savoy Ballroom, Chicago by playing a Sunday-night dance (again sharing billing with Floyd Campbell's band).

*Down Beat* commented on Louis Jordan's snowballing success, noting that in a period of eighteen months the band had become 'one of the highest-paid, if not *the* highest-paid cocktail combo in the business'. It went on:

> Their records have been such a terrific hit that the outfit is probably the only cocktail group in the business that can play ballroom one-nighters. Louis not only plays them with five pieces, he breaks attendance records. His 'The Chicks I Pick' is directly below Bing Crosby's version of 'White Christmas' at the top of Decca's sales list. Decca is 'knocked out'.

The magazine picked 'Knock Me a Kiss' b/w 'I'm Gonna Move...' as one of its top vocal discs of the year, saying, 'Jordan's dry humour plus his ability to sing blues with a great feeling and a new sense of style put him right up there.'[13] *Down Beat*'s readers also expressed their approval of Jordan's group by voting them into sixth place in the band section of their annual popularity poll. The listing read:

1. Duke Ellington
2. Tommy Dorsey
3. Hal McIntyre
4. Woody Herman
5. Harry James
6. Louis Jordan

Despite having only recently recovered from a throat infection, Louis showed no signs of easing up on his work schedule. His night off from the Garrick Stagebar fell on New Year's Eve, so he took a lucrative gig for the band at the Sherman Hotel in Chicago. At the Garrick, Joe Sherman was insisting on the maximum hours possible from Louis Jordan, so it was decided to implement an opt-out clause in Louis's contract which said that Sherman was to provide a radio line so that the band could broadcast from the club. Sherman had not honoured that clause, so the band left the booking on 10 February.

Louis went to hospital to see a throat specialist, then moved on to New York to open at the prestigious Loew's State Theatre.

This booking was the first leg of a big tour that grossed Jordan and Adams a huge amount of money. The itinerary included weeks in Newark, Philadelphia, Baltimore, and Bridgeport theatres, preceding a nightclub booking in Toronto, Canada. The band then journeyed down to play the Oriental Theatre, Chicago from 16–22 April, achieving the biggest pre-Easter gross that the box office had taken in seven years.

But Louis's enormous income took a sudden dive when he was asked to honour his pledge (made a year earlier) to entertain servicemen. He became part of a tour of service bases organized by his former patron Ralph Cooper, under the sponsorship of the Pabst Blue Ribbon Beer Company. Louis worked as a single on this month-long tour while his musicians went off to fulfil a previously contracted engagement (commencing 3 May) in Omaha, Nebraska. Louis's place as the bandleader was taken by his early inspiration, alto saxist Pete Brown. Louis's musical companions on the Pabst Blue Ribbon tour were Earl Hines's orchestra (containing two young musicians already being hailed as jazz giants: saxophonist Charlie Parker and trumpeter Dizzy Gillespie). Billy Eckstine was singing with Hines then, and so too was a newcomer, Sarah Vaughan. Usually for Louis's brief spot in the show Sarah played piano, alongside Hines's bassist Jesse 'Po' Simpkins and drummer Rossiere 'Shadow' Wilson. Louis enjoyed the accompaniment the trio provided and some while later both the drummer and the bassist joined the Tympany Five. Off-stage, Louis and Sarah vied with each other to establish which of them was the better mimic.

The whole unit, billed as the 'Blue Ribbon Salute', consisted of a quartet of female dancers (the Four Blue Bonnets), Pearl Bailey's brother, dancer Bill Bailey, and the Patterson and Jackson duo. Most of the venues the unit played were army camps in the South, and Ralph Cooper insisted that the show must play only to integrated audiences, because previous touring packages had performed segregated concerts, one for white troops and a separate one for black personnel (and often when only one show was possible the black troops were excluded altogether). Cooper recalls:

I not only insisted that there should be no segregation at all, I also insisted that the seating should be on a free-for-all basis, so that no one automatically got the best seats. This acted as a big boost for morale for all the black troops, who previously were often denied the chance to enjoy a touring show.[14]

Initially the backstage atmosphere was generally happy, with Louis, as usual, keeping to himself, but always making a point of listening to Charlie Parker, who was temporarily playing tenor sax; at one jam session he borrowed Louis's King alto sax. The two men got on well, but Louis was astonished that Earl Hines allowed Parker to get on the bandstand late, and made no effort to reprimand him, even when he fell asleep in full view of the audience. Halfway through the trek, however, a sourness developed among the musicians over the financial arrangements. Payment for the tour was to be in line with a scale laid down by the Musicians' Union for USO bookings: $84.50 cents per man per week, and $115 for the bandleaders, with free accommodation, transportation and food. But when it was discovered that more than those amounts had been guaranteed by Pabst, the resultant disputes disrupted the tour and eventually caused it to be curtailed. Charlie Parker, who usually earned $105 a week with Hines, left the tour in Washington, DC and Hines himself dropped out in Texas and made his way home. Louis Jordan left soon afterwards.

Any ill feelings that Louis experienced on that tour instantly evaporated when he received confirmation that because of his chronic hernia problem he had, after all, been rejected for service in the US armed forces.[15] This meant that Berle Adams was able to go ahead with ambitious plans for Louis, including a trip to Hollywood.

After a tour of the South took the band through Texas, Louisiana, Mississippi and Arkansas, they played a return booking at Loew's State Theatre in New York, where Barry Ulanov said in his review: 'Jordan concluded his show with "Old Man Mose" for which he donned preacher's garb and ad libbed some fabulous, flavorsome and most engaging sermons.'[16] Following a two-week stay at the Tic Toc Club in Boston, the band briefly returned to New York just as a series of riots were occurring in Harlem. They were not directly involved, and moved out to tour their way across to California, where they opened at the Swing Club in Los Angeles on 18 August.

Racially, the summer of 1943 was a tense time in many places in the USA, but somehow Louis's on-stage personality soothed away any hint of a problem at all the venues he played. Police had closed the Savoy Ballroom in New York in an attempt to eliminate fighting between white and black service personnel. In Little Rock, Arkansas a bubbling cauldron of tension overflowed, resulting in a near-riot at a dance, causing all black dances there to be temporarily banned. Even in Los Angeles, an increase in racial friction caused many club operators temporarily to stop booking black bands.

But Billy Berg, the white owner of the Swing Club, continued with his policy of booking mainly black groups to play for predominantly white audiences. While at the Swing Club, plans were mooted for Louis to appear in an all-black Universal movie, with Lou Levy (then head of the publishers Leeds Music) as associate producer. Levy promised that 'the Uncle Tom slant that was notable in MGM's *Cabin In The Sky* and Twentieth-Century-Fox's *Stormy Weather* would be avoided'.[17] Unfortunately, the film was never made, but the initial plans for it stimulated other film-world interest in Louis Jordan, and he and the band spent three days at Universal Studios for their spot in the film *Follow the Boys*.

During his stay in California, Louis added an important new song to his repertoire, 'Is You is or is You ain't My Baby?', written by Billy Austin, a native of Denver, Colorado, who described himself as a 'sailor, lumberjack and construction worker', but who was, according to Berle Adams, working as the superintendent of an apartment building at this time. By featuring the song in the *Follow the Boys* movie, Louis gave it a perfect launching, and it was to become one of his most popular numbers.

The film itself featured a pot-pourri of entertainers and musicians assembled to publicize the functions of USO tours for the troops. Orchestras led by Ted Lewis, Charlie Spivak and Freddie Slack were featured, as well as film stars such as Jeanette MacDonald and George Raft. On the set, Jordan was involved in a curious incident with George Raft, who had been a visitor to Hot Springs, Arkansas in the 1930s. Jordan and Raft had never met before, but they soon discovered they both had fond memories of that Southern spa city. As a friendly gesture, Raft saw to it that Louis's part in the film was expanded. It was unusual for Louis to mention his days in Hot Springs. He once made the mistake of telling a club owner that he remembered seeing him there in the early 1930s. The man suddenly looked grim and said emphatically, 'You've got the wrong guy, mister!'

Because Louis had helped Billy Austin to polish up 'Is You is or is You ain't My Baby?', he was granted a half-share by the composer. Jordan played the song to good effect at Billy Berg's and when he left that club in mid-November featured it on his first big West Coast theatre date at the Orpheum in Los Angeles. It was soon obvious that the song was a winner. To add topical interest, Louis used to dedicate it to movie star Errol Flynn, who was then embroiled in a paternity suit. Happily, the recording ban had recently ended, and in October 1943 (after a fifteen-month gap) Louis resumed his Decca career, making one of his first tasks the recording of 'Is You is or is You ain't My Baby?' This Los Angeles date also produced another big-selling record, 'Ration Blues', on which Louis soothed wartime nerves with his light-hearted vocal, backed with the deliberately exuberant 'Deacon Jones'.

One of the big Hollywood film successes of this period was *Here Comes Mr Jordan* (about a reincarnated boxer) starring Robert Montgomery and Claude Rains; the title of the movie was enterprisingly incorporated into Louis's billing. When the topicality of the film diminished, Louis was advertised (in 1944) as 'The King of the Blues' or 'The King of the Jukeboxes'. Jukebox plays remained an important part of Louis's career, but an equally important factor developed during this trip to California, namely, his initial participation in 'Soundies', brief 16mm films, showings of which could be seen for ten cents on the visual equivalent of a jukebox.

The innovation was first marketed in 1940. Several companies produced the apparatus for showing films (on a 24x18inch screen) that usually featured a band filmed from a minimal number of angles, performing a three-minute number. The early models offered eight numbers, all on a continuous 1,000-feet reel of film, so order selection was impossible, but innovations later allowed the customer to choose an individual item. Wartime manufacturing restrictions caused a halt in the production of new machines, but Soundies continued to be seen in hundreds of outlets throughout the USA. By 1946 the Soundies Distribution Corporation of America (based in Chicago) was able to offer 1,200 in its advertisements.[18] Louis Jordan's dynamic presentation was ideal for soundies. His photogenic qualities and his ability to convey enthusiasm on to film made him one of the star soundie performers, greatly enhancing both his record sales and his fees.

At the end of 1943, Louis could survey a year of enormous professional progress, but domestically he suffered a setback in the matrimonial courts, where Ida Jordan won a decision for maintenance payments. Judge William Baird ordered Louis to pay her twenty-five dollars a week, and to settle attorney fees and court costs.[19] Thereafter, Ida decided to make some extra money out of Louis's growing fame by taking engagements on which she billed herself as 'Mrs Louis Jordan, Queen of the Blues, and her Orchestra'.[20] Louis objected to this and stalled on paying maintenance. Another court case ensued at which Ida produced the receipts for the timps and the piano that she had bought. Finally, Ida was awarded a lump-sum settlement of $50,000.

Louis began the year at Fay's Theatre in Philadelphia, then played the Royal Baltimore before returning in triumph to the Apollo, New York. The run of theatre bookings spun on and on and it was something of a relief for the band to play a club date at the Bali, in Washington, DC, before they again worked at the Regal Theatre, in the city that Louis now thought of as home, Chicago.

By 1944, managing Louis Jordan was a full-time occupation, so Berle Adams decided to quit the GAC agency and set up his own offices on La Salle in Chicago. When Louis was out on tour he rarely saw Adams, but during this period the two met regularly, as Adams recalls:

Louis wasn't a typical musician, he didn't smoke and he didn't drink. In those days he had a weakness for ice cream, which he said gave him energy for the show. I don't recall that he was a gambler, and he never went crazy over any particular hobby, though he spent a lot of money on shoes – he couldn't resist them and if he saw some that were only slightly different from any he owned he'd have to buy them.[1]

Louis's bassist, Jesse 'Po' Simpkins, had been called up for service in the US Navy and his place was taken by an ex-Cab Calloway star, Al Morgan, a lively showman originally from New Orleans. Shadow Wilson had also moved on and his place at the drums was taken by the ex-Fats Waller percussionist Wilmore 'Slick' Jones. By now Louis was paying his musicians top money, so he had no difficulties in filling any vacancies that occurred, but any newcomer had to be both a fine musician and an enthusiastic showman. Eddie Roane (trumpet) and Arnold Thomas (piano) were with the band, but a new addition to the troupe was the Trinidad-born singer, Peggy Hart Thomas. Pianist Arnold Thomas's life was made easier when Louis agreed that it was no longer vital that he stood up to play.

This line-up played Flint, Michigan and Louisville, Kentucky before moving west to take up a month's residency at the swish Trocadero Club, in Hollywood, California, from 9 May to 5 June. During this period Louis and the band took part in a movie entitled *Meet Miss Bobby Sox* (which starred Bob Crosby); for the two days' work at the studio Louis received $2,700.[2] The group also recorded various items for the World Transcription Service, and appeared on the 'Command Performance' radio shows; in between all this activity they also found time to appear in some new Soundies, and to make some new sides for Decca, including one of Louis's biggest hits, 'GI Jive'. This had been written and recorded by Johnny Mercer who, seeing the prospect of harvesting more royalties, sent the song to Louis Jordan who took up the suggestion that he should record it.

Louis put his own inimitable stamp on Mercer's song, relaxedly delivering the slick lyrics over a slow shuffle rhythm, and contributing a scorching twelve-bar alto sax solo, which he resolves with a series of daringly conceived notes; Eddie Roane's cup-muted answers are perfect. The topical nature of the song, dealing with army jargon, caught the attention of many disc jockeys, so with lots of radio plays (and a Soundie to back it up) Louis's recording became a mega-hit and reached the number one spot in the *Billboard* chart (and stayed in the listing for twenty-five weeks).

Another big recording event that summer was the duet session that Louis Jordan and Bing Crosby shared (backed by the Tympany Five) in July 1944. The idea of recording a duet by two of Decca's best-selling singers (one long-established and the other a recent addition) was hastily planned, both artists having heavy work schedules, but luckily a chance telephone call to Crosby paid off. Louis Jordan recalled the circumstances: 'Bing was with Dixie [Dixie Lee Crosby, his wife] at home having a party, but was told, "We have Louis Jordan here." He said, "I'll come in tonight" and he just came down. Nothing was pre-planned and when Bing walked in they said, "Here's the music." '[3]

The resultant two sides are charming without being sensational. Bing sings an out-of-tempo verse on 'My Baby Said Yes', then Louis (on tenor sax) lays down the tempo of the bouncy chorus which the singers share, with Eddie Roane providing a dainty obbligato. Louis sounds slightly pedestrian in his eight-bar tenor sax solo, but Roane blows confidently to usher in the two singers for the final chorus, and then joins them vocally to make up a three-part harmony team. Bing Crosby apparently cut a solo vocal of the same number which was never issued.[4] On a second take of the duet version Bing offers encouragement by singing 'Come On Lou' and is answered by some fine, robust tenor sax phrases.

'Your Sox Don't Match' is the better side, featuring as it does a series of jocular exchanges between Louis and Bing (again accompanied by Roane's cup-muted trumpet). Louis plays alto on this track and takes an effective sixteen-bar solo before he and Bing relaxedly share the light-hearted lyrics, taking alternate lines then combining for a harmonized vocal ending. The two never recorded together again, but this one coupling gained an enormous amount of air plays over the years and helped broaden Louis's appeal even further. The record was released on Decca's 'Popular' label, whereas Louis's previous issues had been issued on the less well-distributed 'Sepia' series. This move also helped to bring Louis's sound to new listeners. *Down Beat*, reporting on the session, said, 'It took Bing and Louis Jordan only three hours from 6 to 9 p.m. to record "Is You is or is You ain't", "Don't Fence Me In", "My Baby Said Yes" and "Your Sox Don't Match"'.[5] Neither of the first two of these titles was issued, but Bing scored heavily by recording both of them with the Andrews Sisters.

July saw Louis add another city to his run of successes; this time the 'sold out' notices applied to his stay at the Golden Gate Theatre in San Francisco. By now Louis's popularity had spread all over the country; there were no blank regions and his appeal continued to fall evenly between black and white audiences. Echoes of the previous summer's racial friction caused promoters in many states to hesitate about booking black groups for mixed dances, but *Down Beat* outlined a compromise that was adopted:

Due to the Louis Jordan band's popularity with both white and colored audiences, promoters in larger cities are booking the quintet for two evenings, one to play a white dance and the other a colored dance. The initial experiment came in Oakland, California where Jordan's Tympany Five drew 4,200 at a colored dance and pulled 2,700 through the turnstiles at an ofay function. Jordan begins his two-nighter tour in September and will play Oklahoma City, Chicago, New Orleans and Kansas City.[6]

Louis was now considered to be a top-of-the-bill attraction, so a package show was formed around him and the Tympany Five, consisting of comedians, dancers and George Hudson's sixteen-piece band. Hudson (a former Jeter–Pillars band trumpet player) led a St Louis-based unit which had impressed Louis when they worked with him at the Plantation Club in that city. Jordan decided to sign them up for his forthcoming 'around the world' theatre tour, commencing at the Apollo Theatre in October 1944. Hudson believed in employing promising youngsters and during the coming years he featured many future stars, including Clark Terry, Ernie Wilkins and Tommy Turrentine.

While playing the familiar theatre circuit, Arnold 'Tommy' Thomas (Louis's long-time pianist) was taken ill in Baltimore with ptomaine poisoning, and he died shortly afterwards on 26 October 1944, aged twenty-eight. Louis and the band had to fulfil existing contracts, so a replacement for Thomas was soon found. The new man was William 'Bill' Austin (not the composer), who joined the band in New York and played dates with them in Boston and Newark before moving on with them to Fort Wayne, Indiana, Columbus, Ohio, Detroit, Michigan and Chicago. It was a time of upheaval for the band; Slick Jones had left to be replaced by the former Savoy Sultans' drummer Alex 'Razz' Mitchell. A serious problem manifested itself in late 1944 when it was found that trumpeter Eddie Roane had tuberculosis. Louis offered a life-line to Roane by promising to keep his job open in the hope that rest, fresh air and a healthy diet might defeat the disease. Arkansas trumpeter Lee Trammell worked with the band briefly, as did Leonard Graham (later known as Idrees Sulieman). Another important change in the band's line-up then came when Louis decided to augment the group by adding a tenor sax player. The newcomer was Freddie Simon, a twenty-five year old ex-Alabama State Collegian, and although his presence made the unit into a sextet, it continued to be billed as The Tympany Five.

In January 1945 the new line-up recorded three highly successful numbers, two of which became huge sellers: 'Caldonia Boogie' and 'Buzz Me'. The third title, 'Somebody Done Changed the Lock on My Door', was a Bill Weldon number which the band had attempted to record before, but here the version is entirely successful with Louis underlining his admiration for Weldon's original version by making a close copy of it. The words of 'Buzz Me' were written by the ex-*Down Beat* journalist Dave Dexter, using the pseudonym of Danny Baxter, because he was then working for Capitol Records, a rival to Decca. Dexter, an old friend of Berle Adams, mailed the blues lyrics to Adams in Chicago from his home in Hollywood, more in hope than expectation. He heard nothing from Adams for several months, then he received a note saying, 'Jordan recorded your "Buzz Me" and it's a winner.'

Adams's prognosis proved all too true; the record was soon a smash hit with jukebox fans (Dexter estimated it went into 400,000 machines) and rose high in the charts. Dexter did not look a gift horse in the mouth, but he was slightly bemused to discover that he had gained a co-composer, namely Fleecie Moore – the maiden name of the woman who was by now Louis's wife. Dexter did not know of this connection and so assumed that the name Moore was a pseudonym for Louis Jordan. He therefore readily agreed to the deal, commenting philosophically, 'Half of something is better than all of nothing'.[7] But the time would soon come when Louis himself bitterly rued the day he ever agreed to allow Fleecie's name on this song, and the all-important tune from the same session, 'Caldonia Boogie'.

Louis's subsequent bitterness over his decision to 'donate' the rights and royalties of several songs to his then loving companion, Fleecie Moore, was not the only powerful source of ill feeling springing from these compositions. The founder of Leeds Music, Lou Levy, who had published several of Louis Jordan's successes, told Arnold Shaw,

> Louis Jordan was controlled in those early days by Berle Adams and a fellow called Lou Levy. I told Berle that if he would quit his

job at GAC I would give him my piece of Jordan. When I got out I said, 'I'll publish the songs and you manage him.' Then Mr Adams forgot to remember. They put Louis Jordan's wife's name on the song and gave it to another publisher.[8]

Forty-six years after the initial release of 'Caldonia', Lou Levy remained decidedly vexed over the whole affair. In 1991 he said he still felt too angry about the matter to discuss it in detail, but said firmly, 'I set the whole Louis Jordan deal up, and I blame Berle Adams and Louis Jordan equally for what happened.'[9]

In later years Louis accepted his part in the strategy: 'I didn't write under my own name because I was signed with another publishing company, so I put her name on it, Fleecie Moore. Ha, she didn't know anything about music.'[10] There is no doubt that Adams and Jordan felt it to be in their best interests to register the song 'Caldonia' in Fleecie Moore's name, since they could then negotiate deals not subject to the various ongoing restrictions and limiting clauses that would have automatically been part of Louis's existing contracts with music publishers. They were able to make 'Caldonia' the title piece of a new short film, knowing that Fleecie Moore would raise no objection, and they were also able, via Fleecie's name, to make a deal with Broadcast Music Incorporated, which meant that BMI subsidized the making of the film in the certain knowledge that it would be able to recoup revenue from music-licence earnings when the short was shown in cinemas.

Berle Adams and Bill Crouch, a Soundies executive, organized the making of the band film, then took it to Robert Savini, head of Astor Films, for him to arrange distribution. Astor Films, with twenty-six offices in various regions, then enticed various cinema operators to show the film as a short second feature a few days before Louis Jordan played in their locale (for a low rental fee of about forty dollars a week). In so doing they went against the usual practice of the major distributors by hiring the films out to individual cinemas rather than to chains. The 'Caldonia' movie proved to be a huge success with both white and black audiences, causing *Billboard* to comment, ' "Caldonia" has been one of the very few all-Negro productions to get bookings in Southern white theaters.'[11] It was, they added, better to be featured in a well-produced short film than to perform one number that was buried in a poor full-length movie. Jordan links

110

with Astor continued and resulted in several further films, the showing of which added to Louis's in-person drawing power and lifted record sales even further. Louis and Berle Adams also gained because their company Preview Music published many songs featured in the Astor films.

Louis Jordan's gramophone record of 'Caldonia' was not the first version to be released; it was preceded by a highly successful issue from the white bandleader, Woody Herman. The intriguing background was explained by Berle Adams:

Decca seemed to be slow about releasing 'Caldonia'. Woody Herman was an old friend of mine and one night I met him in Lindy's restaurant and he said, 'You've got all that good junky material, get me something hot to record', so I suggested that Woody catch Louis's show at the Paramount. He did and flipped over 'Caldonia', so much so he went and recorded it as soon as he could, I say within hours, but certainly very quickly. [Herman recorded it for Columbia on 26 February 1945.] Then Erskine Hawkins followed up with a version for RCA Victor, and then Decca decided to issue Louis's record and that was a hit too.[12]

'Caldonia' became one of Woody Herman's most popular recordings. His treatment of the blues theme, and his emphatic stressing of the song's line 'Caldonia, Caldonia, what makes your big head so hard?' proved to be a powerful hook for the public, and the trumpet section's boldly phrased unison figures (devised quickly and without music in the recording studio) delighted all those interested in new jazz developments. Herman's version of the song was quite different from Louis Jordan's. Louis summed this up by saying: 'He did it up, real fast; mine was medium-tempo.'[13] He could afford to be nonchalant, because royalties from both versions were being paid into his publishing interest.

The actual origins of 'Caldonia' are elusive, as Milt Gabler pointed out:

The basis of 'Caldonia' came from a Hot Lips Page record, 'Old Man Ben', from back in 1938. On that, Lips sings, 'Caldonia, Caldonia, what makes your head so hard?', but pinning down the source of blues lines can be tricky. One thing's for certain, 'Caldonia' wasn't a 'cotton-field' blues, it was a 'bar-room' blues. Louis Jordan was thrilled to think that a big bandleader had recorded his material, but I was mad as hell. It's bullshit to say Decca held up Jordan's version; it was just that Woody Herman deliberately moved so quickly.[14]

A recording by the Spirits of Rhythm in 1941 also used the 'Caldonia, Caldonia what makes your head so hard' line, but Hot Lips Page's part in the origins of the song was specially mentioned by Louis Jordan:

'Caldonia' started a long time before I came to New York. There used to be a long, lean, lanky girl in Memphis, Tennessee, where Jim Cannon used to have a gambling place where people used to come to shoot a bale of cotton because they didn't have too much money to gamble. This long, lean, lanky gal used to hang out in this place and she wouldn't do anything you asked her to do. That's why they said, 'Your head was so hard,' and, God bless the dead, Hot Lips Page was very young then and I met him and he said, 'You should make a tune out of that, just a plain old blues.'[15]

Years later, a dancer, Marie Reynolds, claimed that Louis Jordan had written 'Caldonia' about her. In 1945, soon after the song had been issued, blues singer Sippie Wallace claimed that the song was based on her 1924 recording 'Caldonia Blues' (composed by George Thomas). Many years after this initial complaint, Sippie explained that she had started to take legal action over the song but her lawyer died and the complaint subsided. To an impartial ear the only obvious similarity between the two works seems to rest on the use of the word 'Caldonia', but Sippie went through life feeling she had been plagiarized.

During the spring of 1945, another hugely successful theatre tour took the Louis Jordan Show around the Baltimore, Washington, Detroit and Chicago circuit, but despite all the admiration and revenue Louis was becoming increasingly disenchanted with his band's performances. He was also again suffering from a persistent sore throat, so after completing a two-week booking in Chicago on

17 May 1945, he decided to enter hospital for a tonsilectomy. This gap in the band's working life presented him with an ideal opportunity to carry out a complete reorganization of his group: he fired everyone in the Tympany Five and began recruiting new personnel.

Louis gave, as his reason for the dismissals: 'I was dissatisfied because the band didn't jump in its usual style', adding that it 'lacked co-operation'.[16] One of the reasons he did not cite was that this edition of the Tympany Five did not take too kindly to his dictatorial ways. As a result, some of the musicians questioned his right to govern their lives by calling extra rehearsals and insisting on having first call on their spare time. They were also keen to play solos and felt disgruntled at their subsidiary roles now that Louis was featuring himself on practically every number. When a reviewer pointed out that the group's leader was excessively to the fore, his sentiments were endorsed, although not publicly, by Louis's sidemen. Louis's high rates of pay had a soothing effect on this discontent, but word was out in the profession that he was reluctant to let the spotlight linger on any individual sidemen. Indeed, when Clyde Bernhardt formed his band, he told the musicians, 'Just because my name is up front it doesn't mean I'm taking all the solos like Louis Jordan.'[17]

Louis's drastic revamping of his sextet was a result of the weed of discontent seeded in his psyche; once in a while it broke ground in random places, at random times. It was this broody side of his nature that caused him, every so often, almost dispassionately to carry out changes both in his musical and his personal life. Not long before he decided to disband in 1945, he seriously considered forming a big band, at the very time his group was being hailed as the most popular small band ever. Fortunately, Berle Adams was able to talk him out of the idea.

In forming his new outfit, Louis employed his former drummer Eddie Byrd, who had been leading his own band. Louis also asked his former bassist Dallas Bartley to rejoin, but by then Dallas was a successful bandleader and making records under his own name so he declined, but he recommended a young tenor saxist, Joshua Jackson, who had recently worked for him. Louis approached Jackson (then working with pianist Sonny Thompson in Chicago) and found that the young musician jumped at his offer. Louis heard that another of his former bassists, Jesse Simpkins, was about to be medically discharged from the US Navy, so he offered him a job, but Simpkins could not give the exact date of his release from the service, so Louis employed a temporary bassist, Carl Hogan, who had formerly been a member of the Jeter–Pillars band. Simpkins duly obtained his release from the navy and took over bass duties, but in the intervening time Jordan had heard Hogan practising the electric guitar and realized that he would be a great asset to the band on that instrument. Accordingly, Louis stretched the group to a seven-piece unit, but still retained the Tympany Five billing.

Louis's choice as his new pianist was William Davis, who had studied music, first at Tuskegee then at Wiley College, Texas. Davis, who later gained the nickname 'Wild Bill', was a fine all-round musician and a skilful arranger. This last attribute was to prove particularly useful to Louis, who felt that the recent erosion of his disciplinary powers had been partly due to the fact that a miscreant musician felt secure in his job knowing that it would take any replacement weeks to learn the repertoire since few of the new numbers had been written down. Jordan knew that the public usually liked to hear a faithful reproduction of a hit record on an in-person appearance, so he had, at times, to bite the bullet and appear more lenient than he wanted to be when a sideman became unruly. With Davis's arrival, Jordan had on hand a staff arranger who was eminently capable of writing new arrangements, and of transcribing all of Louis's previous recorded successes, thus making it relatively simple for a new musician (or a temporary substitute) to familiarize himself with the band's repertoire.

Bill Davis recalls those early days:

> I first met Louis Jordan in Chicago. He was in the process of making a complete change-over, so he asked me if I would write out some of his previous hits from the recordings so that the new men would be able to just read them off. This led on to me arranging new material for the band, and as he also needed a new pianist I took the job. 'Caldonia' had just happened by the time I joined, so everyone was trying to book the group. After rehearsals we started out in Detroit then moved into the Paramount Theatre in New York. As far as the new arrangements, our working scheme was that I sat at the piano and Louis played through his

ideas on alto sax; this was a regular occurrence because Louis was all the time searching for new material. He was always listening, wherever he was, for the next idea for a new recording. He never sat at the keyboard and demonstrated any ideas that way, he played what he wanted on sax; he was a good alto player, not too good on tenor. I never knew of him having any hobbies; his life was music, and finding new material. As far as I know, he didn't have any close buddies. I don't remember him hanging out with anyone, either in the music business or out. He might go out to hear someone perform, but only to check them out. When we got to a town, we were likely to go to our own individual hotels, and meet up later either to work or to rehearse. He could be jovial, but he never let that affect the business relationship he had with the musicians in his band.[18]

Louis's choice of trumpeter was Aaron Izenhall, who was to remain a mainstay of the band for the next six and a half years. He recalls the background to his joining:

Louis knew of my work with Ernie Fields so he called me here in Detroit and asked if I wanted to join the band. I said 'Yes!' because I knew most of the Jordan records and was very familiar with Eddie Roane's playing on them. Louis explained that when Eddie Roane was fit again the job was his, and as long as I understood that, everything was OK. So I went down to Chicago and we got the new band into shape at rehearsals somewhere downtown. Bill Davis wrote out some new stuff and the group started to sound fine. I hadn't been in the band long before news came that Eddie Roane had died, so I stayed with the band for years.

Louis was an excellent reader, but somehow he couldn't arrange, he couldn't write out musical ideas, even if he'd thought of them. He'd spend hours sitting backstage in his robe, and when an idea came to him he'd pick up his sax and call for Bill Davis. So many of Louis's hits were born just like that. He was a genius at thinking up these things. I didn't realize it at the time, but I know it now.

Louis couldn't stand any monkey business or sloppy playing, and if anyone smoked pot or took drugs they were fired on the spot. He was a very strict bandleader. Everyone had to behave like gentlemen, be clean, be smart and behave themselves. He didn't drink or smoke in those days; maybe he'd have a single glass of champagne if we'd finished making a movie, or at the end of a big show. But you couldn't fool him; if you'd been up all night at a party or had too much to drink, he'd know it. If nothing went wrong he'd let it go, but if it messed up the music – look out! He'd holler out loud, saying how embarrassed he'd been on stage having to listen to all the wrong notes. He was temperamental like that, highly strung. Some guys couldn't take it, but it was nothing personal and I always remained pals with Louis.[19]

The new band's first dates were in Detroit, then they moved into New York City for a three-week season at the Paramount Theatre (commencing 4 July 1945). With a schedule that involved several shows a day at the Paramount, appearances on the popular 'Chesterfield Music Shop' radio show, transcription recordings and sessions at Decca, the new group became a highly polished outfit. At the Paramount, the band shared billing with Stan Kenton's Orchestra; Kenton made the tactical mistake of trying to meet Jordan's music halfway by singing a semi-cod version of 'St James Infirmary Blues', which *Down Beat* reviewer Frank Stacy found disappointing. But Stacy was full of praise for Jordan's band: 'The music of this clever group is really delightful, though with its extra emphasis on cuteness it doesn't play as much jazz as it once did on records. It's Jordan himself who's the whole show, with his irrepressible wit and good jazz singing. "Caldonia" brought down the house.'[20]

The same issue of *Down Beat* contained another reference to 'Caldonia', but this made less satisfactory reading for Jordan because it contained details of the $100,000 law suit that Lou Levy was bringing against him, Berle Adams and publisher Buddy Morris. Levy claimed publishing rights on 'Caldonia' through prior agreements. Jordan countered by saying that 'songwriter' Fleecie Moore had penned the song and had placed it with the joint Louis Jordan–Berle Adams publishing company Preview Music. Berle Adams tried to laugh the matter off by saying, 'My mother is very proud of me. Now that I'm being sued for a hundred thousand dollars I *must* be a big man.'[21]

116

Neither Adams nor Jordan allowed the law suit to interfere with existing plans and the band travelled to California, where they spent two days (30 and 31 July) filming for a Monogram picture entitled *Swing Parade of 1946* (featuring Connee Boswell and Will Osborne's Orchestra). On the following day they began a week's booking at the Golden Gate Theatre in San Francisco and played that city's Plantation Club until 22 August. The band had already recorded 'Don't Worry 'bout that Mule' (written by Louis Jordan and Bill Davis) at one of their July Decca sessions, and its sales were to be considerably boosted by the release of the film. Another popular item from these same sessions was 'Salt Pork, West Virginia', composed by William Tennyson, a twenty-two-year-old from New Orleans who was just beginning his song-writing career.

In October 1945, after the band had returned to New York, they took part in another celebrated duet session for Decca, this time with Louis's old friend, Ella Fitzgerald. Milt Gabler reminisced about the date:

> This was an era when teaming acts was becoming very popular, so I thought of the idea of pairing Ella with Louis Jordan. It was simply a question of finding the right songs, because there was no jealousy at all between Ella and Louis. Then Ella came to me and told me about a song that her hairdresser had sung to her. It was 'Stone Cold Dead in the Market'.* That was easy to trace because I had recorded the composer Wilmouth Houdini's version some while before. Ella wanted to do the song and Louis could do that West Indian dialect perfectly so it paid off.[22]

The flip side of 'Stone Cold Dead' was 'Petootie Pie' (which had also started life under a different name: 'Miss Sally Sue'). The Ella–Louis recording of it got a rave review from an unlikely source, bandleader Benny Goodman who, while being interviewed by George T. Simon, suddenly said, 'You know what I like? That record

---

*Frederick Wilmoth Hendricks (1901–73) originally recorded the song in 1939 as 'He Had It Coming'; Wilmouth Houdini was a stage name.

Ella and Louis Jordan made of "Petootie Pie". To me that's the best jazz record of the last ten years. And it's relaxed, too. I've been playing it every morning now for about six weeks, almost as soon as I get up, and I still think it's great.'[23]

The coupling became a hit, and Ella wowed her audiences by impersonating Louis and singing both roles on stage. A week after the recording with Ella, Louis's band tried making its own version of 'Petootie Pie', but it remains unissued. However, that session produced a minor hit in the shape of 'Reconversion Blues', a topical number that had been well received by all of Louis's audiences during the preceding months. In his heyday, Louis Jordan tried out almost everything he recorded on a variety of audiences to help him establish the song's potential. If the response was consistently indifferent that number was eliminated from the repertoire; if it was enthusiastically applauded it went on a short list of material to be recorded, but even then it was not a certainty, since Louis often readjusted the arrangement and sometimes the lyrics, just to see which version the public preferred. Berle Adams and Louis were in total agreement about this method of judging reaction. Adams said, 'We did our market research by trying out material on the road. I might send Louis twelve songs and they'd all be tried out on different audiences.'[24] Small wonder that Louis did not spend much time enjoying the local nightlife; he never used written cues on stage, which meant he had the task of learning hundreds of new songs each year, knowing full well that only a small percentage of them would become fixtures in his repertoire. Louis continued to be a demanding bandleader, and Fleecie observed, 'Louis rehearsed an awful lot. You talk with anyone who played with him and they will tell you. He was really rough on the band.'[25]

The most prestigious booking of this period for Louis Jordan's Tympany Five was a residency at the Zanzibar Club in New York, playing opposite Duke Ellington's Orchestra, in a show that featured (among others) Louis's old favourite Mantan Moreland. Duke Ellington opened on 11 September and Louis was due to begin sharing the engagement on the 12th, but a last-minute dispute surfaced that almost caused a row between the managers of the two bandleaders. It had not been clearly established with the Zanzibar's managers, Carle Erbe and Joe Howard, who was to receive top billing, Ellington or

Jordan, and for a time neither of the managers seemed willing to take second place. Berle Adams, shrewd as ever, saw publicity possibilities in the situation and had an 'open letter' from Louis Jordan printed and distributed to music-magazine editors, disc jockeys and band bookers. It read:

Dear Duke,
    You probably know that old saying: Heaven protect me from my friends, my enemies I can take care of myself!
    Ain't it the truth. Imagine my surprise when I got in from Chicago last week, just in time to open at the Zanzibar with you, and found out I was feuding with you about our respective billings, or so they told me . . .

Louis's letter went on to say how proud he was to appear with Duke, who he called 'the master of modern music', adding: I'm still young enough to play second fiddle to the Duke. I don't mind admitting that your accomplishment as a musician and composer have always been an inspiration to me in my own bid for success. You understand Duke, I'm not claiming I'm a shrinking violet; with the help of all the other great performers in the Zanzibar's New Revue we'll keep giving the customers the greatest show on the main stem. You dig me, Duke?[26]

Years later, Berle Adams commented on the misunderstanding:

The row over the billing at the Zanzibar worked out like this. Cress Courtney, who was Duke's manager at the time, was a good friend of mine, but billing hadn't been agreed so he said, 'We've got to have Duke at the top.' Eventually I agreed, saying, 'Sure, Duke is absolutely great, but Louis Jordan has got to be billed as an EXTRA ADDED ATTRACTION in the same-size type, but to make a contrast his name has to be in white letters on a black background.' Cress agreed with the idea, but (as I surmised) when the ads came out, Louis's name jumped off the page and this caught everyone's eye, more than the name Duke Ellington. Duke was greatly amused by this; he came up to me chuckling and said, 'Berle, you did it. You did it again.'[27]

During Louis's stay at the Zanzibar he gave an interview in which he had some pertinent things to say about showmanship: 'A showman must "intrigue" the customers. He must hold their interest from one minute to the next to keep them guessing as to what's coming.'[28]

One of the band's big successes at that club was 'Beware', a number that allowed Louis to banter with his audience, warning unmarried men to avoid being rushed into matrimony. One of his set pieces within the song went: 'Hey, you there. You there in the front with the lovely blonde. I'm trying to *save* you brother, and you're laughing. Don't laugh too long boy, or it'll be too late.'[29]

The Zanzibar booking turned out to be enjoyable for all concerned. It enabled Aaron Izenhall to achieve his ambition of sitting in with Duke Ellington, which he did a few times when a regular member of Duke's trumpet section was absent. It was also the venue at which Duke Ellington became aware of Wild Bill Davis's various skills, eventually leading to Duke commissioning arrangements from Davis. But for Louis Jordan, the most significant event at the Zanzibar was romantic rather than musical. It was there that he first met Florence Hayes, who danced in the show's chorus. Though still married to Fleecie, Louis began dating Florence (who preferred to be called Vicky); it was a move that almost cost him his life.

# *Look Out!*

During the war years, Louis Jordan and his Tympany Five took part in several V Disc sessions, making records intended solely for distribution to service personnel. As a result he developed a solid following among all branches of the US armed forces. By late 1945, many of these servicemen and women had returned to civilian life and were eager to see the band they had heard on record. So another influx of Louis Jordan fans swelled the queues that formed up in front of every venue at which the band appeared; some theatres took to billing Louis as 'The Global GI Favorite'.

The famous record producer and writer, John Hammond, never forgot Louis's wartime morale boosting. In his autobiography, he wrote:

Although he was playing at Lake Charles, some 200 miles from New Orleans, Louis Jordan was willing to come to Plauché, if we provided transportation. I persuaded the camp officers that Jordan was worth the effort. We used my old Hudson and one camp vehicle. The band was a sensation. Louis was tired, as all entertainers who travelled the South were in those days of gas rationing and separate-but-unequal accommodations, but he couldn't have been more co-operative. He had a fine young trumpet player, Aaron Izenhart [sic], whom I remembered hearing some five years earlier in Fort Wayne, Indiana. A kid then, now he was a star.[1]

Louis finished his booking at New York's Zanzibar Club on 5 December 1945, and two days later opened at the Apollo. Such was the demand for tickets at the theatre that the management booked the band for two consecutive weeks, a highly unusual occurrence. Louis's supporting cast there included his old friend Hot Lips Page, who despite being a fiery and inventive trumpet player and a superb blues singer, could not gain a large following among the general public. Louis may have looked at Lips Page's career and thought 'there but for the grace of God' – the two men remained good friends.

Another of Louis's friends, though they never developed any real degree of closeness, was Nat 'King' Cole, who had emerged as a top recording star at about the same time as Louis Jordan did. Cole, regarded as one of the best young jazz pianists in the world, virtually abandoned his keyboard improvising to concentrate on singing, with enormously successful results. Louis firmly believed that he had persuaded Nat to concentrate on vocalizing by offering him the song 'Hit that Jive Jack' in 1941 (when they were both in Chicago). Dozens of other people have made similar claims, but the story of Nat 'King' Cole suddenly becoming a singer by chance (as relayed in several biographies) is untrue. As early as March 1939 'King Cole's Vocal and Instrumental Trio' was billed on NBC's West Coast broadcasts.

Cole remained one of Louis's favourite artists, and was an inspiration for his style of ballad singing. The two men formed a mutual admiration society, and Cole said of Jordan: 'He's one of the great performers. I would give top rating to anything he does in the novelty class. He can take a nothing piece of material and make something out of it.'[2] But there was no sense of rivalry, as Louis explained: 'Nat wasn't in competition with me. He was in another field – the pop field.'[3] Like Louis, Nat became slightly indignant when jazz lovers hinted that he had sold out, and said, 'I'm in the music business for one purpose – to make money. I'm not playing for other musicians. We're trying to reach the guy who works all day and wants to spend a buck at night. We'll keep him happy.'[4] Louis fully endorsed these sentiments, commenting: 'I wanted to play music on stage that made people forget about what they did today.'[5]

There was no question that Nat Cole was the more popular of the two, and this was confirmed in the *Down Beat* 1946 readers' combo poll which was topped by Cole with 3,064 votes, while Louis came second with 1,031 votes and Eddie Heywood third with 460. In 1946 Cole's overall popularity brought him rewards in the shape of his own

Wildroot-sponsored radio show (later he was to have his own television series), but despite Jordan's across-the-board appeal (and regular guest appearances on many radio shows) he was never granted his own radio series.

But in the long run, Louis's influence was to prove a greater force in the music profession than Nat Cole's. By 1946 echoes of the Tympany Five's music were already becoming apparent in the work of small groups throughout the world. Some simply impersonated the sound of the records as closely as they could, but others began using various facets of Jordan's music, such as the shuffle beat or the riff-filled arrangements, as important ingredients in their performances. Carl Hogan's electric guitar playing had added a new dimension to Louis's group, particularly apparent on 'Salt Pork West Virginia' where his solo (with its modern signposts) and his flexible way of floating in and out of the ensemble created an appealing and highly musical effect. Hogan remains one of the unsung pioneers of rhythm and blues playing (contrasting with either pure blues, or pure jazz); although his name is not celebrated, he was cited by Chuck Berry as an early vital influence.

Indeed, the music of the Tympany Five generally was all-important for Chuck Berry, who said: 'I identify myself with Louis Jordan more than any other artist. If I had only one artist to listen to through eternity it would be Nat Cole. And if I had to work through eternity, it would be Louis Jordan.'[6]

Like Chuck Berry, Carl Hogan was raised in St Louis, Missouri, where he had worked with various bands on bass and on guitar, including the Jeter–Pillars band and George Hudson's Orchestra. Aaron Izenhall reminiscing about him, said, 'He was full of weird musical ideas, but he was a fine player. He was always working on inventions, including one that involved only using one central peg to tune all six strings on a guitar. God knows how that would work, but he continued experimenting.'[7] Drummer Chris Columbus also spoke of Hogan: 'He was not only inventive musically, he was also inventive mechanically; he was always devising new material to make guitar strings from, and at one time he played an Hawaiian guitar, using the steel on the strings.'[8]

Musical excellence was only one of the appealing factors in Louis Jordan's continued success. Louis's flamboyant on-stage personality and the showmanship of his musicians also played a major part in establishing the group. Listeners, charmed by a recording they hear on the radio, often feel let down when they see the artist in person, because of a listless presentation or a lack of stagecraft, but there was never any inkling of disappointment when people saw Louis in action. The band was always smartly, if flamboyantly, dressed; all their stage suits and uniforms were provided by Louis, which led to an ex-member wisecracking: 'When you left Louis you left in your underwear.'[9]

One of Jordan's 1946 hits, 'Beware', provided the perfect showcase for the group's panache. After some bold phrases from the trumpet and apt fill-ins by the guitarist. Louis begins preaching a mock-frenzied sermon warning his male listeners about feminine guile. The band join in with vocal encouragement while Louis ladles out broad humour in a harangue that blends quips, bitter advice and teasing in a superbly timed routine. It was an immediate sensation with record buyers and with the audiences that packed theatres in Newark, Philadelphia and Detroit. By the time the group played a return booking at New York's Paramount Theatre in June 1946, they had honed the 'Beware' routine to perfection. Reviewing their appearance there, George T. Simon wrote specifically about 'Beware', describing it as 'just about the most entertaining music I've ever seen on any stage. It brought the house down.'[10]

Looking back, Aaron Izenhall commented:

What Louis was trying to do was to present his audiences with a Technicolor picture of a live band, getting the musicians to imitate a movie on stage. The wild colours, the movement, the exaggerated gestures, the whole thing came over like a scene from a movie and that's what Louis wanted. We were the first ones to wear those bright colours and that became an automatic part of rock, and even now you can go back to our version of 'Beware' and realize that it's the earliest sort of rap.[11]

All the visual effects, rehearsed movements and musical excellence were supplemented by Berle Adams's and Louis's advance planning. To coincide with the group's return to the Paramount they organized a timely release of a nineteen-minute short film, 'Caldonia', which featured the band playing various recorded successes. It was an early example of using a screen to promote record sales in much the same way that videos were used many years later. *Metronome* magazine commented, 'The short is set for first-run distribution and will be given equal billing with feature pictures as well as being used for theatres where Louis will appear.'

Louis's schedule remained as hectic as ever, but during yet another return booking at the Apollo he was again overtaken by a throat ailment. After playing the opening performances on 19 July, Louis suffered what was described as a severe case of laryngitis, but instead of remaining in New York he flew back to Chicago to see his own doctor, returning to New York later that week to play the final two days of the booking. Louis felt that he was more likely to be ill at the Apollo than anywhere else, and his sudden departure from the 125th Street theatre was symptomatic of the love-hate feelings he had for the place. He later explained: 'Every time I used to go to the Apollo I'd get hoarse. Why? Because it was a filthy theatre. The same dirt was there from year to year. To tell you how I know – I used to put a mark in it – and I'd come back to play there again and my mark would be there.'[12]

But despite complaining about Frank Schiffman, the owner of the Apollo, being unwilling to improve backstage conditions, Louis acknowledged his expertise, calling him 'one of the best managers of theatres I have ever worked for; he could get out of you what you think you can't do . . . made a lot of Negro stars. A great manager! But as for the theatre – it stinks.'[13] Schiffman's son, Jack, in his book *Uptown, the Story of Harlem's Apollo Theatre*, described Louis Jordan as being 'temperamental', commenting on an incident that involved Louis complaining that the theatre was too cold, then, next day, that it was too hot. When Louis read this he said, 'His father didn't care how you felt as long as you did the show.'[14]

In another book, *Harlem Heyday*, Jack Schiffman wrote unstintingly about Louis: 'When performing, Louis Jordan would stare down at the audience with eyes popping; he would feign anger, terror – any emotion – and make you believe it. Louis wanted to make you laugh – and he did – but his alto saxophoning was serious.' Dozens of aspiring performers watched Louis's every move, and learnt as much as they could from him, among them James Brown, the 'Founder of Funk'.

When asked if Louis Jordan was an influence on him, Brown said without reservation, 'He was *Everything*.'[15]

An Apollo contract often called for thirty shows a week, which meant that a booking there could prove gruelling if a performer was not in the best of health. But despite his misgivings, Louis Jordan returned again and again to that theatre to play to an audience that adored him. Ralph Cooper, long-time master of ceremonies there said: 'Louis was so successful at the Apollo because the audience loved him from the moment he walked on. As far as I was concerned, Louis always conducted himself in the right way and we always remained friends. He was more than a good musician, he was an artist.'[16]

Although most of the Apollo's audiences were black, there was always a fair sprinkling of white faces. Record collector Norman Levy used to play truant in order to enjoy Louis Jordan's performances there:

> Louis had a stage presence that was unforgettable. He was always devising new ways of opening his act and one time the stage lights went up and Louis was standing on this podium playing 'Knock Me a Kiss', then suddenly he jumped off and still carried on playing, he didn't miss a beat, carried on phrasing smoothly; the audience loved it. This was in the early 1940s, and there was never any trouble between black and white there.[17]

Louis's 'Beware' recording was given a huge boost by the release of his first full-length movie, which bore the song's name. The film (which had been shot at the Filmcraft Studios in New York during December 1945) was premièred at the RKO Hamilton cinema in Harlem, and Louis managed to attend by being rushed there from his last show of the night at the Paramount. Among many well-wishers who turned out at the 11 p.m. première to greet Louis were his former bandleader, Joe 'Kaiser' Marshall, plus the Nicholas Brothers, actor Canada Lee, singers Maxine Sullivan and Thelma Carpenter and pianists Pete Johnson and Willie 'The Lion' Smith.

The hour-long film, which had an all-black cast, concerned Louis Jordan (playing himself) returning to his old college to prevent its dissolution. He is successful in his mission, wins the heart of a beautiful woman (Valerie Black) and lives happily ever after. Writer

John E. Gordon's plot simply acted as a vehicle for ten songs from Louis, including several of his hits. *Down Beat* gave it a favourable review: 'There's not too much to the picture, a one-week quickie. Mostly the camera and mike are trained on Louis Jordan, who sings, plays and dishes out lines. But Louis happens to be such a terrific performer that the results are more satisfying than plenty of elaborate Hollywood super-productions.'[18] The film was directed by Bud Pollard, and produced by Astor Pictures, which was owned by Robert M. Savini, Berle Adams and Louis Jordan.

Because he donated the proceeds of the *Beware* première to the Riverdale Children's Association, Louis was later given an award by them (along with Frank Sinatra and Irving Berlin). Jordan could drive a hard bargain when he wanted to, and was sometimes surprisingly direct when asking about specific expenses, but he had no miserly traits. He paid his musicians more than almost any other bandleader, and was always quick to foot any restaurant or bar bill. He did, however, get slightly irked when he saw his sidemen needlessly wasting money on something he felt they did not need, and he did his best to encourage them to be thrifty, as Aaron Izenhall recalled:

When the sax player Josh Jackson and me joined Louis we were getting $140 a week, which in the 1940s was tremendous money. I was twenty and Josh was twenty-three. The first theatre we played with Louis was in Detroit and he called us both into his dressing room and said, 'I want you guys to look after your money. So here's what I'm going to do. You bring me your bank book in a year from today and whatever you've saved I'll double.' We could hardly believe our ears. I made up my mind to start saving straight away and pretty soon I had $2,000, but then I was young and wild and I spent it on girls and having a good time and Louis's offer went right out of my mind, whereas Josh was smart and saved his money. I forgot all about the deal, then one day in Cleveland, Ohio, Louis called me in and said, 'The year's up, show me your bank book.' Well, I had less than a hundred dollars in it. Louis gave me a long look then said, 'I'll give you another year – same deal.' But the money just flowed away and a year later there was nothing to double – after that Louis didn't continue with the offer.[19]

Louis's Decca recordings continued to sell in vast numbers; 'Buzz Me' had sold 800,000 by March 1946 and his royalties were given a fillip by the success of the duet sides with Ella Fitzgerald, a coupling which soon sold 250,000. Another half-million pressings were eventually purchased. 'Choo-Choo Ch'Boogie', which was to prove Louis's biggest-selling single, was already a huge success, despite being given the thumbs-down by a *Metronome* reviewer who wrote, 'It gains its effect entirely from the title, lifted bodily out of "Hamp's Boogie".' The same writer also panned the coupling 'That Chick's too Young to Fry', calling it 'a cheap exercise in *double entendre*'.

Admittedly, 'Choo-Choo' is a slight composition, but Louis's rocking interpretation gives the maximum impetus to the blues framework on which the song is built. Milt Gabler, the record's producer, who collaborated on the piece, gave the background to his fellow composers; 'Denver Darling was a country-and-western singer on WNEW radio in New York, and Vaughan Horton was a steel-guitar player (and a fine songwriter) who worked at WNEW in the house band led by Irving Ross.'[20] Gabler instantly saw that the original idea for the song the two men offered had strong commercial possibilities. Gabler had the gift of linking a song with the sound of an artist in his head, and conjectured that 'Choo-Choo' was something for Louis Jordan. Recalling his first sight of the song, Louis said, 'We came in on the train from Atlanta, Georgia to New York to do the recording. They brought the words in and I said to Bill Davis, "Leave the chords in the blues vein, and let's see what we can do with it."'[21] From this informal beginning a record that sold over two million copies developed.

In those days there were few well-equipped studios outside of the main cities in America, so for most of Louis's career the majority of his sessions took place either in New York, Los Angeles or Chicago. Jordan's June 1946 New York studio date produced four sides, two of which, 'Ain't Nobody Here but Us Chickens' and 'Let the Good Times Roll', were hits. The first was one of many songs Louis devoted to domestic fowl, but its lyrics were a shade sharper and more humorous than his other salutes to the feathered world. The record was often played on the American Forces' Network and became a great favourite with US troops stationed abroad. 'Let the Good Times Roll' had been a long time taking shape. Its creator, composer-comedian Sam 'Spoo-De-O-Dee' Theard (who also wrote 'I'll be Glad when You're Dead You Rascal You'), had first outlined the song to Louis when they were working the Chicago club circuit in 1942. The wait was worthwhile, because the song proved a winner with both listeners and dancers. Although most of Louis's dates were in theatres, he still usually managed at least one tour of Southern ballrooms each year. Louis always liked to see at first hand how tastes were changing, and he was happy to note that his group could lay down a beat that instantly brought young and old on to the dance floor.

Louis also made a point of continuing to play nightclubs, though at this stage of his career, only places with expensive tariffs could afford to book him. One such venue was the 400 Restaurant on New York's Fifth Avenue, which reopened in September 1946 after some elaborate renovations. Previously only one black band – led by Duke Ellington – had played there before Louis Jordan (sharing the bill with the Modernaires and trumpeter Randy Brooks's big band) provided the music for the restaurant's reopening.

While at the 400, Louis made an important change in his personnel. His long-time drummer Eddie Byrd had decided to leave, so Louis was busy auditioning prospects in New York. One seemed promising, but he could not quite create a shuffle rhythm effectively, so Louis decided to ask an old friend, drummer Joe Morris, professionally known as Chris Columbus, to pass on advice to the percussionist. Chris recalls the situation:

I got a call from Louis, who was at the 400 Club, saying he was having problems with his drummer and would I go down just to show the man what Louis wanted. At the time I had my own band at Smalls' Paradise in New York. Louis knew this, but he said, 'Please come down here and just sit in to demonstrate to the drummer what I want.' So I did this and asked my son, Sonny Payne, who was then a teenager, to take over on drums at Smalls'. Louis was pleased with what I played and offered me good money to join his band. I hesitated and he said, 'Well come and play with the band for a couple of nights.' That two nights turned into a stay that lasted for almost six years. You see I knew how important Louis regarded the shuffle beat. The shuffle beat was a big part of

Louis's style and I used to complement that rhythm in a way that didn't overshadow anything else. I never made it weighty, always light, and the listeners liked that and so did the dancers. Louis liked what I was doing and we stayed pals.

I first met Louis when he was working with Charlie Gaines in Philadelphia; I was living and working in Atlantic City, only sixty miles away. Everyone can get moody, and Louis could get a little mean at times, but I only worked with him, I didn't have to sleep with him. He was a great showman on the bandstand, and always, whatever the circumstances, he did a superb job. He was a good alto player and baritone sax too. Of course when he got rich he changed some, but there's hardly anyone that money won't change.[22]

Not long after Chris Columbus joined the band, they made a return visit to the Regal Theatre in Chicago and broke the house record there. Next came Detroit, then it was back to New York for another booking at the Apollo. This time his support band there was led by a young, up-and-coming leader, Johnny Otis, a drummer of Greek origin who had spent most of his professional life working with black musicians in California. Otis remembers with gratitude Louis's help in securing bookings for his big band:

I had seen Louis Jordan often on stage and regarded him as a master showman, but I first got to know him in Chicago in 1946. He learnt that we (my band) were being forced to lay off there. We had just finished a successful ten-week stay at the El Rado Club (which was in the basement of the Pershing Hotel). We were offered another ten weeks there but because we were an out-of-town unit (from Los Angeles) the Chicago union stepped in and said we couldn't do the extra weeks. This meant we were stranded, but Louis Jordan gave me four hundred dollars and said, 'Get your band to Detroit and I'll add you to the show I'm doing at the Paradise Theatre.'

It was a very kind gesture, and I'll never forget him for it. After that we appeared with him at the Apollo for the first time, and that introduction led to a whole series of bookings there. Now I've heard bitter complaints from some musicians who worked for Louis, saying how strict a disciplinarian he was, but when I got to thinking about this I came to the conclusion that the guys who complained loudest were the guys who were prone to fuck up.[23]

For Louis the box-office grosses were bigger than ever, and he also gained an increase in his record royalties earnings when Decca (on 1 December 1946) upped the retail price of recordings to seventy-five cents per disc (previously most of Louis's work had been on the thirty-five cent label). The move did not drastically diminish Louis's sales, so he gained a percentage share of the extra forty cents. So the money was rolling in, but looming in the distance was the 'Caldonia' suit, which had reached the US Supreme Court. Leeds Music were seeking $400,000 from Louis Jordan, Berle Adams, Preview Music and Edwin H. Morris Music, claiming that an injustice had been done over the assignment of various songs. Any thought about the litigation sent Louis into overdrive, greatly exacerbating his usual workaholic tendencies.

One big task was the recording of the soundtrack for another Astor Productions movie *Reet, Petite and Gone*, which at seventy-five minutes' duration was the longest film in which Louis had starred. It was directed by William Forest 'Bill' Crouch. The plot concerned Louis's screen-father (played by Louis himself) stipulating on his death bed the vital statistics of the girl that Louis must marry in order to inherit his father's fortune. Several songs later (some by heavy-weight June Richmond, some by Louis) Louis and Bea Griffith (whose measurements fit the requirements exactly) marry. Also in the all-black cast were Vanita Smythe, Mabel Lee, Milton Woods and Lorenzo Tucker. The lively title song was recorded and issued on Decca, as were some of the other songs in the film, including 'Ain't that Just Like a Woman'. It was not a big hit for Louis, but for years afterwards he featured it in his act.

The band moved out to California to begin a residency at Billy Berg's Club on Hollywood's Vine Street, commencing 15 January 1947, for a guaranteed $3,500 a week. This was a listening club (not a dancing one) often visited by movie stars and show-business people. Berg continued to specialize in booking black combos, and later that same year he presented the first club appearance of the recently formed Louis Armstrong All Stars.

During the first week of the booking the Tympany Five went into

Decca's Los Angeles studio to record 'Friendship', returning there a few days later to wax 'Open the Door Richard', which was proving to be a hit for tenor saxist Jack McVea, who wrote part of the song. McVea, describing this period of his life, said, 'In the middle of my band starting, here comes Louis Jordan, the new thing, and I jumped on the bandwagon. I got our group to sound like Louis and my work just went up.'[24] In recording 'Open the Door Richard' Louis thus had the easy task of copying a record by a band that copied him. The song became a hit for Louis, and for other artists, with rival versions by Clinton 'Dusty' Fletcher (who wrote part of the song) and Count Basie.

Because Louis always had a vast trough of possible recording material, he rarely showed any interest in making 'cover' versions of successful songs; occasionally he featured a current hit like 'Pistol Packin' Mama' on a radio show but, in general, he wanted listeners instantly to identify him (and only him) with a particular song. He had no part in the composing of 'Open the Door Richard', which was basically a revamp of an old vaudeville routine, so was not concerned with the subsequent ownership disputes that arose over the song. Charlie Chaplin once said, 'Where there's a hit, there's a writ' and this proved to be the case with 'Richard'. Louis felt that he was finished with *contretemps* of that nature, but he himself was soon to be involved in a bitter dispute over who owned several of the songs he had recorded.

Louis's romance with dancer Florence 'Vicky' Hayes had blossomed since they had first become enamoured of each other during the band's 1945 booking at the Zanzibar Club, New York. Louis's wife, Fleecie, rarely accompanied him when he toured with the band, so Louis often took Vicky on the road with the troupe. However, in January 1947 Fleecie decided she wanted to visit California again, so she accompanied Louis to Los Angeles for what was scheduled to be a long booking. Fleecie's ostensible reason for making the trip west was so that she could spend the winter months in a warmer climate, but those close to the Jordans suspected that Fleecie had somehow got wind of her husband's extra-marital activities with Vicky. Fleecie herself gave no indication of rancour during the first part of the band's booking at Billy Berg's, but on Sunday 26 January her fury erupted.

After returning to their apartment in Pasadena, Louis got into bed alongside Fleecie, who was sitting up, having just finished paring the hard skin from her feet with a sharp knife. What was said will never be known, but, Fleecie suddenly lunged at him with the blade. A contemporary magazine reported, 'She cut Louis across the right side of his face and stabbed him numerous times in the chest and stomach. When he tried to protect himself with his hands she stabbed them also.'[25] Another account gave even more explicit details: 'Jordan received several cuts on his hands and face and one gash missed his heart by about an inch. His left hand was cut badly with the possibility he may lose the use of the fingers. He also received a three-inch cut starting at the corner of his mouth and running diagonally downward.'[26]

Louis was taken to the Huntington Memorial Hospital, where he was later pronounced out of danger, but he was shaken and badly scarred. He told a reporter, 'This is the second time Fleecie cut me. There's not going to be another time.'[27] Fleecie was arrested and charged with 'assault with a deadly weapon'.[28] One of the first things she did when released on bail was to file a suit against Louis for separate maintenance.

The details of the stabbing incident were slow to emerge, because all of that day's newspapers had already been printed, but eventually the nation's radio stations began broadcasting the news. Berle Adams, far away in Chicago, remembers the circumstances clearly:

One Sunday evening I was sitting at home. I'd been to a football game and I was relaxing after dinner sipping a brandy and listening to Walter Winchell on the radio when suddenly they broadcast the words: 'Louis Jordan has been stabbed.' I immediately got on the telephone, but I couldn't find out anything, I didn't know whether Louis was alive or dead. Finally I decided to telephone Billy Berg, the club owner, and all he could say was, 'How could he do this to me? All week people have been standing in line around two blocks, business couldn't have been better and he has to go and get himself stabbed.' From various sources I found out that Louis certainly was alive and not as badly hurt as was at first feared, but it was a terrible experience for him.[29]

Louis's band, unaware of the incident, turned up for work as usual, Aaron Izenhall recalled:

> We were getting our things ready when the band's road manager Wilbur Brasfield rushed in and said, 'Louis has been stabbed, he's not expected to live.' Then the story came out. Louis and Fleecie were staying at an undertaker's house – in those days a hotel accommodation in Hollywood for black people was out of the question. Fleecie had found out about Vicky, who had been travelling with us a lot, and as Louis lay down to rest Fleecie got the knife she was using to pare her corns with and stabbed Louis. She waited until he got into bed so that the sheets would make it difficult for him to move fast. Happily, he wasn't cut as badly as he could have been. We were laid off for about six weeks and I came home to Detroit.[30]

Originally it was hoped that the band would be able to play for the remainder of the booking, using various substitute front-men. Comedian Timmie Rogers came in to work with the Tympany Five, but at the end of the week the idea was abandoned and Louis's musicians went their separate ways to await further news from their bandleader. Meanwhile, almost every newspaper in the USA carried details of Louis's experiences, including the *Brinkley Citizen*. Louis's home-town friends were deeply shocked by the news; they had met Fleecie when she had visited with Louis, and several of them knew her relatives in nearby Brasfield.

Louis gradually recovered from his injuries and took stock of his domestic situation. The pain from his stab wounds was almost equalled by his receiving the news, via Fleecie's attorney, that his wife intended to keep every cent of the royalties that had accrued on all the songs he had registered in her name. There was a terrible irony in this manoeuvre, because the only reason the copyrights had been allocated to Fleecie had been to make more money for Louis. Now he was faced with a situation where the royalties earned by some of his most successful songs would not reach him at all. To add insult to injury, Fleecie's claim for maintenance had been resolved in an out-of-court settlement which netted her $15,000 in cash and another $15,000 in property assets.

# 10
## It's a Lowdown Dirty Shame

Louis decided not to press charges against Fleecie concerning the 'assault with a deadly weapon', and as a result the case was dismissed by the Pasadena Justice Court. After announcing that he was in the process of securing a divorce, Louis left for a vacation in Mexico.

After a few weeks' rest Louis felt well enough to return to work and was able to fulfil a previously contracted engagement at the Paramount Theatre, New York, commencing 19 March 1947. His reappearance prompted the press to carry reminder stories about the recent domestic mayhem. Under a headline: LOUIS JORDAN IS BACK ON STAGE WITH THE BLUES BUT SANS THREE FINGERS, the *Chicago Defender* carried a story by Dolores Calvin, who had visited Louis backstage at the New York theatre:

> It was after the first show at the famous Paramount and we were just dying to see how Louis Jordan, making his 'debut' after the recent knife-slashing incident with his third wife, was taking it. Outside of not being able to use three fingers of his left hand and having fourteen stitches in his chest, and some few other places, plus a deep cut under the lip, he was ready for action. 'After I rest up about two months I'll be sailing again. I'm a free man as of yesterday, you know. Now I can walk up and down the street and take my pick again. And this time – ha ha.'

One senses that Louis was laughing to keep from crying, but he miraculously summoned up enough energy to fulfil the rigorous schedule at the Paramount and performed with such abandon that the audience instantly forgot about his injuries. Trumpeter Ralph Porter, a friend from early Arkansas days, met Louis in the street at this time and, seeing that he looked far from well, offered him advice: 'You should go to Hot Springs for the waters. You know only too well that they will do you a power of good.' Louis replied, 'Porter, when I had the time for that sort of thing I didn't have the money, and now I've got the money I don't have the time.'[1]

A week after opening at the New York theatre, Louis attended a special Decca reception where he was presented with his first gold disc – for the million sales of 'Choo Choo Ch'Boogie' – and told that four of his other discs were rapidly approaching the million-seller gold award. By this time Louis had a new tenor saxist, Eddie Johnson (originally from Louisiana but raised in Chicago). Johnson (who replaced the Brooklyn tenor saxist James Wright) later said unequivocally, 'Louis Jordan was rocking and rolling when the Rolling Stones, the Beatles and Elvis Presley thought the only rock was in a baby's rocking chair.'[2] His first date with Louis was at the Paramount, as he recalled:

I got a call from Louis Jordan's manager and about the same time I got an offer to join Duke Ellington, but I chose Louis because the money was much better. Duke was offering about a $100 a week, but in a full week Louis was paying nearly $300. We travelled comfortably in cars; all of the instruments went in the truck which was driven by a guy from Texas. The road manager was Wilbur Brasfield (who I believe was still in the business working as a road manager forty years later). Louis was the strictest bandleader ever. He was very particular about dress, about shoes being shined and especially about being on time. On a date we played in South Carolina he actually fined me $10 for having muddy shoes. We did all sorts of work, a lot in theatres where George Hudson's band worked alongside us.[3]

Louis took a brief respite after his Paramount booking then resumed touring with a vengeance, scarcely allowing himself a day off during May and June, playing theatres in Cincinnati, Cleveland, Indianapolis, Columbus, Dayton, Baltimore, Washington and New York (at the Apollo). He also had to keep his record-buying public happy by waxing new material. In April 1947 he returned to familiar territory in recording 'Barnyard Boogie', he also sang a song about another of his favourite subjects, food, entitled 'Boogie Woogie Blue Plate', which features an elegant, 'locked-hands' twelve-bar piano solo from Bill Davis, and completed an up-tempo set with a brisk, humorous piece, 'Every Man to His Own Profession'. The final two items on the date were calypso numbers, 'Early in the Morning' and 'Run Joe'.

Louis had long been fascinated by music from the Caribbean; during his days at the Elks Rendezvous he always did his best to play numbers requested by West Indians who had settled in New York. His interest had been stimulated by the advent of Peggy Thomas, a Trinidadian singer and dancer who had featured in many of Louis's shows since 1944. She was always humming songs from her childhood, and Louis was constantly saying to her, 'That's a pretty tune, teach me the lyrics.' The success of his duet with Ella Fitzgerald on 'Stone Cold Dead in the Market' further kindled his interest in the exotic sounds, but it was not until Dr Walter Merrick became his regular physician that Louis seriously considered regularly featuring calypso music.

Dr Merrick, born in 1896 on St Vincent, a small island a few miles from Trinidad, was a recognized expert on the history of Caribbean music and a successful composer. In 1928, during early medical work in Washington, DC he had written an operetta entitled *Black Empire*, and later he had songs recorded by various performers, including Louis Jordan and Dinah Washington. Merrick and his lyricist, Joe Willoughby, from Trinidad, demonstrated their songs to Louis and were delighted when he decided to record 'Run Joe', whose success made it the first in a long line of West Indian themes that Louis featured for the remainder of his career. Louis thus gained a large number of fans in the Caribbean, some of whom were deceived by Louis's convincing accent into thinking that he too was a West Indian; those who were not fooled were flattered, so everyone ended up both satisfied and amused.

'Early in the Morning', a Caribbean-flavoured number written by Leo Hickman, Louis Jordan and bassist Dallas Bartley (who had recently rejoined the band), became the reverse side for 'Look Out', which Louis recorded in June 1947. 'Look Out' was conceived as a sequel to 'Beware'. This time, the lyrics were a female catalogue of complaints about the opposite sex, with Louis camping the lead role, aided and abetted by high-spirited shouts from the band. The reviewers were lukewarm about the pairing, but *Down Beat* said it was 'still a good deal better than the stuff his numerous imitators keep dishing out'. This comment highlighted the fact that an army of Jordan copyists was growing. Their task was made easier in the summer of 1947 when Times Square Music published a series of small-band arrangements based on Louis's recorded hits such as 'Beware', 'Caldonia', 'Reconversion Blues', 'Salt Pork', 'That Chick's Too Young' and 'Choo Choo Ch'Boogie'. So for fifty cents an orchestration, any combo in the world could read off a printed score and do its best to imitate the Tympany Five, but precious few came anywhere near capturing the sound of Louis's group, or of his saxophone playing. Occasionally reviewers in this period praised Louis's work on alto sax, but in general his instrumental excellence was taken too much for granted by many people in the music business. However, many young players who were just starting to make their way in the profession were full of admiration for Louis's playing. Among them was Art Pepper, who recalled, 'I heard Louis Jordan on alto; he knocked me out.'[4] Sonny Rollins also spoke of his early admiration for Louis Jordan: 'He was like a bridge between the blues and jazz – he had a great big sound on the alto and I just loved him.'[5]

Besides inspiring many youngsters to take up the saxophone, Louis was also primarily responsible for making the general record-buying public aware of the sound of the alto, preparing the way for future big sellers by Earl Bostic and Tab Smith. The great alto saxist Charlie Parker occasionally dropped in to see Louis Jordan, but their friendship temporarily withered after an incident in Chicago when Parker tried to sell Louis an alto sax that had just been given to him by the white bandleader Jimmy Dorsey. Dorsey, horrified by the decrepit state of Parker's instrument, carried out an act of spontaneous generosity and gave him his own brand-new Selmer saxophone. Parker thanked Dorsey from the bottom of his heart, left the club and immediately tried to sell it. No pawn shops were open that late, so he decided to see how much Louis would give him for the instrument. Louis did not want any part of the deal and said so; Parker cursed him and left. Later, the two men resumed their cordial friendship.

On 8 August 1947, Louis and the band began an engagement at the newly-opened Club Troubadour in New York, but for once a Jordan show failed to attract a large influx of customers. It was obvious to any potential patron that the club was in an unfinished state; the plaster was still wet, the lighting had not been fully installed, nor had the air-conditioning. Business was so poor that Louis was able to secure a release from his contract there, allowing him time to enter the Edgecomb Sanitarium in New York for a minor operation. Work, it seems, took precedence over everything, including his own health.

Louis was still not totally fit and this caused him to curtail his usual allocation of alto sax solos on several of the 1947 recordings. Fortunately, Eddie Johnson was on hand to play some eminently satisfactory tenor sax solos and he is heard to good advantage on the pot-boiler 'You're Much Too Fat', where he takes a lusty thirty-two-bar chorus, and on the lively 'Chicky-mo, Craney-crow', where his contribution is a good, free-wheeling forty-bar excursion. The same session produced a new number from Billy Austin (the writer of 'Is You is or is You ain't My Baby?') but his faintly amusing story of a protesting drunk, 'Have You Got the Gumption?' did not clock up big sales, despite another fine tenor sax solo. One of the best numbers from this batch is a sophisticated blues, 'We Can't Agree', written by another Trinidadian musician, Wilhelmina Gray, who also composed 'Barnyard Boogie'. Louis does not play alto sax at all on 'We Can't Agree', but provides a silky vocal, perfectly accompanied by the subtle piano figures created by a newcomer to the band, Bill Doggett. Bill Davis had gradually found that Louis's ever-increasing demands for new arrangements meant that he was spending many hours devising new scores as well as playing piano in the group. He let it be known that this was an unsatisfactory state of affairs, so Louis decided that the answer would be to get a new full-time pianist, allowing Bill Davis to submit arrangements as a freelance writer.

After completing a theatre tour on which they were supported by George Hudson's big band and guest star Sarah Vaughan, Louis and the band travelled to California to play a series of West Coast dates, including return bookings at Billy Berg's club (commencing 29 October). Louis planned to sign a new pianist during this trip, apparently having a particular West Coast musician in mind, but he was advised to listen first to Bill Doggett (also a highly experienced arranger).

Bill Doggett supplied the background:

In 1947 I was working with Lionel Hampton's Orchestra in California, but strictly as an arranger, travelling with the band but not playing piano. We were scheduled to play two weeks in Oakland, but after the first week the club owner was slow paying Gladys Hampton (Lionel's wife), and that was that – Gladys pulled the band out there and then. We travelled by train down to Los Angeles and I learnt on the grapevine that Louis Jordan was looking for a pianist and arranger. I heard that he liked some of the arranging I'd done for Sarah Vaughan. I didn't know Louis personally, but I'd known about him since we'd both played in Philadelphia during the 1930s. I went along to Billy Berg's club and got the job and played my first date with the band at the Golden Gate Theatre in San Francisco. It was the start of a long association. His hand had healed by this time, but you could still see the scars where he'd been cut.[6]

I remember the first day I went to rehearsal, he said, 'Bill Doggett, I want to tell you something, that was one of the greatest solos I've ever heard – but – as long as you're in my band don't ever cover up my words.' So I started to learn the lyrics so that I knew when to fill in. I marvelled at how he could remember those lyrics each and every night and play the same solo that he played. Louis used to tell us, 'Don't play anything you can't play twice. Because if I like it you've got to keep it in.' He was a stickler for that. He'd say, 'Fellows, some days we're going to jump 400 miles and have to play the same night. But, if you're experimenting with your solos, some nights you're not going to be able to invent and we're going to have a sad show. But if you play the same thing all of the time it will always sound right.'[7]

Doggett and Jordan never had a serious disagreement during their years together; the equanimity that existed between them was built on similar musical beliefs. Like Jordan, Doggett believed in satisfying the audience:

After all, what is music for? It's a thing to make people happy. Take the guy that spends money to hear us. He brings his old lady and they expect and deserve to hear what they like. A lot of musicians think it's corny to play the blues. What they really want is some kind of chord changes that will give them an opportunity to show off. The blues are simple, musically, but they have a feeling all their own, and that's not simple. Some people can play them, and some can't. I can sit and listen all night to someone who really knows how to play the blues.[8]

This trip to the West Coast was proving enormously successful; using his Tuesday night off from Billy Berg's in Los Angeles, Louis took the band to play a one-night stand at the Oakland Auditorium on 4 November, picking up $4,700 for this one engagement. The 7,000 crowd Louis drew to the dance was almost double the number that had attended similar functions featuring such top names as Lionel Hampton, Woody Herman and Stan Kenton.

Louis seemed to have made a good recovery from his injuries, but in late 1947, much to the surprise of the band, he issued a public statement saying he was 'temporarily breaking up his band due to ill health'.[9] In its 17 December issue, *Down Beat* gave the details: 'Due to an arthritic condition in one arm, Louis Jordan has cancelled all engagements for the next twelve weeks on doctor's orders.' Louis had been plagued by arthritis for some while, and indeed the condition proved to be chronic, but his sidemen had not noticed a deterioration in his general health and came to the conclusion that there were probably other reasons for what they regarded as an unwelcome, unpaid lay-off.

Tenor saxist Eddie Johnson recalls that soon after they attended a farewell party at Billy Berg's on 8 December, the band were formally given notice, and told that Louis did not want to work any more at that time because he did not want to pay most of what he had earned in taxes. The burden of income tax was only one of the financial problems bearing down on Louis. Since various of his earnings had been detailed in print, he was becoming increasingly vulnerable to further alimony demands. He still provided for Julie (in Chicago) and her daughter, and had commitments to Ida in New York (which he eventually settled with a lump-sum payment), but the financial problems connected with Fleecie's departure seemed insurmountable. To the astonishment of both the music business and the general public, Louis and Fleecie decided on a reconciliation, and to show the world that all was well again they packed their bags and paid a visit to Arkansas in late December 1947, where the *Brinkley Citizen* published a photograph of Louis and Fleecie, with Mack and Lizzie Reid and Louis's father.

One of the band's last get-togethers was at Decca's Los Angeles studio, where they recorded four sides, including 'Don't Burn the Candle at Both Ends', a jocular sermon in which Louis issues streams of rhymed advice. The other notable side from the session was a duet between Louis and Martha Davis entitled 'Daddy-O'. Martha Davis, a fine singer and pianist (from Wichita, Kansas), had long been a friend of Louis's. For about three years they had been promising each other they would make a record together, and they finally got around to it just before another dispute between the Musicians' Union and the record companies resulted in a further ban on recordings from 31 December 1947 until 14 December 1948. On 'Daddy-O', another advice song, Martha is heavily featured, taking five vocal choruses to Louis's two. This number later became a speciality for one of Louis's transient vocalists, Bixie Crawford.

Louis told his musicians that he was unable to say how long the lay-off would last, and this led three of them, Dallas Bartley, Eddie Johnson and Carl Hogan, to tell him that they were unwilling to wait about for an unspecified period and that they planned to find regular work elsewhere. Before Louis began his vacation, he earmarked the men's replacements, a move that later brought into the group guitarist Roosevelt James Jackson (known to all as 'Ham'), who had been working in Loumell Morgan's trio at Billy Berg's; bassist Billy Hadnott, who had been recommended by Bill Doggett; and tenor saxist Paul Quinichette, previously with Johnny Otis's band.

During the lay-off, Louis underwent plastic surgery to remove facial scars, then spent a few weeks recuperating in Florida. Returning to Los Angeles, he rehearsed the new line-up, then began working in February 1948, playing a series of West Coast theatre bookings. There was no easing in; the band immediately launched into a full schedule which included the making of a new Astor movie, *Look Out Sister*, a sixty-seven minute picture that featured Louis as a musical cowboy who discovers oil (Louis was able to utilize the riding lessons he had taken in Hot Springs years before). Some of the scenes in the film were shot at Louis's home in Phoenix, Arizona. When the movie was released, early in 1949, it was said to be the first feature film in which all the music had been provided by a seven-piece band.[10]

The short break in Louis's career had not impaired his drawing power at the box office, and for a two-week booking at the Golden Gate Theatre in San Francisco (February 1948) he grossed $70,000. In April, when Louis took on a string of one-night stands that extended into Vancouver, Canada, the tour promoter, John Burton, said, 'Louis Jordan will make me more money than any other four attractions I can get.'[11] With big money again flowing in regularly, Louis decided to buy a new Fleetwood Cadillac, but in order to keep the peace with Fleecie he also bought her a similar car. Louis employed a chauffeur (Mickey Collins) and a valet (Collis Wilburn), in addition to his long-time road manager, Wilbur Brasfield. Usually the musicians travelled in a De Soto (later replaced by a Chrysler Suburban).

Some of the 1948 tour dates were in theatres, others in dance halls, where Louis and his musicians were given the chance to improvise extended solos, often using a repertoire that incorporated old jazz standards and evergreen ballads (which Louis enjoyed singing), but Louis always made sure that recent record hits were sprinkled throughout a dance-hall date. By this time, modern jazz (or bebop as it was called), had won over the tastes of many jazz fans, ousting the swing style. Those who preferred older concepts plumped for traditional jazz, causing a revival of interest in that music which existed alongside (sometimes in open rivalry) the new bebop style.

Louis was careful not to appear an old fuddy-duddy, and in a March 1948 interview said:

Like bebop? Man, I love it. That's for me. You know Dizzy Gillespie's my boy. I worked with him back when I was with Chick Webb and he was with Teddy Hill at the Savoy Ballroom. That was when Dizzy was first starting. We've got seven or eight bebop numbers in the book right now, but you can't put them over on the stage. Not now. Maybe in a couple of years when people get educated to it. We play them at dances now.[12]

In fact, Louis did his utmost to keep any trace of bebop from his recordings. As a token, the band played quasi-bop themes at dances, and occasionally on radio shows, but he specifically asked his drummers not to interfere with the steady shuffle rhythm that had become one of the Jordan trademarks, and he vetted all his arrangement to make sure that no vestige of the revolutionary new jazz concepts had seeped into them. His sole concession was occasionally to quote a bop cliché or two in his solos, but he did this only when he felt the audience would be hip to the joke.

Louis's attitude to bop created a certain amount of antagonism in his new tenor saxist, Paul Quinichette, who later likened Louis to 'a dictator with Uncle Tom qualities'. Recounting his memories to Stanley Dance, he told him, 'He really wanted Wardell Gray, but Wardell had told him, "Fuck you, you Uncle Tom, I ain't going to work for you." ' In another interview, later in his life, Quinichette said:

> Wardell Gray was working somewhere and his wife didn't want to go, so I went with Louis Jordan and came to New York. I hated all the time I was with him. I didn't like the type of thing he was doing, it wasn't swing. I think Louis was a prelude to this rock thing. I didn't like all those tunes, 'Deacon Jones', 'Caldonia', 'Run Joe' and all that, but they were all hits. The money was great with him.
>
> We went all over the place, all over the South, all over New York, everywhere; we even made a little old movie, a three-reeler. I got sick of wearing those sequinned, Christmas-tree-type uniforms, red pants, vivid green coats, sequinned ties and boots, and we had to stand up there and dance and play those tunes. We fell out. I told him one time, 'Listen, you were doing much better when you were playing alto with Chick Webb than doing this.' He didn't like that at all, so that was the parting of the ways right there, I joined Hot Lips Page.[13]

There is no doubt that Louis was vexed with Quinichette. He felt that Paul had let him down because he had known what the band's style was before he joined, and what the job entailed. The tenor saxist had shown no qualms in accepting more money than he had ever earned before, but repaid Louis by getting drunk and being late on the bandstand. Bassist Bill Hadnott feels that Louis might have forgiven Quinichette for his attitudes had it not been for a particular incident. He told Peter Vacher in 1979, 'Paul was a handsome cat, fooling around with Peggy, the little vocalist, and Louis didn't like that. Louis caught him and fired Paul.'[14] At the time of his dismissal, Quinichette said, simply and tersely, 'I couldn't clown; he fired me.'[15]

Trumpeter Aaron Izenhall saw the conflict develop:

Paul Quinichette and those bebop disciples didn't like the idea of wearing really bright, wild-coloured clothing and moving around while they played, or putting on a show. Louis decided enough was enough. A little later on, Charlie Rouse came into the band on tenor sax; he didn't create any problems at all, but he was just too modern for what Louis wanted and they parted amicably. Louis himself liked bop, and he was crazy about Charlie Parker, but he didn't want it in his band. His motto, which he often said, was: 'Keep it simple.' He wanted music that a working man could relax to. One reason why Louis was so strict with guys like Paul Quinichette was because in those days the stage managers at various theatres were also so strict, and they insisted on everything being just as the contract stated, so if one man was late going on stage Louis was liable to forfeit money, or be fined at the end of the week.[16]

Although being called an 'Uncle Tom' irked Louis, he tried not to show he was hurt if the charge was made in public. But on more than one occasion his musicians witnessed a backstage explosion of fury as Louis countered such allegations by pointing out that all of his showmanship had been learnt from black performers, all of his tricks of the trade mastered while he was playing to black audiences. If, later, white audiences also found them funny this was not, in his eyes, a disgrace. Louis was particularly proud that he was popular at the Apollo Theatre, which boasted the hippest audience in the world, and pointed out that the audiences there were 'too damn busy laughing at me, and at themselves, to make any complaints'. It was a good point, because while Louis had, from his own experiences, shrewdly observed what black city dwellers found funny about their country cousins, he also knew how to make rural people laugh about life in a big city. He thus acted as a middle man and made his points in a vernacular that all parties understood, wrapping his lyrics up with music whose beat attracted unstinting approval from every section of society.

With Paul Quinichette's departure, Louis brought back Josh Jackson on tenor sax. Bill Hadnott temporarily returned to California and his place on double bass was taken by the Philadelphia musician, Bob Bushnell. The vacancy was first offered to Stanley Gaines, the bass-playing son of Louis's old mentor, Charlie Gaines, but Stanley was then with the successful group The Cats and the Fiddle, so he declined the offer. Arranger Bill Davis had left the fold by this time and all the arranging duties were in the hands of pianist Bill Doggett. In February 1949, the new line-up produced an unusual coupling, 'Safe, Sane and Single', a mock 'hoe-down' romp brought to Louis by a young songwriter in Omaha, Nebraska, and 'I Know what I've Got', a ballad by the experienced composer Sid Robin, which produced a sensitive vocal from Louis, and also some brief but poignant alto sax playing.

The singer Peggy Thomas continued to work regularly with Louis, still intriguing him with her seemingly limitless store of West Indian themes. It was she who encouraged Louis to record the Trinidad-inspired 'Push-ka-pee She Pie', which was composed by the familiar team of Dr Merrick, Joe Willoughby and Louis Jordan. The exuberance of this piece was almost equalled by the band's recording of 'Beans and Cornbread', which apart from a few pedal notes on the tenor saxophone, is a wild gospel number, with Louis exhorting his congregation to new heights by hollering out a menu comprising perfect food combinations. The voices of the band were able to rest during the next item recorded, an instrumental entitled 'Onions', featuring Louis and Josh Jackson. As if to prove to the world (and Paul Quinichette) that he was not a stick-in-the-mud, Louis decided to record this number, one of the bop-tinged arrangements he played at dances. The same applied to 'Psycho Loco', which begins with Louis showing that Charlie Parker did have a temporary effect on his playing. The first of his three blues choruses reveals his admiration for Bird, but as he brings the solo to a climax he reverts to his own licks.

Jim Jordan (conductor and cornetist) with the Brinkley Brass Band c. 1919

Above: Louis Jordan's childhood home in Brinkley, Arkansas

Below: Brinkley railroad station, 1991

Above: Trumpeter Charlie Gaines's Band, Philadelphia, 1934. Louis Jordan is the end figure on Gaines's right (Frank Driggs Collection)

Left: Louis Jordan c. 1935 (Frank Driggs Collection)

opposite page

Top: Chick Webb with his reed section 1937. Louis Jordan on alto saxophone
(Frank Driggs Collection)

Bottom: Chick Webb's Orchestra on tour, Chicago 1937. Louis Jordan (alto
saxophone) kneeling (Frank Driggs Collection)

Above: Louis Jordan's Tympany Five c. 1940

Above: Ella Fitzgerald and Louis Jordan (Frank Driggs Collection)

Below: Louis Jordan and Bing Crosby (Courtesy Decca Records)

Above: Louis Jordan (alto sax)
Hot Lips Page (trumpet) July 1946
(Peter Vacher Collection)

Right: The Jordanettes
(Peter Vacher Collection)

Top left: Fleecie Moore (Courtesy of the Jelks family)

Top right: Berle Adams

Bottom: Louis Jordan and Florence 'Vicky' Johnson

Top: Dinah Shore and Louis Jordan with Ezekiel of the Hoosier Hotshots during Command Performance radio show 1944 (US Army photograph)

Bottom left: Louis Jordan and George Raft in *Follow The Boys* 1944 (Danny Garçon Collection)

Bottom right: Jackie Davis, Dottie Smith and Louis Jordan

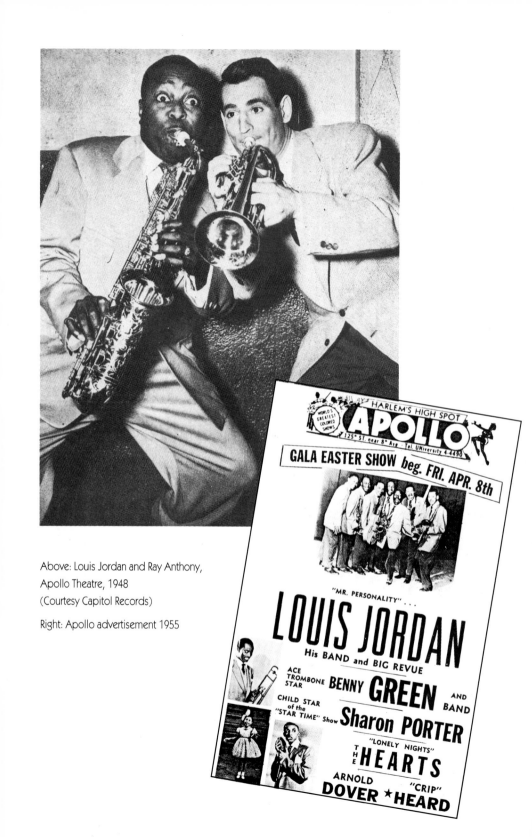

Above: Louis Jordan and Ray Anthony,
Apollo Theatre, 1948
(Courtesy Capitol Records)

Right: Apollo advertisement 1955

Aaron Izenhall (trumpet)
(Peter Vacher Collection)

Carl Hogan (guitar) (Courtesy Ralph Porter)

Chester Lane (piano) (Peter Vacher Collection)

Johnny Kirkwood (drums)
(Courtesy Johnny Kirkwood)

Above: Louis Jordan's Tympany Five, Jamaica 1951
(Courtesy of the Gleaner Co. Ltd)

opposite page

Top left: Louis Jordan opens the batting, Georgetown 1951

Top right: Louis Jordan wearing his Deacon Jones outfit

(Photograph by Warren Rothschild)

Bottom: Louis Jordan's Tympany Five with Peggy Thomas during the
1948 filming of *Look Out Sister* (Courtesy Astor Films)

Above: Louis Jordan's Big Band, 1951 (Frank Driggs Collection)

Below: Louis Jordan's Tympany Five (Frank Driggs Collection)

Above left: Louis Jordan visits his home town, Brinkley, Arkansas in December 1959
and presents an album to Hi Mayo of radio station KBRI
(Courtesy of the *Brinkley Argus*)

Above right: Louis Jordan, December 1962 (Photograph by Val Wilmer)

Below: Chris Barber, Ottilie Patterson and Louis Jordan. London, December 1962
(Photograph by Val Wilmer)

Above: Louis and Martha Jordan, Los Angeles,
1960s (Photograph courtesy of Martha Jordan)

Right: Louis and Martha Jordan, August 1970
(Photograph courtesy of Martha Jordan)

By the time that session took place Louis had implemented one of his more bizarre instrumental ideas by adding two trumpeters to the band's line-up, creating an unusual front line of three trumpets and two saxophones. The two newcomers, Bob Mitchell and Harold 'Hal' Mitchell (no relation) were vastly experienced players, but even they had never been part of a similar line-up. Hal Mitchell recalled his stay in the band:

> I had worked with Chris Columbus when he had his own nine-piece band at Smalls' Paradise in New York, so he recommended me to Louis Jordan when he heard that Louis was planning to augment. Chris said to me, 'This guy goes in for bullshit but stick with him.' I soon realized that Louis wanted to create a big-band effect without paying for a big band. Aaron Izenhall was on lead trumpet and he told us what the running order was, and what Louis was about to play because we sure as hell wouldn't have known from Louis himself. He didn't give many indications, but this was because most of his guys had been with him a long time and they knew all about his show routines. It wasn't the greatest or the worst, but it was interesting from the beginning to the end. Louis Jordan being an entertaining instrumentalist and me being a musical instrumentalist meant I didn't quite fit his mould. I'm sure I wasn't the greatest singer and dancer he ever had, but I did the best I could, which it seems wasn't good enough.
>
> It was a very odd group. I wrote two arrangements which the musicians liked and which Louis played twice, but forgot to pay for. My engagement with him was for a twenty-seven day RKO theatre tour, spread over four or five weeks. Appearing with us as part of Louis's show was the Will Mastin Trio, featuring Sammy Davis Jr. Also on tour was Paula Watson, who'd just had a hit with 'A Little Bird Told Me'. We travelled by cars for the tour, which took in the Royal, Baltimore, the Howard, Washington, the Regal, Chicago and the Apollo, New York. Louis also forgot to pay me at the end of the tour, but I collected all of it later.[17]

During his brief sojourn with the band, Hal Mitchell took part in the second Louis Jordan–Ella Fitzgerald duet session for Decca. It produced two satisfactory sides, 'Baby It's Cold Outside' and 'Don't

Cry Cry Baby', a coupling which stayed in the charts for several weeks without getting near the top. Louis and Ella worked long and hard at a written arrangement of 'Baby It's Cold Outside' without producing a satisfactory master recording, but after they decided to ad-lib it they wrapped the song up very quickly.[18]

Louis regularly hired the Will Mastin Trio (featuring Sammy Davis Jr) as a support group when he played theatres, and later he proudly observed Sammy gradually achieving international fame. But for some reason Davis chose to forget the help and encouragement that Louis had given him during the early stages of his climb to the top. In 1965, when Louis read Sammy Davis's autobiography *Yes I Can*, he was astonished and hurt to see that he did not rate a single mention, but he sensed it would be so, because Sammy had deliberately kept out of his way for some while before the book was published.

Perhaps, in looking back, Sammy had been irritated by memories of Louis's ability to top any previous performer's efforts, no matter how well they had been received by an audience. Jordan's was always an immensely tough act, one that refused to be outshone. There was nothing malicious in Louis's attitude, but on stage he was usually fearsomely competitive. His former manager, Berle Adams, can cite many instances of Louis demolishing nationally-known performers who tried to steal the show from him or who had insisted on appearing after Louis had done his stint. Only once during this period did Louis come close to suffering a setback, and this was at the hands of the Texan pianist-singer Ivory Joe Hunter, who worked in a similar groove to Louis, holding the view that 'rock and roll is nothing but the blues hopped up'.[19] The audience at the Regal Theatre, Chicago went wild over the huge, bespectacled boogie specialist, and though Louis closed the show he could not equal the response given to Ivory Joe.

The short-lived experiment of augmenting the band ended, and Louis resumed recording with his usual small line-up. Bassist Bill Hadnott had returned to the Tympany Five, and it was through him that Louis created another everlasting favourite, 'School Days'. Hadnott and Josh Jackson worked up a song similar to 'School Days' but found they could not copyright it because it contained too many references to nursery rhymes that were in the public domain. Louis lingered on the idea and decided to record 'School Days' complete with a band vocal; the move produced another hit.

At a Decca session four months later the band continued its winning run by waxing what became Louis's most requested numbers 'Saturday Night Fish Fry' – the pinnacle of all of his eating-partying songs. Louis developed Ellis Walsh's song, and was bold enough to visualize it as a double-sided 78 r.p.m. issue, which meant the listener had to turn the record over to hear the second half of the piece. Again three trumpeters were booked for the date, but this was principally to match up the sound of the band for 'Hungry Man' so that it could be the 'B' side of 'Push-ka-pee She Pie'. It was decided also to use the bigger band on the 'Fish Fry' sides. Bill Doggett recalls this as being an impromptu head arrangement for which no music was used, though Berle Adams feels that the song was tried out in public for about eight weeks before the recording date.

By this time Bill Doggett had fully assumed the role previously played by Bill Davis. Doggett, a fine pianist and a skilful arranger, found that he too had to spend many hours in Louis's company, writing down the framework of arrangements and providing harmonies for various embryo songs. The two men got on, but no close friendship ever developed. Doggett explained:

I always felt that Louis didn't want anyone to get too close to him. For instance, we'd finish a job and prepare to move off to the next date, say 120 miles away (or maybe further), and he'd say, 'Hey Bill. You gonna ride with me?' Then the next night he'd keep silent and his chauffeur would drive off with him. Louis rode in his Cadillac, the rest of the band travelled in a De Soto, and the instruments and the uniforms went in a big truck – all that side of things was looked after by the road manager, Wilbur Brasfield. Maybe I'd ride with Louis three nights running, then he'd say, on the fourth night, in a matter-of-fact voice. 'You ride in the De Soto tonight.' He just didn't want to get too friendly.[20]

One time in Atlantic City we were living next door to each other and he would come down to the beach and my wife and I would be down to the beach and he'd call me over and we'd sit down and talk. And I can remember one talk in particular. Louis must have been really down in the dumps. For about two hours or more, he told me all about the business and the tax problems he was getting ready to get into. He said, 'Bill, this is just a terrible situation. My manager is taking 20 per cent and my booking office is taking 15 per cent, so I'm losing 35 per cent of my money before I even pay my expenses.' And then next day he walked to the beach and waved his hand. Then one night we played a dance in Kansas City, Missouri and we filled that auditorium with people. We only had to go on to Columbia, Missouri, which wasn't that far. We all got down to the bus to leave at ten or eleven o'clock in the morning. We were talking on the bus as sidemen do; 'Louis filled that auditorium. Man, I know he's gonna give us a tip on payday.' Louis got on the bus and said, 'Harma shaba,' went back in his seat and didn't say a word to the band from Kansas City to Columbia, Missouri. That was his mood swing. We figured he was going to come down and be happy and jolly. Nobody had done a thing to him. Instead of saying, 'How you all?' he used to come in and say 'Harma shaba.' We knew that meant: 'Good morning.'[21]

Decca, still extremely satisfied with Louis's sales figures, renewed his recording contract in January 1949. They, like other major recording companies, were preparing the way for the introduction of micro groove recordings – within a few years, all releases would be made on 45 r.p.m. or 33⅓ r.p.m. discs. Louis's overseas sales were encouraging, particularly in Britain where he had built up a durable following, larger than that of Nat 'King' Cole, because initially Capitol (the company that issued Cole's recordings) could not find a suitable UK release outlet. Jordan's records also enjoyed healthy sales in Australia, despite the Federation of Commercial Broadcasting, which kept a strict watch on lyrics to eliminate any hint of suggestiveness. They had originally banned all versions of 'I'm Gonna Move to the Outskirts of Town' because of the reference to the iceman.[22]

In the late 1940s, bowing to editorial pressure from music magazines, most American labels gradually dropped such trading appellations as 'Race label' or 'Sepia label', but this did not mean the old ogre of prejudice had vanished, as Louis Jordan and his band found out when they broke new ground by playing a booking at the Thunderbird Hotel in Las Vagas from 8 to 21 February 1949. Henry

Miller, formerly a booking manager at GAC, thinks that the Delta Rhythm Boys vocal group were the first black act to work Las Vegas, with Louis Jordan's Tympany Five becoming the first black band to be employed there.

In those years, Las Vegas was just beginning to expand, and was then only about a tenth the size it is now. Even so, it attracted some powerful, rich gamblers from the South. The various hotel and casino managers had no wish to alienate these big spenders by allowing black musicians to mingle with them – it was the same sort of situation that Louis Jordan had experienced many times in the 1930s. Aaron Izenhall remembers that engagement clearly:

We did a spot in the show, only three numbers, then we had two hours off between shows, but in those days we were not allowed into the casino. The management were very polite to us and offered us anything we wanted to eat or drink, but they pointed out that they had gamblers in there from Texas and Mississippi and so we were not allowed to go in. The only black allowed to go in there in those days was the dancer Bill 'Bojangles' Robinson. He could go to the tables and gamble, but he was the exception. Often during that two-hour break we went across town to the black section. You could relax there and you could gamble there too, if you wanted.[23]

Eventually Louis was granted the full facilities of the gambling rooms, but this proved to be a costly privilege for him, because he almost became a compulsive gambler. Having lost a hundred dollars playing craps he did his utmost to win it back, but ended up losing over $10,000 during one of his Las Vegas bookings. He borrowed enough to pay the band their wages, then set out to drive to New York. But in Sweetwater, Texas he wept so bitterly, he recalled, that 'my eyes swole up and I couldn't see to drive'.[24] Louis was in such an emotional state that he had to hire a chauffeur for the rest of the journey. Some months later he had to steel himself to play a return booking in Las Vegas. He decided to return to the gambling city early to test his willpower before the engagement began. He kept away from the dice, but wagered twenty dollars on the fruit machines, lost that, and pronounced himself cured.

The trailblazing that Louis and his band did in Las Vegas during 1949 paid off, because within a year other established black groups (like the Nat 'King' Cole Trio) were playing regularly at the Thunderbird Hotel; Louis and his musicians also returned there many times. During the coming years they became the first black band to play at many previously denied venues, both in the North and in the South. The breakthrough was especially timely for Louis, because so many of the theatres where he had triumphed (and earned enormous fees) were either closing down or changing over to a 'movies-only' policy – the death rattle of vaudeville had begun.

# 11
## Work, Baby, Work

Louis still tended to take on work schedules that were much too heavy, and as he sang almost every number the wear and tear usually affected his voice first. In February 1950, just as he was about to open at Bop City on New York's 52nd Street, he again became ill with laryngitis. This meant cancelling a proposed trip to the West Indies and a long, lucrative tour of the South; instead he went home to rest. Bassist Billy Hadnott recalled:

> Early in 1950 Louis took time off because he was exhausted, and he genuinely was; you see, at a dance or in a club Louis would play and sing one number after another for hour after hour, then after a thirty-minute break he'd get back on the stand and work just as hard. He couldn't coast or pace himself, he wasn't like that. He was a fine entertainer, singer, dancer and comedian but he was also an excellent musician, and remained, always, a perfectionist. He believed in keeping you on your toes. Though every arrangement was written out he expected you to memorize each one so that there would be no music parts on the bandstand. I left New York when he temporarily disbanded and I returned to Los Angeles. When he formed up a few months later he asked me to rejoin, but I had had enough of touring and I said, 'No thanks.'[1]

Bassist Bob Bushnell became a permanent member of the band, as did the left-handed guitarist Bill Jennings, who took 'Ham' Jackson's place.

By this time Louis and Fleecie had purchased a luxurious home in Phoenix, Arizona. On the rare occasions that spare time became available Louis went there to relax and to indulge in one of his favourite pastimes: basking in the sun (which he found beneficial for his arthritis). The house (on Purple Drive), with its 40 x 20 ft swimming pool, was a potent attraction in itself, and the clear air and warmth of Phoenix appealed to both Louis and Fleecie. But dark clouds were again gathering over the couple's relationship, despite the fact that in July 1950 Fleecie threw a huge forty-second birthday party for Louis, attended by more than 200 people. The basis of the trouble was that Louis was again seeing his old flame Vicky regularly.

Fleecie had little desire to tour with the band, occasionally travelling to a booking if it was in a city where she and Louis had mutual friends. But Vicky, younger than Fleecie, still felt the glamour of the road and was usually willing to tag along knowing how much Louis appreciated feminine company when he was on tour. Perhaps because Louis had spent a good deal of his childhood in the company of women (his father being away on tour), he found it easier to relax with them than with men. He was cagey enough not to show all of his cards to anyone, but after he had completed his work he liked to unwind by chatting with dancers and singers, even when there was no question of a sexual liaison. Trumpeter Aaron Izenhall said, 'Louis liked women, but he wasn't a womanizer.' It was not unknown for Louis to take his entire female chorus line out for an unplanned celebration, putting three hundred dollars down on the table to show them that they could order anything they wanted.

Ann Bailey, who sang and danced in Louis's chorus line the Jordanettes, spoke warmly of Louis's generosity:

Louis paid for all the dancers to have tuition and made sure we never went short of money, clothes or food. When the Jordanettes were offered the chance to play the London Palladium, as a separate act, Louis insisted we took the booking. We appeared there with comedian Tommy Trinder. It was fun, but I guess Britain was still suffering from the after-effects of World War II because we couldn't get the sort of food we liked; we had to put up with dried eggs and ice cream that never tasted quite right. Louis got to hear of this and sent us all care packages. That was really such a kind gesture.[2]

154

Ann Bailey's husband (who sang and compèred) was with her on most of Louis's tours; within the troupe several of the dancers were linked (some matrimonially) with members of the Tympany Five. Chris Columbus's wife, Jessie Morris, was with the show for a long while, as was Elaine Robinson (formerly the wife of Bill 'Bojangles' Robinson) who married bassist Bob Bushnell; Aaron Izenhall and Jean Hooper were close friends. Singer Peggy Thomas was also becoming increasingly involved with a musician who wasn't part of Louis's shows, namely the celebrated jazz pianist Erroll Garner (she eventually left the Jordan set-up in the summer of 1951 to become a full-time travelling companion to Erroll).

Louis's 'new' band made their first recording together in June 1950, producing two unsensational sides, 'I Want a Roof over My Head' and a joky 'Show Me How You Milk the Cow', another barnyard frolic and one that did not please the critics; one reviewer described it as 'tiresome mooing'. The same session yielded the slow, bouncy 'Blue Light Boogie', which featured a group vocal by Louis, Josh Jackson and Aaron Izenhall, backed by the four-piece rhythm section. Its 'party' theme was intended to create a follow-up to 'Saturday Night Fish Fry', and like that hit it was also spread over a double-sided record release, but the story line was nothing like as effective and that too got a lukewarm reception, typified by *Metronome*'s 'mildly entertaining' description. The most significant part of 'Blue Light Boogie' was created by Bill Jennings's supple guitar playing, echoes of which cropped up in the work of several musicians.

Even Louis's new recording with Ella Fitzgerald, 'Ain't Nobody's Business' and 'I'll Never be Free', failed to attract either critical acclaim or big sales, but another duet session made that same month (August 1950) had a sensational effect on reviewers and the general public. Louis's partner here was none other than Louis Armstrong, who moved into top gear, instrumentally and vocally, stimulated by the infectious swing of the Tympany Five's accompaniment. The two Louis' vocals and horn work combine perfectly to produce a euphoric climax to 'You Rascal You' and a series of ingenious inflections on 'Life is So Peculiar'.

Unfortunately the two men never recorded together again. No reason has ever been established for this state of affairs, but it was

rumoured that Armstrong's manager, Joe Glaser (who was slow to
forgive any slight – real or imagined), still brooded over Louis's
success at the Capitol Lounge in Chicago some twenty years earlier,
feeling that one of his acts should have been offered the booking.
Many years after the recording with Armstrong, Louis Jordan passed
on his vivid recollections to Steve Allen (then a producer at the
British Broadcasting Corporation):

> Louis came in town and his lip had busted on him – had busted all
> the way down, and he says, 'I don't care if I don't have a lip; we're
> going to record today.' So we got in the studio at six o'clock in the
> morning. There's a couple of places around New York called
> Chock Full of Nuts, one not far from 50 West 57th Street where we
> recorded for Decca, and Louis says, 'Let's go down to Chock Full
> of Nuts and get a sandwich and some coffee and then we'll see if we
> can find some fruit. I said, 'What's this about fruit?' and he said,
> 'Well, I find that if we can get some white grapes and eat them and
> rest awhile probably my voice will clear.' He was real hoarse and
> he says, 'And I'm going to make it anyhow. Don't worry about it,
> I'm gonna make it.' We were supposed to start recording at seven
> o'clock, but we didn't start until 10.30 a.m. We went out and had
> sandwiches and got the fruit. We came back and sat around in the
> studio for hours just talking. He'd pick up his horn and blow a
> couple of notes and say, 'No, I ain't ready yet.' And we'd keep
> right on talking, and we started the session about 10.30 or 10.45 and
> we were through in ten minutes. We had talked it over and he'd
> looked at the music and we knew what we were going to do, but
> we had to wait on his lip. Finally he says, 'Let's go,' and we went
> and played it. He even played those high Cs and things with his lip
> busted. He was magnificent.[3]

Time had mellowed Jordan's memories of the date, because Bill
Doggett recollected that Jordan was 'mad – fit to be tied'[4] over the
late start to the session.

The couple proved to be a big seller, both in America and in
Europe. Jazz pianist Joe Bushkin, reviewing 'Life is So Peculiar' as
part of a 'blindfold test' told Leonard Feather, 'If this record becomes
number one on the Hit Parade it will put all the psychiatrists out of

business, and also all the other trumpet players. I love that King Oliver break there, in the middle.'⁵ The break Bushkin referred to is a scintillating two-bar blend of alto sax and trumpet, beautifully played and effectively harmonized which climaxes a musical chase between the two stars, each of them taking four bars apiece. Their vocal duetting is no less effective.

'I'll be Glad when You're Dead You Rascal You' (written by Jordan's old buddy Sam Theard) had been recorded years before by Armstrong, but here he tackles the song with an exhilarating freshness, first by answering Jordan's lively vocal with vigorous, apt trumpet phrases and then by imparting a free-wheeling swing to his singing (Jordan answering first on alto sax then vocally). Then Armstrong blows three epic choruses, rising to his top register to answer the fervent riffs created by the Tympany Five, capping a stupendous endeavour with a triumphant final high note.

Louis Jordan was delighted that his duet session with Armstrong (whom he always addressed as 'Pops') had turned out so well, but the success of those two sides did nothing to quell another bout of his periodic restlessness. Despite the fact that the Tympany Five was still doing excellent business wherever it went, Jordan skidded through a patch of despondency before hitting on a new idea. His innovative plan was to feature the band's former pianist, Wild Bill Davis, on organ with the Tympany Five. Davis, a pioneer of jazz Hammond organ playing, was excited by the idea:

> My main reason for leaving Louis was so that I could specialize on organ. It was a gamble because I spent over two thousand dollars on the instrument, and I actually took a drop in wages to carry out my plan. I was on $175 a week with Louis; when I started my own trio on organ I was only getting $75 a week, but I was gradually learning more about the technique of organ playing, and I was happy. Later, when Louis offered me the chance to make records with him on organ I was pleased to accept the challenge.⁶

The link-up created 'Tamburitza Boogie' and 'Lemonade', the success of which inspired Louis to revamp his stage show to include Davis on organ, while Bill Doggett remained on piano. The new package began life at the Howard Theatre in Washington, DC during Christmas week 1950, and then played week-long bookings at the Royal, Baltimore and the Earle, Philadelphia. The audiences responded to the full-blooded sound of the powerful organ but the theatre circuit was by this time so diminished that the idea of keeping the show together permanently was abandoned, though Louis used Bill Davis on several subsequent recordings. Davis was relieved at not becoming a permanent part of Louis's presentations once more, because he was already establishing a following which eventually led to him selling millions of his own albums.

The tour dates with Davis had their effect on Bill Doggett, however, who noted, without rancour:

> Louis paid Bill three times what he paid us. I liked the sound of the organ, so I thought, 'That's for me.' I went out and put a deposit on one at the Steinway showrooms, and began practising as hard as I could. But I had to keep all this a secret, because if Louis found out that I'd bought an organ he'd know that I had eyes for moving on and leaving him, and I needed the money that Louis was paying me to finish off paying for it.[7]

Several of the songs that Louis recorded for Decca in the early 1950s were unissued: Louis was finding it more difficult to obtain the right material, despite maintaining his practice of keeping the door open to any budding composers. Berle Adams never ceased to be amazed at Louis's willingness to see anyone who arrived saying they'd written a song for him – though Adams had to admit that good material had arrived in that way during the past. He said, 'A songwriter would always leave him feeling buoyed up. Afterwards I'd ask him: "How could you say those nice things when you knew it was a piece of junk?", and Louis would say, "If I said something negative they'd argue with me and I'd never get them out of my dressing room. So long as I say a good word they leave."'[8]

Even songs that were accepted sometimes needed tailoring and altering, but Louis was content to sit down by himself for hours permutating ideas for a new song. Often the hopefuls had simply copied one of Louis's previous hits, but even then Louis would patiently hear the piece through. Nevertheless, at least two of his songwriting callers were memorably original. One brought in a ventriloquist's dummy and sang a poor call-and-answer blues with his prop, prompting Louis to say that the song was not for him because he was not a ventriloquist. The man merely beamed and said, 'Don't worry, it won't take long, I'll teach you.' The other was a young, shy-looking girl who began her audition with a loud scream, so piercing that some of the show's cast came running along the passage to see what the trouble was. Louis, considerably agitated, asked, 'In God's name, girl, what made you do that?' The demure visitor answered, 'It's the start of my song "I'm Screaming My Head off for You".' Yet Louis still continued to encourage songwriters to bring their material to him, saying, 'As long as they write 'em and are willing to sell 'em, I'm willing to do business with them. I can't write everything myself and I'm not greedy for all of it.'⁹

Back in the summer of 1950 Louis realized that his own domestic affairs would soon result in a showdown, but he cast thoughts of that impending situation from his mind to deal with another problem. His long-time manager and adviser, Berle Adams, had decided to quit. The background to this decision was outlined in a *Down Beat* story, published in its issue of 11 August 1950: 'Berle Adams, personal manager of Jerry Gray and Louis Jordan, has dropped out of the personal management field to join the Music Corporation of America where he will concentrate on building new talent.'

Years later, Berle Adams recalled how daunting it had been in 1950, having to tell Louis Jordan of his decision to leave:

Breaking the news to Louis was very difficult because we had worked so closely for nine years, without any serious disagreements, but I was suffering a lot with my back, and I wanted to move to California permanently with my family. The offer from MCA came at a crucial time and I decided to accept it even though business with Louis was still booming and my other work with Mercury Records was going well. I had to start afresh, so I relinquished my previous interests, but Louis definitely thought I was moving on because I'd sensed he was losing popularity. He looked at me very sadly and said, 'So I've hit the top and now I'm sliding down. That must be it, because you're too smart to walk away from success.' He was demoralized and nothing I could say changed his attitude, but difficult though it was, I stuck with my decision.¹⁰

Louis hit the doldrums and announced in the musical press that he was seriously considering quitting the music business to retire to Phoenix, Arizona, but a few weeks of inactivity rekindled his enthusiasm, and he was greatly heartened when Decca again renewed his recording contract early in 1951. His mind began racing with new plans.

The only persistent bone of contention between Louis and Berle Adams had concerned Louis's long-held desire to form a big band. Adams was firmly against the idea, pointing out that Louis had developed a unique, instantly recognizable sound with The Tympany Five. It was all right to make occasional records where the tone colours were augmented, or duet singers brought in, but the public had consistently shown that it liked the small band best of all, and promoters too were content to rebook the group time and time again. Louis was not totally convinced by these arguments.

Part of the disagreement stemmed from the fact that Louis felt that his musicianship had never been taken seriously, even with Chick Webb, where he had been featured as a singer and comedian more often than as an instrumentalist. He had always wanted the opportunity to prove himself capable of being the premier soloist in a big musical aggregation. He naturally enjoyed the prominence he got with the Tympany Five, but felt that by leading his own big band he would be able to cock a snook at various detractors and win new audiences at the same time. So when the Carter hotel chain let it be known that they would consider booking Louis if he used a big line-up, he resolved to carry out the ambition he had expressed in 1944, when he had said, 'With my ideas and ambition my best possibilities are with small combos, but after the war, with such a solidly-built nucleus, it will not be difficult to organize a larger band.'[11] The depature of Berle Adams in 1950 precipitated him into carrying out his plans, but his decision (borne partly of vanity) was to prove costly. Louis later admitted, 'I threw away a hundred thousand dollars fooling around with that.'[12]

Organizing a new big band takes a lot of time and money. Arrangements, uniforms, transport, bandstands and publicity all have to be paid for; there is the expense of contacting promoters and persuading them to take a chance on a new attraction; then the bookings have to be co-ordinated in a way that makes it physically possible for the band to travel the distances in between the various one-night stands. Louis realized the project would take months to organize, so he resumed working at full tilt with the Tympany Five so that the coffers would be ready to withstand the considerable outlay he was facing.

In March 1951 the small band left the USA to play dates in the Caribbean area. On the tour, which Aaron Izenhall described as 'the highlight of all my travelling with Louis', the band received rapturous welcomes and unrelenting demands for all the calypso material that Louis had recorded plus countless requests for his biggest hits. Izenhall recalled:

> We stayed at the Myrtle Park Hotel in Kingston, Jamaica and made that our base, flying to all the dates from there. Most of the jobs were in the open air; we played in Kingston and in Port of Spain, Trinidad; Georgetown, Guyana; and Port au Prince, Haiti. Louis and all of us loved the atmosphere, but somehow we couldn't get on with the food. We thought it would be like soul food but it was something different, with a little too much fish and rice for us, and crude sugar everywhere.[13]

But nothing was going to stop the band enjoying themselves and Louis donned cricket gear in Georgetown for some publicity photographs, even accepting a challenge to face up to some local bowling. Adopting a baseball stance, he swiped several balls into the outfield, feeling mightly pleased with himself.

The band returned home and resumed their itinerary, including a residency at the Club Silhouette on Chicago's West Howard Street which was to become a regular booking for them. Louis also took his '1951 Revue' around the dwindling theatre circuit. This featured the Tympany Five, an embryo version of the big band, Peggy Thomas, the Jordanettes (now eight strong and led by star dancer Hortense Allen), plus various individual acts such as Coco, Steve and Eddy, dancer Teddy Hale (Theodore Hailey) and singer Johnny Hartman. But plans for the formation of a permanent big band took definite shape during the early summer of 1951, and Louis and Bill Doggett spent a lot of time discussing which numbers would be in the repertoire, and who should be in the band. Doggett acted as the band's 'straw boss' (or chief organizer). He was also given the task of arranging many of the Tympany Five's biggest hits for the larger line-up.

Louis got the approval of Dave Kapp, vice president of Decca, to begin recording the big band. Previously Louis and Berle Adams would have negotiated such a deal with Dave's brother, Jack Kapp, long the president and driving force within Decca, but he had died in March 1949. When Louis felt satisfied that all plans for the big venture were in shape he left Bill Doggett to rehearse the musicians and went on vacation.

The original big band had as its nucleus the members of the Tympany Five: Louis on alto sax (he no longer played clarinet), Josh Jackson (tenor sax), Aaron Izenhall (trumpet), Bill Jennings (electric guitar), Bob Bushnell (double bass), Chris Columbus( drums) and a new pianist, Jimmy Peterson. Added to these were: Ermett Perry and Bob Mitchell (trumpets), Leon Comegys and Bob Burgess (trombones), Oliver Nelson (alto sax), Marty Flax (tenor sax) and Reuben Phillips (baritone sax). Arrangements were by Bill Doggett and Oliver Nelson, with Al Cobbs contributing a few. This was the line-up, billed as Louis Jordan and His Orchestra, which made a series of records in June and July 1951.

Almost all the sides waxed were recent songs, most exclusive to Louis Jordan. Among the originals was 'Please Don't Leave Me', on which Wild Bill Davis and Louis Jordan shared the writing and the vocals. Bill Davis (who played organ on some of the big-band tracks) sings a relaxed opening chorus on the song, a composition apparently inspired by Count Basie's recording of 'Take Me Back Baby'. 'Bone Dry' features a humorous call-and-answer routine between Louis and the band, but again the tune is not notably original. 'I Love that Kinda Carryin' On' has a smooth vocal from Louis, some pounding off-beat drumming and a fierce-sounding brass section, but the best moments occur in Louis's effervescent thirty-two-bar alto solo.

'Three Handed Woman' is a blues, well performed by the Tympany Five (plus organ) which has the full band playing only in the final chorus. 'Fat Sam from Birmingham' is a further attempt to create another 'Saturday Night Fish Fry', and on 'Cock-a-doodle-doo' Louis treads the well-worn path around the musical farmyard, his vocal efforts helped by an incisive trumpet solo. On 'Garmoochie',

Louis's singing seems to be imitating Billy Eckstine's vocal style, but by the middle of the song he is, happily, his own man again. Bob Burgess's trombone playing is briefly featured on 'There Must be a Way', which has a superb vocal from Louis and some beautifully co-ordinated phrasing from the saxophone section.

Soon after completing the second of its recording sessions, the orchestra made its official debut at a date in Washington, DC. Louis's diligent advance planning (in liaison with the band bookers at GAC) meant that the unit had a full book of engagements for the rest of the year. They soon began a tour consisting of thirty-two one-night stands taking them through Arkansas, Missouri, Kansas, Louisiana, Texas, New Mexico and Tennessee. Changes within the line-up meant that Harold 'Money' Johnson had been added to the trumpet section, and Alfred Cobbs had taken Leon Comegys' place on trombone. Pianist Jimmy Peterson had taken leave to visit his wife in California, where she had just given birth to a baby son. Peterson's place in the band was temporarily taken by the Washington pianist John Malachi. Irving 'Skinny' Brown came in on tenor sax and Numa 'Pee Wee' Moore joined on baritone sax.

Trombonist Bob Burgess (who later starred with Stan Kenton) was the only white musician in the finalized line-up. He vividly recalled the preliminaries to the tour and his subsequent travels with the orchestra:

> Someone, I can't remember who, called me to say that Louis Jordan was forming a big band, augmenting his small group by bringing in a lot of musicians, and making it a mixed unit: black and white. So four of us white players joined the new band: myself, Morty Trautman also on trombone, Marty Flax on tenor sax and Sol Schilinger on baritone sax. We played the Paramount, the Apollo and various theatres around New York. Louis liked my trombone playing and said, 'I want you to stay on, I'm going to make this big band a permanent thing. I've fixed up a big tour of the South.' Well, the rest of the white guys in the band didn't want to take that on, but I was twenty-one years old and thought to myself, 'I'll do it', so when the big bus rolled down South I was the only white musician in the band.

It was a fantastic and fascinating experience. All the guys in the

163

band were great with me, and Louis was absolutely beautiful. I usually roomed with Oliver Nelson or John Malachi (but John left halfway through my stay). In those days there was no question of black people staying at white hotels in the South, and there weren't many Negro hotels, so sometimes we'd arrive at a place around two or three in the morning and go from door to door in the Negro community to see which people had a bed and a room for us. And there I found the people treated me wonderfully well, and I can honestly say I've never tasted home cooking like it. A couple of times I experienced the other side of the problem, when I was refused admission to a Negro hotel whereas all the rest of the band were allowed in, and on another occasion a restaurant wouldn't serve me because I was white.

On the road in the South the band bus would pull up at a diner – really nothing more than a truck-stop, and the bus driver, who was also white, and me would get out and buy the food. The guys in the bus would pull all the shades down so no one could see in, then the two of us would go into the diner and buy fifty or sixty hamburgers and a case of Coca-Colas. People sometimes asked, 'Who is on that bus?' and the driver would answer, 'It's a bunch of athletes, and they're all sleeping.' That way there were no problems.[14]

Louis was full of optimism at the start of the venture and was jubilant when the orchestra drew a crowd of 7,005 for its 19 August appearance at the Municipal Auditorium in Kansas City, Missouri. Louis took the booking for a guaranteed fee of $1,500 against 60 per cent of the gross take. Working under such an agreement can be risky because freak weather conditions or some extraordinary local event can result in the potential audience not materializing, and the bandleader leaving with only $1,500. But Louis had experience of this Kansas City venue, because Berle Adams had previously booked him into it, so he took a chance and came out with $9,000 for the night's work. He had easily topped his gross of $7,700 for an engagement there a year before, but he was shrewd enough instantly to realize that now his overheads were more than double what they had been when he had had only the Tympany Five to pay.

Tenseness about the financial hazards of touring with a big band aside, Louis genuinely enjoyed working with the augmented line-up, but he was persistently vexed by customers asking mournfully, 'What happened to the Tympany Five?' Louis, as usual, beamed at the question and pointed out that all the musicians from the small band were right there on the stage, but this didn't satisfy everyone, and often people said, 'Gee, but I came to see the Tympany Five.' Louis's response was usually to work twice as hard to win over any doubters, but the questions irritated him and he was therefore no less moody than he had ever been.

Alfred 'Al' Cobbs, Bob Burgess's fellow trombonist, working for Louis for the first time, was struck by the bandleader's changeable nature:

> I think Louis Jordan was more eccentric than any of the other bandleaders that I've worked with. I say eccentric because he was so unpredictable. For instance, he sat opposite me when we travelled by bus, and sometimes we'd ride a long journey, all night, and he'd never say one word. He'd just look through you, then next night he couldn't stop talking hour after hour. I remember one night he told me that he didn't make any money, any profit that is, for the first five years that he ran the Tympany Five. Then he started making those hits and everything came right.
>
> One thing, he always made sure the band ate well. After we finished the night's gig there was always a banquet laid on for us in the dressing room. But that big band wore Louis out. He overworked himself throughout that hot summer tour. When we played Oklahoma City it was 105 degrees and we were wearing uncomfortable corduroy suits. We were soaking wet after one number and so was he. Louis was wearing the same type of suit so he wasn't getting off any lighter than we were and he was doing the full show. He paid for all our suits, but if we wore tuxedos, which we sometimes did, then we provided them ourselves.[15]

Heat wasn't the only problem the band encountered; racism reared up in several places, according to Bob Burgess:

> I think Florida was then about the most dangerous place for a mixed band to be, but Georgia wasn't too far behind. We were due to share billing there on a show with the Nat 'King' Cole Trio. The

agent, a nice guy, came and told us: 'The Ku Klux Klan have sent a note saying, "If the white boys play the show they'll never leave here alive." ' Well, there weren't any white boys – just white boy – ME! The only other white guy in the musical set-up was Jack Costanzo, who played bongoes with Nat Cole, and he immediately upped and went back home. I was determined to stay on, so the band advised me to buy a pistol, which I did. Then I discovered that almost everyone in the band was already carrying a gun. From then on, at any dance date where there seemed to be trouble in the offing, everyone got on the bandstand and laid his gun on the music stand even before he tuned up – apparently the most dangerous times are either just before or just after the dance. Fortunately nothing happened to me. In the dance halls there was usually a rope across the floor – black couples danced one side and white couples the other – but you could sense that things were changing slowly because often a white couple would duck under the rope and go and talk to black friends on the other side.

The most violent scene occurred in Louisiana. We were on an open stage in a big auditorium and a black guy walked immediately in front of the bandstand. He walked so slowly and deliberately he attracted everybody's attention; he was wearing bib-overalls and an undershirt, and he went straight up to a big, fat lady who was dancing and stabbed her. Then the guy who was dancing with the woman immediately pulled out a gun and started shooting. All the musicians dived off the bandstand and remained off until the cops came and restored order. I was shaken, but a local black guy turned to me and said: 'Well, you see, Louis Jordan plays fighting music. It swings so much the people get besides themselves with excitement.'[16]

Business was generally good on most of the tour dates, but there was no wildfire surge of interest from the public, or from the nation's band bookers, who were already planning their schedules for the following year. By now Louis had no Berle Adams to handle promoters' booking enquiries, so he was having to try to organize future work and perform at the same time. He slowly began to realize that the orchestra had not succeeded as swiftly as he thought it might. It was not uncommon for big bands to take a long time to establish themselves, and many previous leaders had been forced to borrow heavily in order to survive until the big break came, but for Louis the constantly nagging thought was how much less worrying, and more profitable, it had been leading the Tympany Five. However, he put on an optimistic front, saying in an October 1951 interview: 'What's wrong with the band business that a good versatile dance orchestra playing imaginative arrangements can't cure? To be successful today, a band must be capable of creating good music and putting on a show. The public want to see all-round entertainers.'[17] Louis went on to say that the tour had helped swell the sales of his two recent record releases, 'Three Handed Woman' and 'Cock-a-doodle-doo', and assured everyone that his band had hit their peak.

It was not in Louis's nature to slack, so even after he realized that his efforts to establish himself as leader of a big band were not likely to succeed, he continued unstintingly to give the public its money's worth. Fortunately, his general health had improved, though Bob Burgess remembered Louis occasionally complaining about stiffness in his legs:

I think he also suffered from some of the after-effects of the stabbing; he still had big welts across his back and marks on his legs, but to me he always seemed cheerful. In fact I found him to be a prince of a guy. On tour I went to him to draw some money as an advance and he peeled off a hundred-dollar bill and said, 'It's yours.' When it came time for me to be paid I got the full amount with no deductions, and Louis said, 'I told you the hundred was a gift.' On another occasion he could see that I was lonely for my wife and children, so when we had a blank day on the tour he paid for me to fly home and back. He didn't believe in entrusting money to Southern banks, so he carried all the cash in a big steamer trunk, which either he or the road manager (a guy called Mickey) used to look after. But at night it was too heavy to carry in to where we were staying, so the guys in the band used to take it in turns to sit up and keep their eyes on it. They had their guns at the ready to guard that trunk throughout the night.[18]

The one concession that Louis made to his own well-being on the orchestra's tours was to share the vocal duties more than he had done in the past. Instead of singing every number, he introduced a new vocalist, Valli Ford, to the personnel and also featured another male singer, Lloyd Smith, usually billed simply as 'The Fat Man'. Valli Ford (from Pittsburgh) had previously sung with Duke Ellington, and with Mercer Ellington, using the name Sara Forde, but Louis Jordan did not think that name looked good on the publicity material. Aaron Izenhall, recalling the name Valley Forge from a schooldays history lesson, suggested the new singer be called Valli Ford and this became her billing; she remained only for the duration of the big band.

After the band had played in New Mexico, Louis made a brief detour west and took Bob Burgess to stay at his home in Phoenix, Arizona:

> Louis and his wife made me very welcome. It was a big, comfortable house, situated in an area where black lawyers and doctors lived. It was a friendly gesture on Louis's part, but when we were back on the bandstand you knew he was the leader. As a bandleader Louis was very strict, but he was paying good money and didn't expect any goofing around. He made it clear that he wanted everyone in the band to maintain a good atmosphere on the bandstand; it was pretty much a happy band. Louis was a fine musician, and a born showman. They would call it 'tomming' now, but he was just selling the show, projecting his own personality. I can still remember how wonderfully he sang ballads on that tour, 'Poor Butterfly' especially. He was billed as 'The Man who Plays the Blues', and he'd come out on stage and shout, 'Mister Jordan's in town, and he's on the town with fifty cents in his pocket' and the people instantly related to him.[19]

Louis's attachment to Fleecie came to an end during the late stages of the orchestra's touring schedule and Louis and his long-time girlfriend, Vicky, were married on 14 November 1951 in Providence, Rhode Island with Vicky giving her full name as Mrs Florence Hayes Johnson. Fleecie decided to move to the Chicago suburb of Harvey, content that she would be able to live there comfortably on royalties from the songs that bore her name.

In late November the orchestra spent two days in the Decca studios in New York producing another batch of effective but unsensational recordings. 'Come on, Get It!' (arranged and composed by Al Cobbs) features a sturdy shuffle beat, some thrustful solos and a common-currency riff that later turned up in 'We're Gonna Rock around the Clock'. 'Stop Makin' Music' is a bouncy ballad that is entirely vocal. 'Slow Down' is a Tympany Five effort, with the big band entering to play a coda, as is 'Never Trust a Woman', where Louis reintroduces a series of one-bar breaks to add drama to his vocal. 'Work Baby Work' has an insistently repetitious lyric, but lacks the charm that makes the hits. The bonus is the uninhibited tenor sax backing, but unfortunately this is poorly recorded. 'All of Me' has some well-phrased singing from Louis and some eager vocalizing from Valli Ford; again the instrumental contributions from tenor sax and trombone are enriching. Louis's ballad singing on the slow 'There Goes My Heart' is quite superb, but the date ended with high jinks from the Tympany Five as they recorded 'Lay Something on the Bar for Me', a fast, joky attempt by Bill Austin (the composer of 'Is You is . . .') to hit the jackpot again.

Unhappily, the prospects of doing a lot of work for the Carter hotel chain faded, and Louis came to the decision that he would soon have to disband his orchestra. Ironically, the final review of the band, written by Leonard Feather during the band's residency at the Rustic Cabin, Englewood Cliffs, New Jersey, was encouraging. Feather was not swept off his feet by the orchestra's music when he heard it during the two-week stay at the Rustic Cabin (commencing 27 November), but gave it some praise, nevertheless:

Jordan has aimed at producing a swinging band that neither strains the brains nor insults the intelligence, and he has done it. Section for section the band rarely does anything remarkable, though here and there as in 'Begin the Beguine', you hear a pleasant passage by the reeds. With the exception of the leader's own humorous booting, Pete Brown-ish alto, the saxes are weakest in solo power. Both trombonists, Al Cobbs and Bobby Burgess, the latter the crew's only ofay cat, contribute many fine solo moments. Always a perfect showman, Louis is in complete command with the enlarged crew. Surprisingly, he did some of his best singing of the evening on ballads. Such tunes as 'Trust in Me', 'Morning Side of the Mountain' and 'Don't Let the Sun Catch You Crying' seem to indicate that this neglected aspect of his personality could seriously cut into the Nat 'King' Cole market. With so few bands around that are even trying to keep a halfway decent musical standard, the Jordan band falls easily on the ears. If it stays together during 1952 it could easily develop into one of the country's top ten.[20]

Louis was tempted to heed this sort of optimistic praise, but the agents, band bookers and ballroom operators remained lukewarm; a hit record with the orchestra would have solved all the problems, but nothing blossomed. The words of Berle Adams, his former manager, were hard to ignore. Adams saw the orchestra in action in Brooklyn and when asked by Louis for his verdict he spoke candidly: 'You sound like everybody else. You were individual, you were the pace-setter. Everybody imitated you.' Initially Berle's words caused Louis to dig his heels in, and he considered keeping the orchestra going, come what may, but gradually he realized that he had indeed abandoned a unique small-band sound for a polished, musicianly, ordinary big band. He decided it was time to disband the orchestra.

# *Slow Down*

As soon as Louis had disbanded the orchestra he went for a medical check-up, and was strongly advised to take a long rest. The strain of leading the big ensemble had taken a heavy toll on his health; his arthritis was continually plaguing him and tests showed that the sugar content in his blood was alarmingly high. Jordan took his doctor's advice and left for an extended stay at his home in Phoenix. *Down Beat* announced that Louis was to 'stay in retirement indefinitely'.[1]

Over the years Louis's sidemen had often been laid off during the leader's periods of indisposition, but this time no one, including Louis, seemed able to forecast how long their period of unemployment might last. This proved to be the last straw for several of the band, including trumpeter Aaron Izenhall, tenor saxist Josh Jackson, guitarist Bill Jennings and drummer Chris Columbus. Jennings and Columbus joined up with another ex-Jordan sideman, Wild Bill Davis, and working under Davis's leadership became an acclaimed trio. Bill Doggett, no longer required as staff arranger, began specializing on organ, gaining himself an enormous following – during the 1950s his records sold over 8 million copies. Doggett never ceased to praise Louis for making him so aware of the importance of presentation: 'Most guys today take a solo then stand like a zombie. Music is supposed to make you happy, and some guys won't even crack a smile for applause. Everything I know about showmanship I learned from Louis Jordan. He was the best. We'd put on our plaid suits and we'd light up the Paramount.'[2]

After three months of recuperation Louis decided to form a new edition of the Tympany Five, this time omitting a tenor saxophone. He offered the job of trumpeter to Bob Mitchell (formerly with

Jimmie Lunceford and the Bama State Collegians), who had worked with Louis in various larger line-ups during the previous three years. Louis retained the services of pianist Jimmy Peterson and made him principal arranger: he also kept bassist Bob Bushnell from the old line-up, but signed a new guitarist, Bert Payne, from Philadelphia. Payne recalled the circumstances of his joining:

> In 1952 I was working at the Oasis Club in Phoenix, Arizona, playing a long residency there in a group led by Nat Cole's brother, Eddie, who played bass. Louis came into the club and sat listening to me play, then he offered me a job; he said he was just about ready to reform the Tympany Five. He also said I could use his swimming pool any time I wanted to – his house wasn't huge but it was luxurious.
>
> When he outlined his offer and quoted an acceptable figure, he told me that record-date money was extra, and he said he believed that his musicians should have a comfortable life, which turned out to be true. We always travelled first-class, and everything was carried for us by Louis's valet Jerry and his chauffeur Charlie. We just had to set our bags and instruments down in front of the hotel and they looked after everything. On a tour of the North West, Louis hired a huge luxury coach, with card tables and piped music – just for the six of us, so there would be plenty of room to relax in.
>
> Louis was OK, he was very good to work for in that he paid top money, but he was strict. If, by accident, anyone went on to the stand without a tie they were fined, and he expected you to observe his dress code in hotel lobbies. You always had to be on best behaviour. He was pleasant to get along with for most of the time, but if he'd had an argument with his old lady, then he'd take it out on the band. He loved to tell jokes. Some were good and some were really corny, but of course everyone listened. From Phoenix I travelled to New York with Louis. We rehearsed there, then played our first dates at a theatre.[3]

Charlie Rice, Louis's new drummer, joined the band at the New York rehearsals, and made his debut with them at the Warner Theatre in New York. He recalled:

> Bert Payne, Jimmy Peterson and Bob Bushnell were all from

Philadelphia and they recommended me to Louis – it was easy fitting in with guys you know. Louis could be nice, but then, for no apparent reason, he could be hard. I remember thinking that I had to find a way of dealing with this, otherwise I couldn't work with him. So my method of getting along with Louis was not to argue, and he quickly cooled down. He'd suddenly get into a temper and say, 'Haven't I told you what to do? Why don't you play like I want it?' This was usually when I'd been doing exactly what he asked me to do, so I'd say, 'Oh gee, sorry about that. I'll get it right this time.' This pacified him and led him to say to the rest of the guys that I was the one in the band that knew him best. Louis had a lot of complexes, he was full of insecurity, I don't know why.[4]

The new version of the Tympany Five made its recording debut in New York on 30 April 1952, completing a further session during the following week. The group was well rehearsed and performed impeccably, but none of the records from these dates seemed likely even to dent the Hit Parade. The main problem was the ordinary quality of the songs. As Berle Adams pointed out, 'Material came to us because he was a big record seller. As he began to slide, the flow of material stopped.'[5]

'Junco Partner' is vaguely exotic, with Bert Payne playing claves in the background alongside an attractive, ostinato bass line. There is no instrumental interlude, and Louis sings throughout with commendable exuberance, but neither the tune nor the lyrics seems worth the effort. 'Time Marches on', is a Caribbean-type opus, written by Louis and his old collaborator, Joe Willougby (Trinidadian, and a keen cricketer). This too is solely a feature for Louis's voice, which is supported by the group singing harmonies. 'Azure Té' is the best tune of the batch (written by Wild Bill Davis) but Louis sounds a bit fey as he tackles the slow, sophisticated song. The bonus here is the leader's alto sax work, clearly influenced by Benny Carter's poised style, with Louis showing that he could eliminate all traces of huskiness from his tone.

The more familiar robust alto sax playing on 'Oil Well Texas' is also well conceived, as is the neatly harmonized piano work, but the letdown is the song, partly written by Louis and heavy with references to Arkansas. Jordan sings it well, but the band's backing vocals transmit a feeling of spirited desperation. The final number from these sessions, 'Jordan for President', is launched with an inviting bluesy introduction, but the mood changes as Louis begins a spoken monologue, in the form of an election address, greeted vociferously by a cast of studio extras. Louis's mock campaigning (which continued on theatre dates) gained him quite a lot of publicity (as did Dizzy Gillespie's similar efforts a few years later) but the 'Jordan for President' routine was based on a 'Deacon Jones for President' sketch popular with minstrel-show audiences in the 1920s and 1930s.

The five titles issued from the new band's initial sessions picked up mildly favourable reviews, but no big sales. In recording calypso material, beat songs, a ballad and a comic monologue it seemed Louis was attempting to trawl over too large an area in his attempts to catch something big enough to enter the Hit Parade.

The new group began work on 7 April at the Warner Theatre on Broadway. While Louis was in New York he renewed his booking contract with General Artists Corporation (GAC had originally stood for General Amusements Corporation, but the full name was changed to avoid its being confused with a coin-machine company). The GAC remained a powerful booking force, split into regions, each controlled by an area manager. In New York the East Coast booker covered an area up to Montreal, Canada, in California the Beverly Hills staff looked after bookings in a territory that stretched from Vancouver, Canada in the north to El Paso, Texas in the south. The Chicago office managed the Central areas and Toronto, Canada, and there were also subsidiary outlets of the agency in Dallas and Cincinnati.

The phrase on most of the GAC's bookings in 1952 was 'rhythm and blues', an expression apparently coined by Jerry Wexler in *Billboard* to describe the musical output of the growing number of small black bands whose vigorous interpretation of blues, and songs with uncomplicated harmonies, was winning over thousands of young enthusiasts. Most of the early examples of the style were issued on small independent labels, and though the performances were often raw and inexpert, many fans found that their rhythmic impetus and emotion-charged singing made up for any technical deficiencies. In May 1952, *Down Beat* began a rhythm and blues section in which it summarized appropriate record releases. Oddly, Louis Jordan's records were not deemed appropriate for this listing, despite the fact that several groups who had copied Louis's earlier hits were regularly included.

As if to avoid becoming too associated with the movement at this crucial time, Louis deliberately moved away from his blues-based material and made a point of featuring several calypso numbers in his shows, including a finale that brought the entire cast on stage to sing 'You Will Always Have a Friend'. This always provided a successful climax and nowhere was it enjoyed more ecstatically than at the Apollo Theatre, where Louis topped the bill in June 1952. By this time, Ann Bailey and Elaine Robinson were a separate act within the show, singing and dancing on a well-received routine entitled 'Natural Man'. Also featured within the Jordan package was a Hammond organ trio led by Jackson 'Jackie' Davis. Louis predicted in the *New York Amsterdam News* that America was ripe for a calypso vogue, and suggested that there was a wonderful future for this type of music in the United States. The *Trinidad Guardian* proudly picked up these comments and published an article on Louis's interest in calypso music, quoting him as saying:

> One thing that has held calypso back in the United States of America is pronunciation. Native Trinidad singers are not easily understood by most Americans. The few successes I have had with calypso tunes show that they will sell if the accent heard is not too foreign. I try to make calypso understandable to Americans and yet preserve that West Indian flavour that makes it unique.[6]

Commenting on Louis's trip to Trinidad in the previous year, the newspaper said, 'He not only met and heard the Colony's champion calypsonians but brought back home a wire recorder which he used to record the best ones.'

For a time the descriptive phrases rhythm and blues and rock and roll were hapazardly interchangeable, which led to bandleader Raymond Scott offering the definition that 'rock and roll is rhythm and blues without the music'.[7] On Louis's Apollo bill an eleven-piece band led by a twenty-year-old black tenor saxist, Willis Jackson (from Florida) was described as a mixture of both styles. His work did not please Leonard Feather, who wrote in his review:

> Willis ploughed his tenor through 'Harlem Nocturne' with clucks and grunts, pausing while he took the horn out of his mouth to utter an almost human groan. He played 'Gator Tail' and proved that a man can blow a horn for three solid minutes without producing a note of music. He wound up this one by removing his coat and tie in mid-chorus. It was a degrading, disgusting spectacle.[8]

It was also, as Leonard Feather feared, the shape of things to come; before a year had passed it seemed almost compulsory for any R & B tenor saxist to cast off a good deal of apparel when playing an up-tempo number. Fine musicians emerged from this volatile era and some fine music (including some from Willis Jackson), but for a time the show mattered a lot more than the sound, and although the alto sax was being featured with huge success by Earl Bostic and Tab Smith, in most of the young groups the tenor sax reigned supreme.

Although some groups did not fit neatly into either category, the term rhythm-and-blues band was usually reserved for black units (or white bands trying to emulate their sounds) while rock and roll applied to white musicians whose groups were presenting a lusty compound derived from several ethnic sources with the basic ingredient being an African American-inspired rhythm. Louis himself was philosophical about the surging popularity of the wild new styles; since he had always vowed that showmanship was essential to success, he understood the youngsters' strategy even if privately he thought that they were not particularly adept at stagecraft. What he did not like was the public's acceptance of poor musical performances. He abhorred out-of-tune playing and the negation of what had always been regarded as good tone on the saxophone. Even so, he appeared outwardly to enjoy Willis Jackson's efforts during their short theatre tour together.

Louis was eager for his new band to play some West Coast dates, so that he could revive the interest of the California-based promoters who had booked him on the memorably lucrative gigs a few years earlier. A tour was fixed but Louis approached it with some sadness because he had heard the news that his old friend, bassist and bandleader John Kirby, had died in California. They had not spent much time together in recent years, but Louis was always grateful to Kirby for befriending him after he had left Chick Webb and for offering him good advice. Kirby had died at forty-three from diabetes; Louis himself had worried about developing this condition after a doctor's warning a few years earlier, so perhaps this added to his feelings of sadness. Twenty years later, he recalled his grief: 'Kirby's death really floored me.'[9]

The band played successful week-long bookings in Sacramento and Los Angeles, during which time Louis enlisted the services of a new personal manager, Maceo Birch, a man who had previously acted in this capacity for Count Basie. After leaving California the band moved across country to play for a week in Philadelphia before beginning an August season in Wildwood, New Jersey.

During this period Louis decided he would bend a little with changing fashion and taste by doubling on tenor saxophone (as he had done some years earlier), but when asked if he would be honking and bleating on the instrument replied, with some spirit, 'The tenor sax isn't supposed to be played that way. It should have the tenor vocal sound and range. Lester Young is probably the greatest creative artist playing the tenor saxophone today.'[10]

In August 1952 Dorothy 'Dottie' Smith joined Louis as a featured vocalist. Dottie, born in Barbados, had lived in Philadelphia for most of her life. She was to remain a regular part of Louis's entourage for the next nine years, doubling on conga drum and acting as band secretary and straw boss, fixing hotels, departure times, and such like. Her joining the band further strengthened its links with Philadelphia:

Louis had finished working at the Earle Theatre in Philadelphia and was looking for a new girl singer. Pianist Jimmy Peterson recommended me, and brought Louis to hear me sing at Spider Kelley's Club in Philly. I had my own band there and was doing OK, but Louis was very persuasive; he said, 'I want you to join me as soon as you can.' So I did, and began working with him at the Beachcomber Club in Wildwood, New Jersey (which is about a twenty-minute drive from Atlantic City).[11]

Though there were no signs of a hit record, the sheer vitality and talent displayed during Louis's in-person appearances meant he continued to win his audiences, and as a result the band kept busy. After playing Oklahoma they headed for Louis's old stamping ground, Little Rock, Arkansas, where Louis's father, Jim Jordan (introduced to the band as 'The Professor'), went to see and enjoy the performance. The band played other dates in the South that year, including a string of one-night stands that took them into Virginia, North and South Carolina and Georgia. They then zig-zagged their way up to Chicago. Working south of the Mason-Dixon line still had its problems for Louis's troupe, as Dottie Smith recalled:

> It was rough on tour in the South, but because I had a fair skin they didn't know if I was Mexican or Spanish. I was raised in the North so I didn't encounter segregation until I went on tour. I could go and order food and take it outside to the musicians. Louis was very strict about dress and conduct on tour. We were travelling and some of the guys in the band tied handkerchiefs around their heads because they had some special stuff they had plastered on their hair and they wanted it to set, but they got out of the band bus still with the handkerchiefs on their heads and Louis was beside himself with rage at them. His strict attitude applied to me also. We had to catch a plane somewhere and I thought I'd wear some smart $250 pants for the trip. Louis looked and frowned, then he said: 'You don't wear pants in my band. You're a lady and I want you to remain one.' Louis was very businesslike in his dealings with his musicians; if he found out that anyone took drugs they were fired immediately. Louis was a very private person, he didn't hang out after shows. I don't think he came to dislike many people because he deliberately didn't get involved with them. If you asked me who his friends were, I'd have to say me. Dan Burley, too, and Ben Waller, who became his manager and Johnny Johnson who owned a hair-tonic company, but no musicians that I can think of.[12]

The last months of 1952 passed in a continuous pattern of touring, so it was a relief for the band to quit travelling for a while to play a residency at the Golden Hotel, in Reno, Nevada during January 1953. Very few black groups had played residencies in Reno before Louis's group, but as with Las Vegas, Louis's pioneering encouraged bookers there to begin hiring other black combos. Accommodation was restricted, Dottie Smith remembered: 'It was a question of going all over town to find some black family who would take you in.'[13]

During February 1953 plans were finalized for a star-studded, coast-to-coast tour featuring Frankie Laine, Ella Fitzgerald, Louis Jordan's Tympany Five, Woody Herman's Third Herd and comedian Dusty Fletcher. Although the show was booked by the New York-based Gale Agency, it played its preliminary dates on the West Coast. It was billed as 'The Big Show of 1953' and its itinerary included twenty-seven consecutive one-nighters beginning in Columbus, Ohio on 18 April and ending on 11 May in Baltimore, Maryland – with thousands of miles of travel in between those two locations.

Not long before the odyssey began, Louis and the band played at the San Francisco Paramount, then moved to Los Angeles to relax for a few days. Taking advantage of this brief respite before facing the avalanche of work, Louis's pianist, Jimmy Peterson, and a white ex-security guard who had just joined Louis's entourage, decided to take a brief vacation in Reno. Guitarist Bert Payne recalled, 'Jimmy and this other fellow made up their minds to drive to Reno, Nevada to see some friends, but just outside Reno the vehicle that they were driving turned completely over and Jimmy was killed.'[14]

The vehicle involved in the fatal accident was Louis's band truck, which careered off the road upside down and came to rest in several feet of water. All the band's arrangements were in the truck and they were rendered useless by the soaking. Louis was thus faced not only with the tragic demise of his pianist and chief arranger, but also by the loss of his entire library of music, and this at the very time he was planning to make changes in his personnel. Louis acted quickly, commissioning tenor saxist and arranger Maxwell Davis to transcribe an entire new library of band parts from his most popular Decca recordings, then he set about replacing musicians in his group, bringing in a pianist, a bassist and a drummer. Thurber Jay, originally from Texas, but then living in Fresno, California, became the new bass man:

Matthew B. Thomas, who was Billy Eckstine's road manager-cum-valet, knew Louis and recommended me to him. So Louis sent for me and for another musician from Fresno, pianist Bill Bigby. We flew to Los Angeles to audition and we both got the job. Almost immediately, in March 1953, we went to Louis's home in Phoenix, Arizona and we rehearsed for almost four weeks there before going to Los Angeles to work as part of 'The Big Show of 1953'. But Bill Bigby had trouble reading music and he left, to be replaced briefly by another pianist, but then Chester Lane joined us permanently while we were on the tour.[15]

Chester Lane, who had worked with Louis in El Dorado and Hot Springs during their early years, remembered the sequence of events clearly:

I was sitting down one Sunday afternoon in St Louis with some friends, and we were laughing about this and that, and someone asked, 'Do you ever want to tour again?' I said, 'No. There's only three bandleaders I'd join, Duke Ellington, Count Basie or Louis Jordan, and as Duke and Count are piano players I guess I'll stay right here.' Within minutes of me saying this, the telephone rang and a voice said, 'Mister Lane, this is Mister Jordan.' (Louis had a way of kidding on the phone.) He went on, 'I need a piano player, can you join me?' I said, 'When would I start?' He said, 'Today or in a year's time.' So I went along with this kidding and replied, 'Well, I can't make it today and a year's time is too far away.' So then we talked hard and fast business details and Louis said, 'I'll get a piano man out of Los Angeles to carry on with this tour and you join me as soon as you can.' Well, I'd noticed that this show was coming to play the Auditorium in St Louis on Sunday 18 April, so I told him that date would suit perfectly. As a result, I joined the band there. That week the show went on to play Cincinnati, Indianapolis, Cleveland, etc, and on the Friday we played Carnegie Hall, which was really something for me as I'd never worked in New York. So in the space of a week all this happened. Then we went on to play all over: Montreal, Syracuse, Buffalo – all over the place, until three weeks later when the show ended with a big party.[16]

Johnny Kirkwood, then in his early twenties, became the third newcomer to the band, and its youngest member:

I got a call from Louis's manager, Maceo Birch, who asked me if I'd be interested in joining Louis Jordan. I said I wasn't sure, because at the time I was young and wanted to play like Max Roach, but I ended up by saying I was interested. I didn't hear anything for a couple of weeks and then Louis Jordan turned up at this little dive-joint where I was working, in Watts, California. He stood near the door and heard two numbers, but left without saying a word to me. Soon afterwards I got a call asking me to go down to Phoenix, Arizona to start rehearsing with the band. Louis had a real nice house there, with a swimming pool and a tennis court, and he had a large rumpus room or den at the back of the house and we rehearsed there. I played the way I usually did but Louis soon stopped me and said, 'You can't play like that with this band.' I felt insulted. Louis didn't want anything experimental and this led to us having a couple of run-ins. I was young and fiery, but he didn't lose his temper, he said, 'Listen to me and you'll be able to play every sort of music.' I gradually realized that he was right. I never had a father and he became like a father to me, and I listened to all the advice he gave me. Usually I travelled in his car. He didn't want me to travel with the rest of the band until I settled in, because they were all quite a bit older than I was and he felt that they might lead me into bad habits. He taught me about travelling on the highways and when he bought a second car he said I could drive it. My first dates with Louis were dances at Bakersfield, California, about ninety miles from Los Angeles, and at San Diego.[17]

Before Chester Lane joined the band, the 'Big Show' (later billed as 'The Biggest Show of 1953') played several tour dates in the West, including one at the Coliseum, Denver on 10 April. Both Johnny Kirkwood and Bert Payne have vivid memories of that trip. For Kirkwood (originally from Texas) it marked the first occasion in his life that he had ever seen snow falling: 'I'd seen it on distant mountains, but never coming down in flakes.' The snow created problems for the aircraft that was carrying most of the show's cast, and it had to make an unscheduled landing at Colorado Springs to be de-iced.

At this stage of her career, Ella Fitzgerald was wary about flying anywhere, and on this tour she was happy to travel by band coach, and play blackjack with various musicians. But it was not feasible to get to Denver by road at this time, so she reluctantly got aboard the aircraft. Bert Payne recalled:

> When the plane was forced down by the blizzard Louis could see that Ella was very upset, so he put on a show, all by himself, to keep her spirits up. He started joking with her, saying it was because she'd put on weight that the plane couldn't make it – Ella used to eat a lot in those days and Louis had been ribbing her about it. Anyway it worked and everyone forgot about the delay. We eventually got going again, and played the show a couple of hours late.[18]

Louis's new bassist, Thurber Jay, recalled, 'On the West Coast we got up as far as Vancouver and on the East to Montreal. When the show got to the East it was renamed "The Frankie Laine Express".[19] This change in billing reflected Laine's huge individual popularity; during the early 1950s his big hits included 'Jezebel' and 'Mule Train.' Frankie Laine admired Louis Jordan's work, describing him as 'one of the greatest entertainers and musicians'.[20]

For Thurber Jay, the tour signalled a change of instrument:

> When we were somewhere in the East an accident occurred to my string bass and the neck was broken. I had to borrow a bass from the guy in Woody Herman's band, but it's hard to play on someone else's bass. Louis realized this and suggested that I try one of the electric basses that were just coming in then, but I didn't go for the idea originally. When the tour ended Louis gave me an ultimatum – that I had to play electric bass from now on. He said he'd pay for it, but also said that I only had two weeks to learn it before we started touring again. He got an early model Fender direct from the factory somewhere near Santa Ana, California, and to be honest I wasn't at all pleased, but I sat at home in Fresno and taught myself how to play it. I did it the unorthodox way, by sticking the neck up slightly, which made it feel more natural for my left hand. In the end everything was OK. I never had a lesson in my life; taught myself to play the E flat brass bass first of all at school, then acoustic string bass and finally electric bass.[21]

The fact that Louis insisted on this change meant that he was keeping a watchful eye on new developments in the music business, even though he had no intention of drastically changing the sound of the Tympany Five. Louis was still licking his wounds over the failure of his big band, but comfort reached him via the packed audiences' reactions to the new Tympany Five when he returned to the Apollo Theatre, yet again, in late May 1952. Box-office business and the Harlem response were so extraordinary that Louis and the band were held over as the top-of-the-bill attractions for a second week.

Bizarrely, a period of smooth sailing was disturbed by a good review. *Down Beat* gave Louis's ballad recording of 'Just Like a Butterfly' a five-star rating, saying, 'Louis gets orchestral background strings and could have a big, big record if Decca pushes it. "Butterfly" is a wistful, simple melody that Jordan sings beautifully.'[22] The song was one of four titles Louis had recorded during the previous February, backed by an orchestra directed by Nelson Riddle. The glowing review for these orchestral sides appeared just as Louis was beginning to feel that he had successfully re-established the Tympany Five. So instead of nonchalantly accepting the praise and doing his best to boost sales, Louis acted as though he felt vaguely threatened by the possibility that a successful recording with strings would undo his recent hard work and hamper the progress of the Tympany Five.

Writer Jack Tracy went to Louis's dressing room to ask about the new release, noting that Jordan appeared 'fretful and slightly worried'. Louis's statements to Tracy conveyed an air of exasperation:

> Will you please tell people that I'm not changing my style, not going on the road with a full orchestra and strings, and that I'm not looking to do a single. That record was just an experiment – I still plan to continue with my little band and do the same type of show I always have. Milt Gabler [Decca recording director] suggested we try something a little different for once. Nelson Riddle did the backing and that was that. People were thinking I was going to quit working with my band, but that isn't the way it is. I'm happy the way I've been working.[23]

Louis resumed recording with the Tympany Five on 28 May 1953, in a session which produced four enjoyable sides, including 'I Want You to be My Baby', written by a young songwriter-vocalist, Jon Hendricks. Louis's version of the song sold satisfactorily, but the tune became a minor hit for Lillian Briggs. Looking back, Hendricks said: 'Louis was sweet, he was amazing, he did everything, he planned all the road trips, he made out the itineraries, he booked the rooms, he made the route charts, he did it all. Then he'd hand it to the road manager, whose job it was to do that, but Louis would do it all himself. He enjoyed his music.'[24]

Maxwell Davis, the band's main arranger, was temporarily working within the Tympany Five and took part in the session; another fine jazz tenor saxist, George Kelly, wrote 'House Party', one of the best things from the date.

Louis continued to regain ground lost during his 1952 lay-off: the Tympany Five played to good business in Washington, Baltimore, Cleveland and Chicago before moving off to play more dates in Reno during August 1953, following this engagement with some trailblazing in Lake Tahoe, Nevada. Louis, like many other top combo leaders, was finding that the increased demand for groups in the various Nevada casino towns was helping to balance the loss of bookings on the ever-dwindling theatre circuits. In late 1953, New York's Paramount, the site of some of Louis's biggest successes, dropped its stage-show policy and installed Cinemascope equipment.

The closure of theatres (or the policy of changing them into movie houses) caused Louis to look more favourably upon venues he had long ignored. In October he played a two-week residency at New York's Cafe Society, his first New York club date in five years. Nat Hentoff's review was full of praise:

> Louis Jordan is a professional showman with a sense of timing and audience control that seems increasingly rare among the younger performers who hit the clubs right from the recording studios. Louis uses the audience like an instrument. After the overture he points out, 'If you want to tell your girl anything, tell her now. You won't have a chance to while we're playing.' He then directs pointed but never offensive comments to ringsiders, generally as a build-up to a song. Louis is still a fine straight ballad singer, with jazz phrasing, and he's a jumping altoist, but his main preoccupation lies with rhythmic comedy – and at that he's a sure-witted master.[25]

After the Cafe Society booking ended, Louis and the band remained in New York to play a two-week residency at Birdland; bookings in Montreal and Philadelphia followed, prior to their Christmas season at the Beachcomber Club, Miami Beach, Florida, where they appeared alongside the veteran 'red-hot momma' Sophie Tucker. This took place only weeks after they had shared billing at Birdland with the brilliant jazz saxophonist James Moody; the juxtaposition gives a clear indication of the band's versatility.

But versatility has never guaranteed big record sales. In late 1953, after examining Louis's recent sales figures, Decca decided not to renew his recording contract. The May 1953 session had produced satisfactory sides, but none had been considered worthy of being accorded a 'plugging campaign', and some had simply been shelved for delayed release. Ironically, the final recordings made for Decca (during a gap in the band's long Miami booking) produced a version of 'Nobody Knows You when You're Down and Out' (arranged by Chester Lane) which (backed with 'Lollipop') achieved good sales figures.

Louis Jordan certainly was not 'down and out', but he was vexed by Decca's decision because he had been recording for that company exclusively since his days with Chick Webb's orchestra, back in 1936. He later wondered if his outburst about the sides with Nelson Riddle had played any part in the company's decision, but he was assured that this was not so. The axing had been formulated before that single had ever been released, and was part of a shift in attitudes that had slowly developed since the departure of the Kapp brothers; Jack had died in 1949 and Dave left the company in 1952. Louis later said, 'Decca asked me to get on that rock thing, you know, with a big beat. They wanted me to honk on a tenor. I was a little too old for that.'[26]

Louis's place in the Decca stable was soon taken by a group led by a white Texas-born guitarist, Bill Haley. A small advertisement that appeared in *Down Beat* during the summer of 1953 announced that Bill Haley and his Comet's version of 'Crazy Man Crazy' on Essex Records was 'The Greatest Dance Beat Ever on Wax'. Suitably intrigued by the group's music (and the big sales they had achieved on independent labels) Louis's former recording director, Milt Gabler, decided to sign them for Decca, initially on a four-sides-a-year contract.

*13*

*Time Marches On*

Before Louis completed his final session for Decca (in January 1954) he had already signed with Aladdin and begun recording for them. As soon as Ed Mesner, the chief of Aladdin Records, heard that Louis Jordan and Decca were due to part company he flew into New York from Beverly Hills and negotiated a successful deal with Louis, which began with a recording session in November 1953 (produced by Mesner). The policy was to continue using the Tympany Five, taping material that embraced humour and rhythm, with an occasional ballad included; several brief instrumentals were also recorded. Coincidentally, in late 1953, for the first time, Louis was listed in the alto saxophone section of the *Down Beat* popularity poll. He gained only twenty-third place (Charlie Parker was voted first), but this was slightly better than the Tympany Five's twenty-seventh spot in the combo section (won by Dave Brubeck).

Louis had always dismissed popularity poll results, regarding a full date sheet as a more important indication of lasting success, and on that score he had nothing to worry about. The group continued to work its way through a succession of lucrative bookings, and in February they played the prestigious, and well-paid, Auto Show in Detroit. Louis's personnel was Mitchell, Lane, Payne, Jay and Kirkwood, and they had, by this time, been joined by tenor saxist Lowell 'Count' Hastings (an ex-Tiny Bradshaw sideman), first spotted by Louis working in the Apollo house band. Socially, the spirit within the group was as good as it had ever been, but this was not a happy period of Louis's life because he had run into a big problem with the US Internal Revenue authorities over the non-payment of income tax.

Johnny Kirkwood spoke of Louis's reaction:

Louis had evil moments. He got to be a bitter man, particularly towards the government over the tax they were claiming from him, going back some years. He felt that he'd been let down by his previous management; he said they should have taken care of these things for him. He also felt deeply about prejudice. A lot of this went back to his early days in Arkansas. He'd talk about things that I guess he hadn't mentioned for years. I know people might speak of Louis as an evil man, but I don't think this is true. He was a nice man, and this always became apparent when you were alone with him. He could be himself then. Similarly, I've heard people say that Dinah Washington was evil, but personally I found she was a wonderful person.[1]

Thurber Jay also had warm memories of his former leader:

Louis was the greatest person in the world. We had our ups and downs and I thought at the time that some of the things he said were crazy, but as I've grown older I see what he meant. He was a heck of a musician, and people just don't realize what a singer he was. If you caught him at a dance, not doing the comedy stuff, but singing ballads, it was fantastic, just beautiful to listen to – he had an awful lot of soul.[2]

In June and July 1954 the group played in Los Angeles and San Francisco, then visited Oakland for an August date at the Auditorium. The promoter there was delighted with the 2,300 attendance, but this was less than half the crowd that Louis had attracted to this same venue during the days of his big-selling records. It was now the younger groups who were beginning to be the big ballroom attractions. Despite having completed half a dozen sessions for Aladdin, Louis had not created a big new hit. Most of the material was well performed, but little of it was catchy – nor was it enticingly rugged. The hooks that magically ensnare a listener's attention, persuading him or her to go out and buy a particular record as soon as possible, were notably absent. Unfortunately the recording quality of the sessions also varied a good deal, often failing to transfer the sound of a well-balanced rhythm section.

Louis was looking for success by ploughing furrows he had found fertile in the past: food songs, party tales, harangue-your-partner ditties, jocular advice themes and repititious-syllable ideas. Innovations were few and far between but one new move was the regular use of the band singing unison vocals, a not entirely successful strategy due to poorly blended voices and some indifferent singing. Another featured the use of more modern-sounding chords at the ending of arrangements, but Louis did not want any wide, dissonant harmonies used and specifically asked Chester Lane, who was then doing most of the arranging, to keep everything harmonically simple. 'He wanted a plain chord, no sixths,' said Lane.[3]

Some of the Aladdin sides were impressive, notably a 'Louis Blues', an instrumental in which Louis takes five impassioned choruses on alto sax. The amusing 'Whisky Do Your Stuff' also has good alto sax work, and 'Private Property' is full of assertive blues singing, enhanced by an apt tenor sax obbligato. 'Hurry Home' (later to be effectively featured by Ella Fitzgerald) is a fine example of Louis singing superbly on a class ballad (written in 1938), supported by a full-sounding arrangement which benefits from an augmented saxophone section. 'I Seen What'cha Done' is lifted by a good old shuffle beat, and 'Messy Bessy' (another song by Jon Hendricks) is bold and lively, but there is often a feeling that everyone is trying too hard, particularly on the fast instrumentals 'The Dipper' and 'Gotta Go'. Louis fails to achieve a suitable 'down home' blues feeling on 'If I Had Any Sense I'd Go Back Home' but sounds full of bravura on 'A Dollar Down' which, with its gospel feel, tenor sax solo and heavy off-beat drumming, sounded a good prospect for commercial success. None of the Aladdin releases sold in huge numbers, however, even though *Cashbox* cited 'I'll Die Happy' as one of the top R & B discs of the year.

The big consolation for Louis was that there was no lack of work. A well-paid tour of Texas, Louisiana and Florida filled in the early autumn, and thereafter things continued to chug along in a lucrative, well-organized pattern. Louis consistently gave a show full of guile and energy, but occasionally something inspired him to perform with messianic zeal. A fund-raising charity dance at the Trianon Ballroom in Chicago (organized by the First Church of Deliverance) proved to be one such occasion. Louis, who had flown in from Florida, presented what he called his 'Broadway Show', which consisted of various bands and singing groups. Perhaps he felt challenged by one of these rival attractions, or the event may have reminded him of his early links with Baptist Church fervour; whatever the stimulus was, he played and sang like a man inspired and carried the 4,000-strong crowd to a state close to hysteria. Even the *Chicago Defender* reporter, veteran of a thousand shindigs, sounded affected: 'Chicago has seldom, if ever, witnessed anything like the Louis Jordan party for the First Church nursery. Witnessing patrons couldn't believe what they were seeing. The Reverend Clarence Cobb couldn't hold up under the strain of the celebration and was forced to retire midway through the proceedings.'4

Still glowing from the Chicago triumph, Louis played a wildly successful week at the Apollo in November 1954, and even managed to keep smiling when he discovered that a thief had stolen the hubcaps from his Cadillac, parked near the Apollo's stage door. Eager to replace the loss as soon as possible, he asked a local if he could get a new set, as the Apollo schedule left him no time to shop. The man was soon back, apologizing that new ones could not be obtained quickly; instead, he offered Louis a second-hand set. Louis was delighted with the speedy service and handed over payment. The brother departed, also delighted, it was only when Louis checked the condition of his purchase that he noticed that they were stamped L.J. Instead of keeping quiet about the transaction, Louis told all and sundry about it; it was part of his nature to be secretive about many things, but he could seldom resist sharing the details of a joke against himself.

For that year's Christmas season the band played a residency at the Sands Hotel in Las Vegas, sharing the billing with Vic Damone (and various other speciality acts and dancers) in a big, glitzy production. But glamorous though the show itself was, Las Vegas had a tawdry side in those days and segregation prevented Louis and his musicians from staying at any of the resort's popular hotels. Guitarist Bert Payne recalled the irony of the situation: 'The funny thing was that when they sealed up a time capsule in Vegas, to be opened at some future, distant date, they asked Louis for one of his saxophones and some music to put in it – yet he wasn't allowed to chose where he wanted to stay.'5

Drummer Johnny Kirkwood remembered:

In Vegas we had to live in a broken-down motel close by the Sands Hotel and we had to eat in the service quarters at the hotel. We could pick up our mail from the front desk at the Sands, but we had to move on immediately. When it was break time during our working hours we had to go to a booth and sit there. We were allocated a waiter so that we didn't mingle with the guests.[6]

Pianist Chester Lane pointed out that things were no better when the band played in Lake Tahoe, Nevada:

In those days black performers could not get any accommodation in Tahoe – impossible. So we had to hire a house; we each chipped in $45 a week, and had to sleep on cots. Louis and his wife had a room and so too did George Kirkby (the comedian) and his wife. But we got by. Soon afterwards Sammy Davis Jr and the Will Mastin Trio played Lake Tahoe and they insisted that they be given proper accommodation, or else they'd walk out. The rules were changed, and from then on we didn't have to hire a house.[7]

A gradual change took place in another Nevada resort, as singer Dottie Smith recalled:

We were due to play another booking at Harrah's in Reno, and I said to Louis, 'Look, your name is in big letters on that marquee and you're still scuffling around for somewhere to stay.' But he didn't like getting involved in that sort of trouble, he was reluctant to do anything about the situation, but me, with my big mouth, I had a different attitude. So before the next booking I wrote in advance, simply giving Louis's name and reserving a suite for him and a room for me, and I asked for a letter of confirmation, which they sent. So when we got there I just walked up to the reception desk and nobody said anything, so we stayed there every time we went back – it was a breakthrough.[8]

Louis Jordan was never a militant – he never made public the anger he felt about prejudice – and in his touring days discussed the issue

only with people close to him, but years later he expressed himself to
Johnny Otis on the subject:

> All through the years of going down South I stayed where I was
> supposed to stay, dealt with the people I was supposed to deal with,
> and I socialized with the people I was supposed to socialize with,
> according to the racist rule. The white crackers, they appreciated
> that, and when I went to deal with them they'd say, 'You're Louis
> Jordan, aren't you?' and I got better recognition from them. They
> did more for me than they would for someone else who was trying
> to lift themselves up before their time came. Let me say this:
> there's many incidents down South where if the people had talked
> different there wouldn't have been an incident. There's one thing I
> learned at home; my grandmother taught me that unless someone
> hits you, words cannot hurt you. I've been called anything you can
> think of, but it never offended me and maybe that's one of the
> reasons why I got along so well in the South with the conditions
> like that. I made a whole lot of money in the South, and the white
> people helped me make more money. So, who's the fool? They
> knew that they didn't have to fight me. I didn't agree with what
> was happening, but I had to take it.[9]

Such sentiments were anathema to many African-Americans and
to many white liberals, but Louis genuinely believed that his method
was right, and would point out that he was the first black performer
to appear at a particular venue, on various radio shows and,
increasingly in this era, on new television shows. During the summer
of 1955 (on 12 July) Louis, Lena Horne and Spanish guitarist Vincente
Gomez were featured on the first of bandleader Stan Kenton's 'Music
'55', CBS television series. Nat 'King' Cole was also doing his own
pioneering on television. During 1956 he began his own NBC series,
which reached seventy-seven stations in all (eighteen in the South),
but no major sponsors were forthcoming, causing Nat to make a droll
comment, suggesting that the advertising agencies were afraid of the
dark.[10]

As usual, Louis's summer tour covered thousands of miles.
Beginning in Ohio, it moved south to Texas and then across to Los
Angeles, but the major part of his annual work was taking place at

three Nevada locations: the Sands Hotel, Las Vegas, Harrah's Hotel at Lake Tahoe and the Golden Hotel, Reno. Each of these places was growing rapidly, and the increased business meant that various hotels could afford to book top-class acts for their lounges. Louis's lively music seemed the ideal fare for gamblers, and he returned to play many engagements at the hotel casinos, most of whom insisted on an exclusive contract extending over a period of two years. The work was lucrative, but playing to a transient audience, often eager to get back to the serious business of gambling, meant Louis was given little chance to follow his long-held strategy of trying out new material and watching for the reaction. The response of a casino crowd was so untypical and variable that it could play no part in helping forecast which tunes were likely to succeed on record.

Decca were at this time still occasionally putting out previously unissued singles by Louis and the band, taken from material that had been recorded and stored. The coupling 'Locked Up' and an instrumental version of 'Perdido' caused one reviewer to comment, 'Sounds as if Decca may have gone into the vaults to get these on the market to coincide with the R & B push.'[11] Louis still collected royalties on such issues, but he would not have grown fat on what he earned from this single.

One of the big problems for Louis was that his current issues were no longer broadcast by the powerful and influential disc jockeys. This was the main reason his Aladdin records achieved disappointing sales. After a year, Louis and the company decided to part company, and Jordan decided to sign for RCA Victor, who originally planned to put him on their new 'X' label. Louis felt that the enterprise looked promising, and hoped that once again his discs would be enterprisingly plugged.

But by this time many new groups were swarming around the Hit Parade hill, determinedly trying to reach the top, and stay there. The most celebrated of these was led by Bill Haley. Haley had begun his professional career as a guitar-playing cowboy singer and yodeller, but a musical restlessness and a desire to blend seemingly disparate styles such as jazz and country-and-western ballads led him, during the early 1950s, through a succession of experiments, to produce what he called cowboy-jive, which became hillbilly boogie and later rockabilly. In 1952 his Saddlemen became the Comets, and a year later, when drums were added to the combination, an embryo version of the music that became known as rock and roll developed.

Based in Philadelphia, Bill Haley and his Comets began to chalk up some impressive record sales. His 'Rock the Joint' sold 200,000 and a 1953 Essex release, 'Crazy Man Crazy' passed the three-quarters of a million mark. Small wonder that all the giant recording companies became interested in Haley's work. Decca won the prize, and within a year Bill Haley's version of 'Shake Rattle and Roll' had sold over two million copies; his 'We're Gonna Rock Around the Clock' became even more popular, having made an impact via the MGM movie *Blackboard Jungle*.

There was no question that, despite creating several mega-hits, Louis Jordan had never consistently achieved sales figures of those dimensions, but it is a matter of contention as to how much influence Jordan's music had on Haley's style. Jordan's expert performances, conceived from various sources, inspired many groups (black and white) to follow in his musical footsteps, both in their presentation of material and in their rhythmic delivery. Jordan's sounds presaged a musical revolution, but it is too simple to cite the Tympany Five as the direct prototype of the Comets; a vast networked diagram would need to be drawn up in order to present Haley's other influences. However, the vital ingredient in Bill Haley's success was his reinterpretation of the African-American rhythmic concepts that had, naturally, been part of Louis Jordan's performances. As writer Nick Tosches commented in *Unsung Heroes of Rock'n'Roll*, 'Jordan did more to define hep and to prepare white folks for the coming of rock'n'roll than any other man of that era.'

Bill Haley specifically cited Big Joe Turner (who had recorded 'Shake Rattle and Roll' before Haley) as an influence, and spoke of the early inspiration he got from hearing black groups in East St Louis. During his formative years, Haley had doubled as a disc jockey and played Jordan's records regularly; his first recording for the Essex label was 'Rocket 88', which had been a hit for black artist Jackie Brenston, so Haley was totally familiar with black small-band music, but he did not acknowledge Louis Jordan as a prime influence. The potent link between the two stars was the Decca recording director Milt Gabler, who said: 'I never played Louis Jordan material to Bill Haley; there was no question of close copying but I used to sing the group riffs from Louis's records. Also I got the tenor sax player and the pianist to think along those lines, and I asked the whole group to project the way that Jordan's group had done.'[12]

Louis Jordan made a succinct analysis of his influence when he said, 'I jumped the blues', but at the time of Haley's successes Louis avoided direct comment on the white emergence, simply saying, 'Music has to go around and around to survive.' However, later in life he had some pertinent things to say on the subject:

> When Bill Haley came along in 1953 he was doing the same shuffle boogie I was. Only he was going faster than I was. But as a black artist I'd like to say one thing: There is nothing that the white artist has invented or come along with in the form of jazz or entertainment. Rock'n'roll was not a marriage of rhythm and blues and counry and western. That's white publicity. Rock'n'roll was just a white imitation, a white adaptation of Negro rhythm and blues.[13]

During the period from March 1955 to April 1956, Louis did four recording sessions for his company RCA, whose biggest star at that time was Elvis Presley. Three of the dates were with an augmented version of the Tympany Five, and one with the usual seven members of the group. The results were varied but uneven, and it was to be many years before some of the sides were issued. On 'Chicken Back', Louis again struts around the barnyard, but this time ends up in the kitchen to present another 'food' song, sharing vocal duties with Dottie Smith. Dottie also joins Louis on 'Texas Stew', which at least has tastier lyrics than many of Louis's other culinary offerings. The gormandizing ends with 'Bananas', which has a charming, light calypso feel. Several of the songs are spiced with rock-and-roll seasoning, but are mercifully not connected with food. 'Rock'n'Roll Call', an up-tempo twelve-bar blues, has crisp off-beat clapping, unison singing and two choruses of lightly honked tenor sax playing, Louis sings well on this track, but somehow a lack of grit prevented it from becoming a solid success.

'Baby You're Just Too Much' also has a heavy off-beat feel; the tenor sax is engagingly extrovert and Louis and Dottie harmonize effectively. 'Slo', Smooth and Easy' is a sixteen-bar theme featuring unison vocals, plus solo work from Louis, singing and playing, but his alto sax efforts (an amalgam of previously manufactured phrases) are a disappointing attempt to force the pace. Nellie Lutcher's song 'It's been Said' sets out as a promising commerical vehicle, with Louis showing how subtly he could interpret lyrics, but midway through (with the inroduction of a silly language lesson) things go awry. 'Hard Head' begins gently, with Louis's vocal incongruously backed by harp arpeggios, but eventually the piece becomes grotesquely frantic. The slow blues 'Where Can I Go?' is sung by Louis all through, but the sophisticated harmonic changes used here sound as out of place as the muted choir. Louis sings 'Whatever Lola Wants' almost without embellishment, but of greater interest is his alto playing; he deliberately blows without using vibrato, somewhat in the manner of the then successful 'cool jazz' players.

The surge of interest in rock and roll had a great effect on ballroom dancing. Jitterbugging and jiving had been common sights in most halls during the 1940s and early 1950s (even when frowned upon by the ballroom owners), but the most popular dances had been waltzes and foxtrots. Young and old mastered the set steps for these, and it was not unusual to see at least two generations on the dance floor at the same time. Rock swiftly changed that situation. Informal, semi-improvised dancing became the order of the day; as a result many people drifted away from what had been a regular part of their lives. Some ballrooms catering to the youngsters' musical tastes thrived, but many other venues which determinedly held on to their old ways went out of business. In general the youngsters wanted to see young performers they could identify with in action on the bandstands.

Louis Jordan had previously enjoyed a big following in some of the nation's largest ballrooms, simply because his infectious beat was so easy to dance to, but he too found that the change of mood caused his ballroom bookings to decline drastically. He was forced to seek other types of engagement in order to keep his work schedule full. The answer seemed to be in playing tours of service camps. Louis had played many one-night stands at army and air-force bases during and after World War II, but in late 1955 he undertook a tour of air bases that began in Alaska and moved down the West Coast via Seattle to finish in Los Angeles. Bert Payne recalls, 'That tour did Louis good, because the receptions were so fantastic. Those guys were starved of entertainment and they went crazy, stomping and whistling. They went mad over our singer Dottie Smith, and Louis was delighted that they did; it all added to the show.'[14]

Louis enjoyed the performing side of the service tour, but hated the intensely cold weather he encountered when the band played the bases in Anchorage and Fairbanks, Alaska. He was fortified by the knowledge that the band would soon be playing dates in warm Miami, Florida. After playing club dates in Detroit and the Mid West the band reached Miami in mid-January. They remained in the South for a few weeks, completing this tour with a Mardi Gras booking in New Orleans, where the band underwent its first personnel changes in a long time. Both drummer Johnny Kirkwood and bassist Thurber Jay decided they wanted to spend more time with their families (each of them had two children). As Louis showed no signs of wanting to lessen his formidable touring schedule, both men handed in their notice, playing two weeks at Carl's Lounge in New Orleans then flying to their homes in California. The New Orleans drummer Frank Parker took Kirkwood's place.

In an attempt to fill the bass-playing vacancy Louis again approached Charlie Gaines's son Stanley, but by this time Stanley was leading his own band and decided to continue doing so. During this period Louis paid a fleeting visit to Arkansas, having driven there from Chicago on his way back to his home in Phoenix. His old friend, trumpeter Ralph Porter, by this time a bandleader in Little Rock, was startled to get a 6 a.m. telephone call:

> I thought it was one of my musicians in some sort of trouble and wanting to borrow money, but it was Louis who was passing through Little Rock and was at a local white service station getting gas. He had a few minutes to spare, so he decided to call me. I was glad he did. I quickly pulled on some clothes and went to see him. He didn't seem in good health and was having trouble walking, more than just being stiff from driving. He'd had a miserable time in Chicago, seeing his ex-wives I think, but he was soon back in good spirits and we had a laugh about old times.[15]

The departure of Kirkwood and Jay caused Louis to rethink his method of employing sidemen. Previously he had hired new musicians on the mutual understanding that they were being offered a permanent place within his organization, and that their stay would continue for as long as they observed his musical and social rules, or until they decided to hand in their notice. Except for unusual circumstances (like the string-laden session with Nelson Riddle), this also meant that the band could expect to be featured on, and paid for, regular recording work with Louis. They could also look forward to regular bonuses; they were, to all intents and purposes, full-time contracted employees of Louis Jordan. But beginning in 1956, Louis usually hired musicians only for set tours, or for pre-defined periods. Thus he could use a good local drummer, or bassist (or any other relevant instrumentalist) and, providing they could read well, Louis knew they would fit in with the rest of the band. The big difference in the new system came when it was time to record again, then Louis felt no great qualms about using top-class freelance sideman, whereas in the past it was understood that current members of the band would automatically be used on a recording session, or on a radio or television date. The new regime and the seemingly ever-longer journeys between club dates, plus what one musician called 'shuffleitis' (prolonged exposure to a shuffle beat), gradually caused the long-time members of the Tympany Five to drop out one by one.

In August 1956, Louis and the band were featured in a spectacular version of NBC's 'Steve Allen Show', part of which was filmed on Market Street, San Francisco. The group were working an eight-week season at the China Trader in that city, so were able to watch the show before they started work, a rare treat in an era when so much television was live. There was still no prospect of Louis being given his own television show, but he was featured on several coast-to-coast productions, including those hosted by Perry Como, Patti Page, Ed Sullivan and Jimmy Durante. Often the band's numbers were shortened for these cameo appearances; on Milton Berle's show, Louis willingly cut an arrangement down several times, but after a further request for brevity he said, smilingly, 'Look Uncle Miltie, I'll just come out for a bow, but please don't cut the money.'

In October 1956, Louis began recording for the Mercury label, using a band comprising some élite New York session musicians, including trumpeter Ernie Royal, trombonist Jimmy Cleveland, saxists Sam 'The Man' Taylor and Budd Johnson, plus an all-star rhythm section. Quincy Jones conducted on the four sessions, and shared arranging duties with Ernie Wilkins. The most important difference between these dates and Louis's efforts for Aladdin and RCA was in the choice of material – other than 'Big Bess' and 'Cat Scratchin'' all the tracks were remakes of songs that Louis had made famous (including 'Caldonia', 'Run Joe', 'Let the Good Times Roll' and 'Beware, Brother, Beware). The result was the album *Somebody up There Digs Me*, which served to introduce Louis Jordan's music to new listeners and also to provide Louis's fans with several songs that had long been unavailable.

Overall, the achievement is impressive, with Mickey Baker's guitar playing providing astute filigree phrases and Ernie Royal's harmon-muted trumpet playing adding a sensitive tone colour. All the arrangements were based on the original recordings, but the extra personnel employed creates a much fuller sound. Louis re-creates his vocals with enthusiasm, if not quite the same elasticity as before, and his alto sax playing remains impressive. But several songs are taken too fast, notably 'Salt Pork, West Virginia', 'Ain't Nobody Here but Us Chickens', and 'Beware, Brother, Beware'; this last suffers notably, because sections of the lyrics become garbled. The only track that benefits slightly from the deliberate change in tempo is 'Caldonia', where Baker's guitar solo opens up proceedings with impressive panache and Sam 'The Man' Taylor's tenor sax solo swings emphatically.

The reason for the changed tempos was to lose the emphasized shuffle rhythm which had been the basis of the originals – simply to re-create the effect in the late 1950s might, it was felt, have given the sides a 'dated' feel, but the loss of the effect diminished the overall charm of the album. In 1956, Sam 'The Man' Taylor had some interesting things to say about rhythm and blues: 'I agree the beat doesn't change much, but I wouldn't want a rhythm section with me that changed every eight bars. If that happens, by the time you're in the groove and swinging, you have to start again.'[16]

At the time of the recordings, Louis was delighted with the results and made a sincere and effusive speech to the assembled musicians, thanking them for their accompaniment. Louis had recently signed with a new personal manager, Ben C. Waller, a black veteran of the

West Coast entertainment world, who had begun specializing in rhythm-and-blues groups during the mid-1950s. Waller gave a formal, optimistic statement to the press about the new recordings, saying, 'Proper exploitation will definitely result in Louis Jordan regaining his place as one of the top recording stars.'

In their launch publicity, Mercury decided to stress Louis's previous eminence by billing him as 'The Original Rock and Roller', but the young people who were being dramatically attracted to the new style of beat music were not interested in paying homage to one of its originators by buying his records. Louis was approaching fifty, but in 1956 most of the emerging stars were less than half that age, with Bill Haley, at thirty-one, a senior contender for popularity.

# It's Better to Wait for Love

In late November 1956 Louis had the rare pleasure of playing close to his home in Phoenix, Arizona. The six-week run at the Ko Ko Club meant a respite from touring life and a chance to enjoy the sunshine and clean air. It was unusual for Louis's wife, Vicky, to have the opportunity to share that much time with her husband; she had come to dislike the touring life and rarely travelled with Louis. The problem was that she, having been a show dancer for several years, got restless in Phoenix, because in those days there was not much organized social life there. She made her boredom plain to Louis, so he offered financial backing for her to achieve a long-held ambition by opening a small coffee shop.

But by this time the couple had become disenchanted with each other, so in 1957 Louis determinedly took as many dates that were far away from Phoenix as he could, touring the East, the Mid West and the South, as well as playing club residencies in Detroit, Philadelphia, San Francisco, Los Angeles and Chicago. While in Chicago he was visited by his ex-wife Fleecie. Dottie Smith observed the reunion and said, 'They seemed to get along OK.' Louis knew that Fleecie was still earning royalties from songs he had written, but was now able to say, 'I guess I'll live a long time without worrying about the money that Fleecie Moore is getting.'[1]

Since the beginning of the 1950s, Louis had found himself becoming increasingly enamoured of Martha Weaver, a dancer from St Louis, Missouri, then in her twenties. Martha, who had enjoyed a comfortable upbringing as the only child in a black middle-class family (her father was an eminent dentist), was always amused when Louis jocularly referred to her as 'the debutante who went astray'. She recalled her first meeting with Louis:

I was introduced to Louis at the Club Baron in New York, which was run by John Barone, for whom Louis had worked (years before) at the Elks Rendezvous. I was in the show there, working with various guest stars such as Ivie Anderson. It was a formal introduction; Louis was with another lady, Fleecie Moore. This would be around 1946. I moved to Atlantic City for a while then returned to my home city, St Louis, and it was there that I first worked with Louis. Each year in St Louis they held the Y Circus Show [for the YMCA], a big event which was split into two halves, the first part being given over to local youngsters and the second headlined by a leading black entertainer. As a kid I'd appeared in the first half when the star of the show was Fats Waller, but in 1951 Louis was the top act; the show had a chorus line led by Hortense Allen and I was one of the dancers. From then on we became friends, and Louis kept in regular touch. We got on marvellously well, and I'd see him whenever it was possible, but Louis wasn't the type of man who would make a woman feel cheap by hiding her away. If he took you out, he gave you the feeling he was proud to be with you. His off-stage personality was entirely different from the wild extrovert his public saw; he was quiet and almost professorial. He rarely discussed show business, and quite early on I remember him saying, 'I make it a rule never to get too friendly with my musicians.' Louis didn't attempt to make close friends, he was really a loner.[2]

With the exception of Dottie Smith (who was singing and playing conga drums), all of Louis's previous musical entourage had moved on by 1957. One of the last of the old guard to go was pianist Chester Lane, who told Peter Vacher: 'Louis wanted me to play the organ. I said I didn't want to play organ, so that meant we disagreed. That's when I came back to St Louis. He got an organ player and two weeks later Bob Mitchell was in Los Angeles and the band had broken up.'

Louis felt that an organist would give his group a fresh timbre and a new lease of life, so he brought Jackie Davis into the band, which usually functioned as a four-piece unit (still billed as the Tympany Five). Another newcomer was guitarist and vocalist Austin Powell, who had led his own band in Chicago before becoming the featured singer in The Cats and the Fiddle. Drummer Roy Porter completed the line-up. Porter, who had enjoyed considerable success in the jazz world, suffered a setback after being jailed for drug offences. Subsequently, he was working with tenor saxist Sigmund Galloway's band in North Hollywood when he learned that Louis was coming in to audition him. He described the scene in the book *There and Back*: 'Louis wasn't sure that I would work out because of my using past and since I was known as a bebop drummer. So when Louis walked through the door I had it worked out with Sig that we would play something with a shuffle and back-beat similar to the style of music which Louis played.' Louis was duly impressed and asked Porter to join; he also offered the band's trumpet player, Clora Bryant, a job, but she had to decline because of other commitments. Porter settled in at a starting wage of $250 a week, which was soon raised to $300 a week. Louis gave his new drummer succinct advice: 'He told me not to play bebop and to just shuffle along, and stay clean.'[3]

After two weeks' rehearsal in Phoenix the new band took off on tour and played a series of dates, sharing the bill with B.B. King, who recalled the bookings:

Most of them were in Texas: Dallas, Fort Worth and Houston. We had a good time, the show worked out nicely and socially we got along fine. Louis was always pleasant but I never got a chance to talk to him regularly. I noticed he didn't go out much. I never saw him rude to anyone but he didn't mix in. But then he'd been a superstar for a long time. He was never off-hand but when there are a lot of people milling around it's not that easy (as I've found out) to sort out who are fans and who are friends. Louis was very clever. I really became aware of this later, when we played the Apollo Theatre together. What set out as a bunch of different acts soon became a show, and a good one. In about two hours of rehearsing Louis had produced a balanced programme. With his own clever ideas he'd put together a fine show – no one could have done it better.[4]

Louis played yet another residency in Las Vegas early in 1957 as part of a Copa Room show headed by singer Howard Keel. Roy Porter liked the working schedule there, which involved only two sets, one at 8.30 p.m. and the next at 12.30 a.m. but when the band resumed touring he gradually wearied of the repertoire: 'I got tired of always having to play "Caldonia", "Let the Good Times Roll", "One Eyed Fish" and "Peepin' Through a Sea-food Store" and so I just split. It was a great experience.'[5]

In September 1957 Louis experienced an unforgettable return visit to his home-town, Brinkley, Arkansas. The *Brinkley Citizen* of 5 September 1957 carried the story:

LOUIS JORDAN TO PLAY BRINKLEY. TUESDAY SEPTEMBER 10th
The appearance of world-famous bandleader Louis Jordan and his Tympany Five in Brinkley promises to be one of he most auspicious occasions in the city's history. Native son Jordan will be making his first appearance since he arose to stardom nearly a decade ago.

Mayor John Deen has officially proclaimed Tuesday as 'Louis Jordan Day'. The celebrated Tympany Five, featuring Capitol recording star Jackie Davis at the Hammond organ, Dottie Smith on vocals and Austin Powell, noted guitarist and baritone singer, will appear at both the National Guard and Armory and the Marion Anderson High School Gymnasium.

Louis enjoyed a happy reunion with his father, and with many old friends in Brinkley. He also visited the Arkansas Baptist College in Little Rock, where he was greeted as a famous ex-pupil, though he had never been a full-time student there. The warmth of the tribute by the College Principal, Dr J.A. Oliver, was not for his scholastic achievements but as a mark of immense gratitude for Louis's generosity as a benefactor. Louis had first met Oliver (then an employee of the Post Office) in Chicago, where their Arkansas camaraderie soon became the basis of a lasting friendship. When Dr Oliver moved back to Little Rock to become the President of the Arkansas Baptist College (from 1953 until his death in 1982), he kept in touch with Louis, who made regular donations to the college and contributed money so that the college choir was able to meet the expenses they incurred on their fund-raising tours. Faced with such kindness, Dr Oliver never issued a contradiction when Louis spoke of graduating from the college.

Highly important issues were in the wind during the period of Louis's visit to Arkansas in 1957. Attempts to implement the Supreme Court's ruling on the desegregation of schools had run into severe problems at Central High, Little Rock where, for the first time ever, black pupils were due to become students. On 2 September 1957, the long-serving Governor of Arkansas, Orval Eugene Faubus, made a speech warning that 'blood will run in the streets' if Negro pupils attempted to enter Central High. As a result of continuing obstacles, President Eisenhower, through his Secretary of Defense, Charles E. Wilson, ordered a thousand paratroopers, white and black, into Little Rock.

What had begun as a joyful return to his early surroundings became for Louis a sad experience, and he left to play his next engagements, at the Sands Hotel in Las Vegas, with a heavy heart. Louis Armstrong let his bitterness overflow in a passionate denunciation of the situation, describing Governor Faubus as 'a ploughboy', but Louis Jordan remained sombre and silent off-stage throughout most of the two months' booking in Las Vegas.

Soon after this engagement ended, Louis decided to dissolve his group. He was suffering a good deal from arthritis and issued a statement saying he was in 'great need of rest'. But his sudden disbandment caused guitarist Austin Powell to make a claim via the Musicians' Union against Louis, alleging non-payment of the stipulated two weeks' money (in lieu of notice).[6] The matter was eventually resolved, but Louis returned home vowing that he had no wish ever to lead a touring band again. As before, however, he soon changed his mind.

Louis still had one more Mercury session to make as part of his existing contract, and this stirred him into forming the nucleus of a regular group. After the relatively disappointing sales achieved by the re-make album, Louis's recordings for Mercury dropped into a pattern that produced a mixture of old standards, novelty songs, lightweight rockers and lively whoop-ups. Most of these were recorded in 1957 by the small group featuring Jackie Davis on organ, but the final June 1958 session used a group similar in intent to the old Tympany Five.

Louis resumed touring, but did not always use the same personnel, relying more on a pool of musicians, including his former drummer Charlie Rice and two other players from Philadelphia, electric bassist Jimmy Mobley and tenor saxist Bill Leslie. Others who played in various editions of the Tympany Five during the late 1950s included drummers Al Duncan and Marvin Oliver, pianist Howard Reynolds and tenor saxist Leroy Lang. Teddy Bunn, one of the great instinctive jazz guitarists, also worked with Louis during this period:

One day Louis calls me and says why don't I come out one evening because he'd like maybe to have me play with the band. So I go out and sat in for a spell. Sure was a tough book, all sorts of fancy arrangements that those guys knew real well but I just know what the guys are going to play, just before they play it. So I wasn't faking too much. Louis says to me, 'How'd you know all that stuff we play? You're hired.'[7]

Looking back, Dottie Smith said:

In the ten years I was with Louis we must have had six or seven complete changes of bands – but often there wasn't a changeover at the same time. If Louis was having trouble with a musician, he'd find someone to take his place while we were on tour and pay off the guy he was firing by giving him his fare home and hiring the new man then and there.[8]

A version of the Tympany Five (Howard Reynolds, piano; Leroy Lang, tenor sax; Al Duncan, drums; Jimmy Mobley, electric bass and Dottie Smith, vocals) played dates with Louis in Baltimore, Maryland, then flew to the Caribbean to play dates in Bermuda and in the Bahamas. Louis's group resumed working at the various Nevada casinos, but elsewhere the demand for the Tympany Five had slackened off considerably. Louis told everyone he had learned his lesson and was taking things easy for the sake of his health but, in truth, he would have liked more offers of work. He became keener to try new venues and in October 1958 played a three-week season at Turk Murphy's Easy Street Club in San Francisco.

Louis's initial reaction to the lessening of demand was to suppose that his long-time booking agency GAC was less intent on selling the band than it had been in the past. Accordingly, in 1959, he decided to break with GAC and sign with Joe Glaser's Associated Booking Corporation. This move led Louis into some new venues where Glaser had strong influence, such as the Metropole in New York, then a famous jazz bar on Seventh Avenue (at 48th and 49th). Louis played a three-week season there (ending 19 June 1960), which won him a review that praised his 'wailing alto and jumping vocals'.⁹ But the Metropole never became a regular booking for Louis; his main New York engagements were still at the Apollo where, despite any changes in musical taste, he remained a tremendous favourite whose annual appearance still drew the crowds.

It did not take Louis too long to realize that changing his booking agency had made little difference to his income; demand had diminished and Louis lashed out at what he now saw as the culprit: rock and roll. In a 1960 interview he said, 'I give it just about one year more. The music is bad, or the words are bad if the music is good. We started it, but it's been changed.' Louis also blamed the payola scandal (whereby some disc jockeys took bribes to play certain records on their radio shows) for a lowering of standards, ending his tirade by saying, 'When a disc jockey tells the kids a record is good they buy it.'¹⁰ On another occasion Louis expressed similarly vexed views, adding, 'Personally, I like sweet music and pretty things like "Clair de Lune".'¹¹

But despite often being on the sidelines, Louis Jordan was still a star in the eyes of veterans of the music world, and he was featured in a March 1960 coast-to-coast Ford-sponsored 'Startime' television show, whose master of ceremonies was Ronald Reagan. Louis sounded as cheerful as ever as he bantered with Reagan about the Apollo Theatre prior to backing Dinah Washington on 'Makin' Whoopee', then Louis made his own introduction to the next number, saying, 'Ladies and gentlemen, here's a little tune that goes with the Tympany Five like red beans and rice – in fact it sold a million records – and here it is "Choo Choo Ch'Boogie".'¹²

Louis's periods of inactivity meant that he and his wife, Vicky, had more time to be at loggerheads. Their relationship worsened after an incident that took place during one of Louis's infrequent tours. Louis had left specific instructions for Vicky to bid for some property in Phoenix, where Louis planned to run a hotel. Louis reasoned that the life of a hotelier would suit him, and that he could delegate the management to someone else when he went off to play any engagements that appealed to him. Unfortunately, Vicky was drinking a good deal during this period, and through a temporary lapse of memory she accidentally missed the time of the auction. For Louis it was almost the last straw, and the relationship steadily worsened.

It became apparent that the two would soon have to move in different directions, and Louis sold his house in Phoenix (the buyer was the religious leader, Elijah Muhammed). Louis left with regrets; 'I saw that town grow from 70,000 to half a million. I like Phoenix better than any other city in America, but musically it hasn't grown 20 per cent in all that time. People come there and buy expensive homes and have parties in them instead of going out.'[13] Louis toyed with the idea of living in San Francisco, but found the climate exacerbated his arthritis: 'San Francisco is too damp for me. I'd wake up aching, even in July and August.'[14] Instead, Louis chose to reside in Los Angeles.

On all of his engagements during the early 1960s, Louis continued to project ebullience and good music, even when he was feeling disheartened. By 1961 he had disbanded the Tympany Five and was appearing as a guest star in a show headed by Debby Hayes, who was featured on trumpet and vocals. Leonard Feather saw the show performing in the lounge of a giant bowling alley in Long Beach, California, and interviewed Louis, who told him about the break-up of his group:

It happened during holiday week between last Christmas and New Year. The doctor had told me to take it easy anyway, but you know how it is around Christmas. And I was in Chicago, where I'd lived for years, so old friends were asking me to play for them at parties, and I had to be back on the job the same evening. Well, you know me; if the job is at 9.30, I'm there at 9. One guy showed twenty minutes later and another half-hour late, and I said to myself I've had it. I gave the guys two weeks' notice. A few weeks later while I was working Basin Street [New York] with a pick-up combo,* Debby Hayes's husband, who manages her, asked if I'd like to join

---

*This was one of the most star-studded groups that Louis ever worked with, consisting of Joe Newman (trumpet), Tommy Flanagan (piano), Al Lucas (bass) and Jo Jones (drums).

her show. I've been with it three months now. I have no health hang-ups, no sidemen to worry about, no responsibilities, no business problems, not even a recording contract; and I can relax on my day off. I've never been happier.[15]

Feather said it sounded as though Louis meant it, but sagely pointed out that it seemed unjust that a 'nation of faddists' seemed unaware of Jordan's immense contribution to popular music. Louis's recording career was certainly in the doldrums at this time; in a Combo Directory that detailed his agency as the Associated Booking Corporation, the final line 'No current records' had an ignominious ring. His sole new releases in quite a while had been a couple of singles on the Warwick label, the issue of which had scarcely caused a ripple on the pop-world ocean, despite one of the compositions, 'Fifty Cents', being perhaps the best food song Louis ever recorded.

To add to Louis's professional disappointments, he was also having health problems, often finding himself slightly breathless. The doctor told him he must diet and Louis took the advice. 'I'm only 5 feet 6 inches and I had gotten up to 196 pounds. My health was affected. I took off thirty-five pounds.'[16] Things began to look brighter in 1962 when Louis signed for Tangerine, a new label owned by singer Ray Charles; soon afterwards Louis began recording with the big band that Charles usually fronted. Ray Charles had long been a fan of Louis's, and years later eulogized him:

He was such a great showman, with a sense of humour and an unforgettable tongue-in-cheek style that, after hearing him once, I couldn't forget him, and I became a great fan. His mastery of the alto saxophone impressed me so much that people tell me that my own alto sax style, in some ways, resembles his. I have to admit that Louis Jordan has had a great and lasting influence upon my appreciation of music and, perhaps, even my performance.[17]

Louis again became professionally optimistic, but domestically he was at a low ebb. In a conversation with Joe Adams, Ray Charles's manager, who also produced the dates, Louis asked Joe if he knew the whereabouts of their mutual friend, Martha Weaver. When Adams said he did, Louis asked him to pass on a message saying he would like to see Martha again, and that he would shortly be working in Las Vegas. By this time Louis's marriage to Vicky had reached a point of no return and she was planning to live permanently in Chicago.

Martha decided to visit Louis in Las Vegas and they quickly resumed the romance they had enjoyed during the 1950s. Martha had driven to the gambling resort to meet up with Louis, and he was delighted with the reunion but horrified by the state of the tyres on her automobile. He promptly bought her a new set. The couple saw each other regularly during 1962, each realizing that it was only a matter of time before they married.

Louis continued to keep in close touch with his father. He visited Brinkley in September 1960, and tried, unsuccessfully, to dissuade him from continuing to work as a part-time caretaker at the Haven of Rest black cemetery there. Otherwise Louis's visit was a happy one, with local friends organizing an outing on the Cache river in his honour. In June 1962 Louis received the dread news that his father had died of a heart attack on the 15th, the eve of his eighty-sixth birthday.

Louis was deeply affected by his father's death, but carried on working through the summer of 1962. By this time he had left the Debby Hayes Show and was back leading his own small band or sometimes temporarily fronting a small existing group, billed either as Louis Jordan's Tympany Five or given smaller separate billing beneath Louis's name. He virtually made himself available to be booked as a guest star, and as a result, ABC fixed a deal with British trombonist Chris Barber for Louis to tour England with Barber's jazz band late in 1962. Louis decided to make his first trip to Europe alone.

For Chris Barber (who brought many American jazz and blues stars into Britain over the years) the tour with Louis Jordan was a happy and memorable one. He had been a fan of Louis's for many years, but had never considered booking him for a tour until he saw him in action in New York. He recalled:

During one of our tours of the States I visited the Apollo Theatre and Louis Jordan was on the bill. He was an extraordinary showman and a brilliant musician and for that booking he had, as a guest star, the saxophonist Sonny Stitt, who was billed as 'Handsome Sonny Stitt'. Louis on alto, Stitt on tenor and a baritone sax player did a round of solos and some tremendous four-bar chases, but they climaxed all this by doing the splits – it was an incredible sight and the crowd loved it. Guitarist Teddy Bunn was in Louis Jordan's band for that booking – that was the only time I ever saw him play. I went backstage and soon found out that Louis was keen to visit Britain, so we put the matter in the hands of agents, and eventually Harold Davison fixed it with ABC and Joe Glaser.[18]

Louis was scheduled to arrive at London Airport on 5 December 1962, but due to adverse weather conditions his plane was diverted to Prestwick, in Scotland. This began a miserable time for Louis. Because his work permit and clearance documents were hundreds of miles away (at London Airport), the immigration officers hesitated about giving him permission to enter Britain, keeping him waiting for an hour in a cold room before they were finally satisfied that he could be allowed in. Since all planes had been grounded Louis's next problem was getting to London. He eventually caught a train, and shivered his way through a long, unheated, unnourished 400-mile journey south. The upshot was a heavy cold that robbed Louis of his voice. Scarcely able to talk, totally unable to sing, Louis retired to his hotel bed while Chris Barber reluctantly cancelled the opening dates of the concert tour.

After a few days' rest, Louis felt well enough to begin the tour, and on Monday 10 December the show billed as: 'Chris Barber's Jazz Band with Ottilie Patterson and America's most exciting vocal entertainer Louis Jordan' opened at the City Hall, Sheffield. Trombonist Chris Barber's Jazz band was already internationally known, with recent hit records to its credit, but for many of Chris's followers, the name Louis Jordan was unfamiliar. For a minority of the audience – Louis's dedicated life-long fans – the concerts were a dream come true, but Barber's supporters remained sceptical until the moment the American whirled on stage. They were instantly converted, as was the *Sheffield Star* reporter, whose review said:

BLUES SINGER STEALS CHRIS BARBER'S LIMELIGHT
Chris Barber's well-drilled group turned in a polished performance at Sheffield's City Hall last night, but it took the appearance of a

fifty-four-year-old, virtually unknown rhythm-and-blues singer from Arkansas to give it real spirit.

Louis Jordan, who arrived in Britain last week and was promptly rendered voiceless by the smog, added vigour to the band the moment he stepped on to the stage. Nattily attired and spritely, he joined the band for such numbers as his own 'Choo Choo Ch'Boogie', which sold a million in 1947, and 'Is You is or is You ain't My Baby'.

Chris Barber retains happy memories of the brief tour:

Louis flew over by himself, no entourage, and he went along with our normal travel plans – we either used cars or a band bus. He was a very organized person. He carried an enormous address book which also contained the birthdays of the wives of every club owner that he'd ever played for, or so it seemed, because he was always posting off greetings cards. He didn't bring any band parts with him, but taught us the routines for ten of his songs in one four-hour rehearsal. They were the ten tunes we recorded later that week, and they turned out all right. I think Ottilie was a bit intimidated, initially, because when they rehearsed a duet on 'Tain't Nobody's Business' Louis wanted a shared coda. Ottilie liked the idea, but felt she wanted to work out a vocal line and asked what the chords were. Louis said, very positively, 'Just sing it. Just sing it.' But everything soon went smoothly, though that number wasn't issued even though we recorded it.[19]

Ottilie Patterson was greatly impressed by Louis's presentation and by his ability to act out a song: 'He was brilliant to watch and to listen to, he was highly mobile on stage, but he made every movement count. I found him to be a lovely man. Intelligent and dedicated. He told me that he'd been at school with a girl called Ottilie.'[20] Barber's trumpeter, Pat Halcox, maintains that Louis Jordan's method of rehearsing a band is the most impressive he has ever encountered: 'He knew exactly which note each instrument had to play within the arrangements, and he also had a marvellous way of showing you how to phrase those notes. He believed in getting things absolutely right, but he had a pleasant way of explaining what he wanted, and of correcting anyone who went wrong. It was a revelation working with him.'[21]

Barber himself also remains full of praise for Jordan:

He was the best thing that had ever happened to us. I learnt a lot from him. He was wonderful at selling a song and a brilliant musician. He was one of the great jazz alto sax players, yet he's never mentioned in this context. Once he'd got over his cold, his health was fine and his energy was prodigious. He was fifty-four and we were in our early thirties, but he pulled us along like a wild horse. His breath control was phenomenal; he could finish a vigorous vocal and immediately put his alto to his mouth and blow an elaborate coda, or vice versa, he'd finish blowing chorus after chorus on sax and instantly begin singing with perfect clarity. He did all this on microphone in the recording studio; no engineering, he just swopped from playing to singing with incredible ease.

During the tour Eddie Smith, our banjo player, badly bruised his thumb in an accident and had to take time off. In his place we got a well-known guitarist; during a concert at Brighton we played 'The Sheik of Araby' and this guitarist lost a beat in his solo. Louis was appalled and said, 'If your guy can't make it for the next gig we'll do without.' Louis came to my home and we relaxed and played records, all sorts of things, but the one he wanted to hear again was 'Carpet Alley' by Johnny Dodds and the Dixieland Jug Blowers (from 1926). He liked Johnny Dodds and he loved the banjo playing on it, saying he'd played some banjo himself when he was young.

The tour didn't make a lot of money, mainly because of bad weather conditions, but wherever we played people were overjoyed to see Louis Jordan in person. Louis gave his all on every gig, but I sensed he was especially pleased when a lot of black people turned out to see him when he played at the Colston Hall, Bristol. They were mostly West Indian families who knew Louis's calypso records, and that night he played with some extra zip.

With Louis we took part in a 'Saturday Club' radio show, recorded at the Playhouse Theatre, London for the BBC. On the same day the Beatles were also there, recording their part – it must have been one of their first broadcasts – but at the time we didn't attach much significance to what they were doing and I don't recall Louis making any comment about them at all.[22]

The tour ended on 16 December at the Fairfield Hall, Croydon, close to London – too close, as it transpired, because the capital was shrouded in one of the last 'peasouper' fogs that occurred before the Clean Air Act took effect, and this prevented people travelling to the concert, so the attendance was disappointing. On the following evening (Louis's last in Britain) Louis socialized with some of the Barber band and other musicians at the Springfield Club in Earlsfield. A jam session took place and so too did a darts match. Louis sportingly took part in this and, as a memento of the occasion, was presented with a dartboard.

Before Louis departed, he gave an interview to the *Melody Maker* in which he said:

One of the things that's destroying jazz is the lack of co-operation among musicians. Too often today an outstanding player goes out to 'kill' the other fellows. He may do it – but in the process he's liable to kill the music too. Another thing is the amount of copying. In this sense Charlie Parker ruined so many alto players. You know I used to hang out with Bird all the time. I was with him the night before he died. I never tried to play like him and I think he liked that.[23]

Louis left behind a great many new friends and followers in Britain, and an album which confirms Chris Barber's view that Jordan lifted the band tremendously. Besides spirited versions of such old hits as 'Choo Choo', 'Is You is', 'I'm Gonna Move' and 'Don't Worry 'bout the Mule', there is also another version of the lively Caribbean-tinged food song 'Fifty Cents' and two swinging instrumentals, 'I Wish I Could Shimmy Like My Sister Kate' and 'Back Home Again in Indiana' (a particular favourite of Louis's, and one that he had featured on various radio shows over the years).

Louis returned, exhausted but happy, to Martha in Los Angeles, determined to rest and to shake off the cold he had been carrying throughout his trip to Britain. He had no long tours planned, just a succession of scattered club dates, but he was philosophical about the future and optimistic about the series of recordings that he was due to complete for the Tangerine label.

# *Every Knock is a Boost*

Louis and Martha had set up home at 6011 Buckler Avenue in Los Angeles, their comfortable house built on three levels, at the top of which was a swimming pool and a bath house. Martha gradually taught Louis how to relax. He went fishing regularly, watched sport on television and bought himself a drum kit and a guitar, practising on both in a casual way. He also purchased a flute, but found that blowing it gave him a headache. He rarely practised the alto sax for long periods, but was still in the habit of sitting with the instrument across his lap then picking it up to blow a few brief phrases of a new musical idea. Louis's old restlessness occasionally bubbled up and, finding himself with so much spare time, he toyed with the idea of becoming a salesman for a wrought-iron company that a friend owned, but after one or two house calls Louis decided it was too late in life for him to change professions.

He listened to emerging talent on television and records and occasionally visited local clubs, but his two favourite singers remained Ella Fitzgerald and Nat 'King' Cole. In his later years, Louis also came greatly to admire Sam Cooke. He said, 'I used to go hear him, but I never played with him. He was on his way to a billion dollars when he got killed.' Louis also liked Shirley Bassey, but in a discussion about his overall choice he said, 'There was one individual, Tiny Bradshaw; he was my favourite entertainer that never got big. He wrote some hit tunes and was one of the great performers of my time, but he never got over the hill. He appealed to everyody, but he never got real big.'[1]

Louis was pleased with the results of most of the items he had been recording for Tangerine and was eager to start helping to plug the issued album. For the first time in a long while he was keenly looking forward to having a record released, but he built up his hopes too high and suffered a disappointing letdown which it took him a long time to get over. Years later he told Leonard Feather:

I took an offer from Ray Charles and began to record for his Tangerine label, but I think he must have just signed me up as a tax deduction or something. I had two or three tunes that could have been very big on an album called *Hallelujah, Louis Jordan is Back*; but you couldn't buy it. They sent a very small supply to Chicago for instance, and I took them to the disc jockeys. I made a tour with Moms Mabley and carried the albums around with me. The jockeys played them and played them, but if you went into a store you couldn't find it; it didn't help.[2]

He returned to the subject in another interview, making disgruntled comments: 'Ray Charles, he did a lot of my things. His first recordings were my tunes, "Let the Good Times Roll", yeah, and before that. He was born in Florida and recorded with a little company down there, and he did "Choo Choo Ch'Boogie".'

Martha Jordan confirmed how upset Louis was about what he considered the shoddy treatment he got from Ray Charles:

Louis just couldn't understand what caused Ray to act the way he did. He had wined and dined Louis and outlined what great new prospects were in store if he signed for the Tangerine label, but after Louis made the records he didn't show any interest, and there were some very good tracks. It was a disappointing time for Louis because he was virtually being ignored by Joe Glaser's office. Louis would have loved to have recorded again with Louis Armstrong but Joe Glaser seemed to veto the idea. I'm certain that it wasn't anything to do with Pops himself, because Louis and I loved Pops and he was always great with us. Joe Glaser somehow saw Louis Jordan as a threat to Louis Armstrong, which was absolute nonsense. I've always felt that Louis's signing with ABC was one of his biggest mistakes; it need not have been, but for Joe Glaser's attitude.[3]

Louis certainly had a case when he complained about Tangerine's lack of promotion and Martha was right in saying that there were plenty of good performances on the album, but as with other sides that Louis had made in his recent past, the material was not uniformly strong. Louis's alto sax is featured on a good percentage of the tracks and he plays well throughout; his tone is not quite as full as hitherto, but his fingers are as nimble as ever as he glides through double-time runs on 'What'd I Say'. His blues playing remained convincing, particularly on 'Time is Running Out', but on this track his blues singing seems light-hearted, leading the listener to expect a joky stanza which never materializes. This approach pays off on the medium-paced 'Hard Head', but again detracts from 'My Friends' (whose lyrics seem to be built on the chassis of 'Nobody Knows You when You're Down and Out').

'Cole Slaw' combines the recurring themes of food and home-state – 'In Arkansas they serve you cole slaw' – but the end result sounds like a long advertising jingle. Most of the neat arrangements were by Ernie Freeman; they are contemporary examples of that period's studio music, redolent of quasi-rock drumming, electric bass figures and punchy brass interludes. The diluted funk feel is typified by the tribute to the highway, 'El Camino Real'. 'Don't Send Me no Flowers when I'm in the Graveyard' is outstanding, fine lyrics attached to a standard sixteen-bar chord sequence. Louis sings this perfectly, subtly emphasizing a macabre line of humour that would probably have ruled it out of most radio shows of the period.

The other memorable side is 'You're My Mule', a slow blues which dispenses with the rock feel, benefiting instead from a Basie-type rhythm section, which enables Louis to give a skilfully relaxed interpretation of the lyrics, backed by some superbly conceived muted trumpet fill-ins (the only time that any other instrumentalist enters the limelight). It remains a good album, but not a great one. Louis was again able to demonstrate his consistency, his undiminished zest, and his vocal and instrumental artistry, but the plan to present Louis in mock-rock surroundings often shrouds his originality.

For his live appearances during the mid-1960s, Louis most often featured a Hammond organ in his line-up, Kenny Andrews fulfilling the role previously filled by Jackie Davis. The new factor in Louis's presentation was the inclusion of Martha's singing and dancing talents. Martha not only played a successful part in Louis's music-making, but after they were married (on 14 June 1966) she acted as the organizer for the band, finalizing details of engagements, paying the musicians and looking after the general administration, thus taking a burden from Louis's shoulders.

Louis wasn't a great businessman, and after we were married I realized how easily he had got himself into a financial mess. He knew it and used to say, 'I just couldn't keep up with business and play music too.' After he'd paid huge sums to the Internal Revenue for past earnings, he didn't obtain, or didn't keep, the necessary receipts, so it was very difficult to know what had been paid and what hadn't. What was certain was that Uncle Sam took all the money that Louis thought was his; I used to kid him after we were married by saying, 'Well I sure didn't marry you for your money, honey.' He didn't have a quarter spare at that time. But Louis felt he'd been let down by others over the tax problems, because when the Internal Revenue Service asked to see the books relating to his big earnings in the past, it took his management three years to produce them, and this made the IRS determined to harass Louis.

Louis's main hobby was photography, and as he gradually found that he had more time on his hands, he used to do all his own developing and printing, but he also took hundreds of slides. He liked fishing and went with various friends, such as George Parker, a restaurant owner, not with people who were in the music business. But generally he stayed in his own bay, he wasn't a boon-coon pal with many people, yet he made friends with the husbands of my friends quite easily and he had a great regard for all of my family, including my aunts and uncles. He got close to them, and they made up for him not having a family of his own.

In these years he always wore spectacles when he wasn't on-stage, and this meant that people didn't recognize him, which suited him. He could be very quiet in a gathering of people, but when he relaxed at a party, people were fascinated by what he had to say, then he would talk and talk in a philosophical way, and he'd be surrounded by interested people. I've always been a television buff, but Louis wasn't, he'd fiddle around the house while I was watching, but he loved seeing football on TV and he tried never to miss a game, particularly if his favourites, the Dallas Cowboys, were playing. He liked playing records, but rarely his own. In fact he didn't keep tabs on them at all and years later I found his gold disc for 'Choo Choo Ch'Boogie' in among a whole pile of 78s that had found their way into the collection of a niece of his former wife, Vicky, and it had been played and played. Can you imagine that? Playing a gold disc? I took it and had it framed. Louis didn't regard such things as important. He liked listening to certain records, and Nat Cole remained his all-time favourite, along with Ella, but he also used to play Julie London records all the time, and he liked Lou Rawls's singing.

Louis liked listening to, and performing, songs with a story. He wasn't enthusiastic about loud, wild groups but he rarely criticized any of them directly, he tried to keep an open mind, and when someone knocked the Beatles' singing once in his presence he simply said, 'Don't judge them as singers or performers, just listen to their songs.' I used to love hearing Louis singing ballads. My favourite was 'Trust in Me', which he always sang for me. I used to tell him what a great ballad singer he was but he'd shrug it off and say, 'You need a gimmick – ballad singing isn't enough.' A lot of musicians used to compliment Louis on the way he played the saxophone, and I can remember Paul Gonsalves, who was in Las Vegas with Duke Ellington, making a point of cutting across each night to hear Louis play. He always requested 'When You're Smiling'.[4]

Louis and Martha continued to play the Nevada gambling lounges, and various hotels and clubs on the West Coast, but in 1967 they undertook their first tour of the Far East, working mainly at US Air Force bases (having previously played Honolulu in December 1965). Martha recalled:

Often we did three different shows at each camp, one for enlisted men, one for NCOs, and one for the officers. We played Japan, the Philippines, Okinawa, Korea, Taiwan, Hong Kong and Singapore, in addition to working a six-week season at a big, plush hotel in Bangkok, Thailand. In Bangkok Louis met up with pianist Maurice Rocco, who made his home there. Louis had worked with Maurice twenty-five years earlier in Chicago and they had a lot to talk about. Some ten years later Maurice was stabbed to death in Bangkok.

Louis liked everything to be on time, but through a series of delays we arrived in Japan with only enough time to go straight to the first gig. There wasn't even an opportunity to check in to a hotel, so we had to go on in the clothes we arrived in, but Louis didn't let this inhibit him one little bit, he just went boldly out on-stage and won them straight over. He could be droll and subtle. When we were in Korea I sang 'Goody Goody' and got one of the greatest receptions I've ever had, and I turned and said, 'OK, follow that, Louis Jordan.' He said drily, 'Well, everyone knows that servicemen will always holler for a pretty girl.' When we were in Tokyo, an army officer asked if we would mind entertaining service personnel who had been wounded in Vietnam, who were in hospital in Japan. Louis immediately agreed and we took an hour's train ride out of the city and were given a fabulous reception. Later we were shocked to learn that a number of American entertainers had refused to play for the wounded.

Louis was determined to enjoy that tour as much as possible and though we were working until 4 a.m. he got up at 7 a.m. to go on a tourist trip to a floating market. We visited as many historic sights as possible and Louis listened intently to what the guides had to tell us. All in all, we were away for several months but when we got back Louis rested and was soon rarin' to go, and began making plans to form up a new group. I think he'd got exasperated by the attitude of some of the musicians on the overseas tour. One of them took so much excess baggage it cost Louis two thousand dollars extra. He wasn't in the band that Louis took to Japan and Korea a year later. Neither was I, because I had to go into hospital for surgery.[5]

In September 1968, former bandleader Paul Gayten contacted Louis and invited him to record for his new West Coast-based label Pzazz. The two men had known each other for years, Gayten having first heard Louis working in the Rabbit Foot Minstrels. Signing a new recording contract raised Louis's hopes and he told Leonard Feather, 'I knew I could rely on Paul to give me a free hand. We agreed on a new sound, using a fourteen-piece orchestra, with Teddy Edwards writing most of the arrangements.'[6] Tenor saxist Teddy Edwards was an admirer of Louis's work, and an old friend of Gayten, with whom he had worked back in the 1940s.

The initial plan was to issue a couple of singles as bait, and then follow up with an album. One of the singles, 'Santa Claus, Santa Claus' (composed by Teddy Edwards) did actually reach the local record charts and gained Louis some welcome air play, but poor pre-planning meant that the disc was issued too late for the Christmas market it was intended to hit. This irritated Louis, who said, 'We got up to Number 41 in the charts and it did real well in Chicago, but it didn't come out until 10 December.'[7] Because of its seasonal message, the song was left off the subsequent Pzazz album, but another single, 'New Orleans and a Rusty Old Horn' (arranged by Carroll Skinner) also got a lot of air plays and was regularly requested by people attending Louis's gigs. It became one of Louis's favourite examples of his latterday work; the only other side that pleased him from the session was 'One Sided Love'. Louis continued to get requests for 'Bullitt' long after he recorded his near frantic instrumental version of Lalo Schifrin's movie-linked composition. The hard-swinging drum work and Louis's long trilled ending gave the track a positive edge, and Teddy Edwards firmly believed that this version was superior to the one used on the original film soundtrack.

Louis's discontent surfaced only after the album was released and it is probable that if the recordings had achieved a good deal of success he would have contentedly refrained from uttering any words of criticism. During his glory years, Louis rarely let disappointment linger when a record failed to live up to his original expectations, simply because he knew that he would soon be back in the studios to try again, but by the time he made his dejected comments about the album he knew that there would be no more sessions for Pzazz. The pity was that he had been so enthusiastic at the time he made the album, as Teddy Edwards noted:

Louis was so happy to be recording again, so much so that when I wanted to do another take on 'The Amen Corner', because the violins weren't quite right, Louis said, 'No, that's OK. You just keep writing 'em like that.' We used an all-star band: Bobby

Bryant (trumpet), John 'Streamline' Ewing (trombone), Al McKibbon (string bass), Max Bennett (Fender bass), Ronnell Bright (piano) and Earl Palmer (drums). I played tenor sax and shared the A & R duties with Jack Scott, who also played guitar; I did most of the arrangements. We didn't use any overdubs; everyone, including the violins and the vocal group, performed live in the studio. Louis was a hit maker, but the album didn't get away – Paul Gayten tried to launch it in LA and New York, the two toughest spots. But 'Santa Claus', which I wrote, almost got through; that was the last thing we did at the sessions, less planned than any of the others. Later I met up with Louis at the Union building and he still seemed happy. I said to him why don't Universal/MCA do your life story – it's your money that built them and of course he was one of the people (along with Bing Crosby of course) that made Decca. He laughed. He wasn't finished and could still kick his feet above his head.[8]

The problem with the Pzazz album is that it lacks cohesion – the spray-shot policy employed left Louis to cover a wide area of popular music in the hope of coming up with a hit. The material ranges from an effective twelve-bar blues, 'You Gotta Go', to a 'Wild is the Night' (which seems to bring out the old 'Ghost Riders in the Sky'). Through this kaleidoscope of styles Louis kept performing to the best of his considerable ability, and on one track 'I'll Get Along Somehow', had Martha alongside him sharing the dialogue, but his alto sax playing is rarely heard throughout the entire Pzazz sessions.

Paul Gayten soon conceded that this omission was a mistake, and said, 'We'll get back to something more like the Tympany Five sound, only with a Fender bass and some of the contemporary combo feeling.'[9] But there was no opportunity to utilise these plans; this was the only album that Louis did for Pzazz and, looking back Jordan was plainly aggrieved:

They wouldn't let me sing like I wanted to sing. I appreciate him wanting to do an album on me, but at least get my full potential. Each one of the arrangers that did a tune wanted me to sing a certain way: 'Don't sing it this way. Do it this way.' That's not the way to treat an artist – so it wasn't really successful.[10]

As the 1960s drew to a close Louis again reverted to using a Tympany Five-style line-up, and was delighted to welcome back his old bassist Dallas Bartley. The rest of the line-up was Herbert Anderson on trumpet, Julius Brooks on tenor saxophone (and occasionally string bass), John Houston on piano and Bill Moore on drums. Louis used this line-up for most of his dates, but for venues that required a more restrained timbre he simply fronted a quartet consisting of John Houston on piano, John's brother Clarence on drums and Dave Allen on Fender bass. Guitarist Leo Blevins also worked with Louis during this period.

Louis was always wryly amused to relate that for the first five years that he lived in Los Angeles nobody offered him a gig there, but by 1969 he was in regular local demand, so much so that in the spring of that year City Councilman Billy Mills authorized a resolution praising Louis for his contributions to the entertainment field. A routine of working for about eight months each year suited Louis. He played a residency in Oklahoma City twice a year, and did two annual month-long residencies in Dallas, Texas. Louis had always had a following in Texas, and Milton Larkin (a Houston-born bandleader) felt that this was because Louis's approach to the blues was basically Texan (despite having been raised in Arkansas). During one trip to Dallas, Louis linked up with Bob Burgess (the white trombonist who had worked in Louis's big band), who said:

Louis came to my home in Dallas one 4 October to help me celebrate my birthday. He was using a rock-type rhythm section to put over his old songs and he laughed when he told me people thought it was something new. He was cheerful but said he'd been taken by some white guys who had advised him to invest money in a scheme that went all wrong.[11]

Besides the Oklahoma City and Dallas bookings, Louis continued to work for at least two months each year at Lake Tahoe and played regular dates in Las Vegas as well as his local Los Angeles bookings. A change in this routine seemed likely in late 1969 when Louis was offered a month's tour of Europe. Bookings covering a period from 17 October to 15 November, including engagements in France, England, Switzerland, Sweden and Denmark, had been set up by the

French promoter Jean-Marie Monestier, but in the late stages of negotiations Louis found it impossible to get out of a contract he had signed to appear in Las Vegas. Sammy Price stepped in to fulfil most of the tour dates.

In a 1969 interview with Leonard Feather, Louis summarized his views on the music scene:

> We emphasized the beat mostly through a shuffle boogie rhythm. The only thing that really changed was the intensity of the beat, particularly in the drums. Later they brought the bass up and then the guitar, which more or less came into its own with the rock-and-roll era. The music didn't change as much as the rhythm. More noise, more amplification – they just put more juice behind everything. On some of the records in the early stages of rock and roll you could hardly hear the melody, nor the singer. Noise can hide a whole gang of faults. That's just about the reason why the amplification got bigger – because so many people made records who couldn't even sing. I've never had a blues album – would you believe it? Here I've been associated with the blues all my life, but the whole time I was with Decca they were so busy making money with my singles that they never thought about albums, so I missed out on that chance.[12]

On another occasion Louis reiterated his dislike of over-amplified music:

> I don't like a lot of rock and roll because it's got too much noise. I went to hear B.B. King when he played here in Los Angeles at the Whisky-a-Go-Go. Well, there was this group on first and they played so loud I had to go outside and give my eardrums a rest and when I went back I couldn't hear B.B. I've heard some groups, they learn five or six tunes and they use the same breaks on everything. If they learn ten tunes they think they're cookin'. They should start from the basics and learn all there is to know.[13]

Financially, things began to look healthier in 1970 and Louis and Martha spent a long, happy vacation visiting Mexico prior to undertaking another tour of the Orient in the latter part of that year. Martha recalled:

> We'd only been back from Mexico a few days when it was time to fly out for the tour. On that trip we did mostly clubs in the countries we'd visited before. It was a tiring schedule but for he most part enjoyable. The outstanding memory from all our tours out there happened in Bangkok. We were playing the cabaret spot at a nightclub and another local band was playing for dancing. Prince Philip was there, relaxing during a visit, and he made it known to his hosts that he wanted to dance to Louis's band. So there were some hasty rearrangements, and word was passed up to Louis on the bandstand. Louis remained on the stage and, not wishing to cut loose too much for the royal visitor, played a slowish, bouncy number, but as the Prince danced by he whispered into Louis's ear, 'I think this would even be a bit slow for Emperor Hirohito.' So Louis broke into 'What'd I Say', and everybody seemed happy.[14]

By late 1970, Louis's group included three brothers (from Philadelphia), John Houston on piano, Leonard Houston on tenor sax and Clarence Houston on drums, but a tragedy occurred that ended the association. During a Christmas booking at Lake Tahoe, Clarence was taken ill and died soon afterwards; his two grief-stricken brothers left the band. For a while, Louis used freelance musicians to play a series of dates in California, including one in May 1971 when he dusted off his big-band charts to lead an all-star-line-up for a date in Studio City.

Louis began planning a new permanent group, and during this time went to a meeting of the Los Angeles Coasters' Social Club, whose guest of honour that day was singer Della Reese. Della's accompanist did not arrive, so pianist Chris Hollis volunteered to back the singer; she did such a fine job that Louis later got on stage and blew a few numbers with Chris, realizing that she would make an ideal member of his new band. But before he formally offered the job to Chris he telephoned her husband Sam for permission to invite her to join. Sam's reply was simple: 'It's up to Chris', but thereafter during his long working association with Chris Hollis, Louis always checked

227

with Sam about Chris's availability, and Sam's answer was always the same.

Imogene Crystal Hollis became a mainstay of Louis's various bands throughout the early 1970s. She was born in Tucson, Arizona (which then had a 20 per cent black population) and was regarded as a child prodigy. As a result, she was invited to sit in when Duke Ellington's orchestra played a Tucson engagement during her childhood. Later she majored in music at the University of Arizona, married Sam, and moved to Los Angeles, where she worked mainly as a solo pianist and vocalist.

Chris looked back on her years in Louis's group with great affection:

We had such a happy spirit in the band; you could think of it as a musical family, with Louis as the father figure. We all learnt a lot from Louis, not only on the bandstand, but during our breaks also, when he'd recall his experiences and what he'd learnt from them. There was a lot of camaraderie, but everyone respected Louis and all of us realized that we were there to complement his musicianship. He was so gifted, and knew exactly how to hold an audience. I remember one night at Donte's in LA, Louis was feeling good and when he played a solo on 'Day by Day' he decided to keep emphasizing one note, on through the various harmonic changes, he kept repeating the note, bending it to fit the next chord. The audience were soon on to it and Louis carried on and on. It became an unforgettable, super musical achievement, and the crowd actually went wild with excitement when he finished the solo.

I played my first gig with the band at the Marriott Hotel in El Paso, Texas, and the others in the group then were drummer Archie Taylor, Irv Cox on tenor sax and Al Hines on bass. Louis didn't hog the show and gave everyone a chance; later on I used to sing a duet with him 'When I Lost My Baby'. Archie Taylor became a dear friend; he was a widely experienced drummer (his son was a good drummer, too). We didn't have a road manager, and Archie used to do most of the driving. We played most of Louis's hits, but also a lot of standards and contemporary songs.[15]

Chris's husband, Sam, who often travelled with the band, soon became a friend of Louis's:

> Louis used to encourage me to cook up a meal if we were away on tour. He just loved soul food, particularly turnip greens and mustard greens. He liked to laugh and joke, and he also liked to sit quietly at times, but everyone respected that. I think the only time I saw him downright grumpy was when he'd bought a new pair of pointed shoes that were too tight. He soon changed out of them and came back and blew his butt off. Octavio Bailly, who came to the States with Brasil 66, joined the band on electric bass, and soon afterwards Louis turned to me and said: 'This is the best band I've ever had.'[16]

Martha Jordan confirmed that Louis was delighted with his new line-up:

> Louis really enjoyed working in that group. The pleasure changed his attitude and he began to socialize with the musicians. When Octavio joined he wasn't too quick at reading music, even though he was a fantastic player. In the past Louis wouldn't have tolerated that and would have hired a good reader instead, but he smiled at Octavio and gave him words of encouragement. We all became friends with each other's families, and it was a lovely atmosphere. Irv Cox was white, and from North Carolina, but Louis was happy to become godfather to his daughter.[17]

The new group won over audiences at the China Trader in Burbank and at Donte's, then temporarily Louis went off to work as a single in a salute to nostalgia entitled 'The Big Show of 1928', which also starred Cab Calloway and the Ink Spots. By this time, Louis had no qualms about being considered as a figure of the golden past. He had come to accept the fact that he was unlikely ever to get into the Hit Parade again, and readily accepted an offer from Johnny Otis to record on Otis's new label Blues Spectrum, which was inaugurated to feature the work of rhythm-and-blues giants, including Charles Brown, Joe Turner and Joe Liggins.

Johnny Otis himself played drums and piano on Louis's album, and his son Shuggie (by means of overdubs) was featured on guitar, bass guitar, piano and organ. Louis's front-line colleagues were his current tenor saxist Irvin Cox, and trumpeter Bob Mitchell (who had resumed working with Louis on a casual basis). Shuggie Otis's propelling bass lines underpin a series of swinging performances as the band re-create seven of Louis's previous best-sellers, including an admirable 'I'm Gonna Move to the Outskirts of Town'. Louis's voice sounds less flexible than it had been, and its range had narrowed slightly. His alto playing remained infectiously lively, however, even if his once prodigious breath control had slackened minimally.

The contents of the album meld together neatly, assisted by the homogeneous nature of three new numbers, 'I Got the Walkin' Blues', where Louis responds to the authentic sounds of Shuggie's guitar work with an impressive down-home vocal, 'Helping Hand', a story song with gospel overtones that rocks away effectively, and 'I'm a Good Thing', a subtle blues written by singer Damita Jo which has a stark, effective alto sax solo. Few of Louis's latter-day recordings were reviewed, but *Down Beat* made a point of noticing this album and described it as 'a joyful record of good, clean, jumping fun'.[18]

Louis's contract with ABC had run its course (Joe Glaser died in 1970), so Louis asked the West Coast booker Harold Jovien to handle his engagements. Jovien, who had worked for *Down Beat* and *Billboard* before becoming an agent, had known Louis for many years:

I first met Louis in Chicago during the Capitol Lounge days and I had dealings with him when I worked for GAC and occasionally after I set up on my own in the summer of 1954. But in the 1970s, I dealt with him regularly. I didn't represent him exclusively, but if a good job came along I'd get in touch with him – we got along fine. He had been one of the great attractions of the 1940s, but had come to accept that he wouldn't reach the heights again. I didn't find him disillusioned; he accepted the fact that show-business people have ups and downs and didn't moan and groan about the situation. However, he was still a force, and when I fixed him into a club like the Playboy here on Sunset Strip he did a wonderful job.[19]

Almost every venue that the new band played was happy to rebook them, but occasionally Louis declined to play a repeat engagement if untoward discomfort was involved. Such was the case when the band played a brief residency at Jackpot, Nevada, a hamlet up near the Utah boarder that attracted gamblers from a vast under-populated area. Chris Hollis recalled the experience:

Archie Taylor drove us as usual, but before we set out Louis called me aside and said, 'Chris, I don't want you to get squeamish, but we're going to drive into an area in which thousands of jack rabbits live, and no matter how carefully or slowly you travel you're going to hit a lot of them.' I said I'd be all right but I had no idea of what was to come. As the light faded, it was as if they had been hypnotized by the approaching car, and they just swarmed over the road for mile after mile. The car continually crunched over the bodies; it was a horrid feeling. Then we got to Jackpot, which was then only four buildings – there weren't any television sets there; it was too far away from the transmitters. We were housed in three bungalows over the other side of the highway and there was absolutely nothing to do whatsoever except read, play cards, dominoes and checkers. The weather was bitterly cold and Louis hated that; he rested up for the whole twelve days. Three of us decided we'd go hiking in the mountains, to fill in time, but then the snows came and settled four feet deep. We could hardly wait to play each evening. The audience were mostly Mormons, who had travelled a long way – I was surprised to see them gambling, and astonished to see them drink a bright-red mixture consisting of three-quarters beer, and one-quarter tomato juice. Louis did his best to keep everybody happy, but on the final night as he was bowing and smiling I swear I heard him say, under his breath, 'Never again. Never again.'[20]

# 16
## I've Found My Peace of Mind

In the 1970s a growth of worldwide interest in all aspects of the blues occurred. The music that had first been recorded almost sixty years earlier was slow to entice vast numbers of the Caucasian public to become devotees. Notable exceptions like Louis Jordan, Wynonie Harris, Joe Turner and a few others had made successful individual recordings of the twelve-bar format during the 1940s and 1950s, but it was not until various white 'beat' groups began propagating (and paying homage to) the work of the American orginators that any fervent widespread interest developed. Records by blues artistes had been avidly collected by a tiny majority since the 1920s, but it was the attention focused on it by the young groups that made millions aware of the ultra-rich heritage of rural and urban blues that existed in the USA.

For a long time the blues purists were suspicious of Louis Jordan, simply because he had been successful – the same type of response is commonplace in the jazz world – but they gradually came to realize what a seminal figure he was in the development of their music. A good deal of this response was posthumous; Louis was never featured at a major blues festival during his lifetime. However, George Wein, the promoter of the Newport Jazz Festival, decided to invite Louis to front a specially assembled version of the Tympany Five for a July 1973 presentation (held in New York City).

Originally the plan was for Louis to take part in a Chick Webb Orchestra members' reunion, but Wein, a long-time admirer of the Tympany Five, also offered Louis a separate feature spot. Louis, who had not appeared regularly in New York for several years (even at the Apollo), accepted Wein's offer with alacrity and flew from the

West Coast in high spirits. Prior to his Tympany Five engagements, Louis went out to Queens, New York on 4 July to take part in a ceremony of dedication for the newly-named Louis Armstrong Memorial Stadium (formerly the Singer Bowl). He appeared there as part of an all-star bill which included Earl Hines, Gene Krupa, Roy Eldridge and Erskine Hawkins. Ella Fitzgerald was one of the guests of honour, and she and Louis enjoyed a warm reunion.

Two days later Louis met up with and rehearsed the freelance musicians who formed the version of the Tympany Five to appear later that day at Carnegie Hall. Sammy Price was originally mooted as the group's pianist but as he couldn't make the rehearsal he had to relinquish his part in the concert, which was taken by Cliff Smalls. Milt Hinton played string bass, Cozy Cole was on drums and Doc Cheatham on trumpet.

The late-evening concert (beginning at 10 p.m.) was styled as a 'Jazz Cabaret', and featured Cab Calloway's band (with guest Dizzy Gillespie), dancer Honi Coles and the Copasetics, Esther Phillips, Nellie Lutcher and Louis Jordan. Appearing immediately after pianist-vocalist Nellie Lutcher's brief set, Louis hit the stage with all his old vigour and rocked the audience through 'Let the Good Times Roll', 'Hard Headed Woman' and 'Caldonia'. His performance bowled the critics over; *Jazz Hot* enthusiastically said that Louis was still '*the* Swingman and Showman', and Richard Williams in the *Melody Maker* wrote: 'Two days short of his sixty-fifth birthday Jordan sang and played like a man possessed, not content to remain a footnote in the histories of both jazz and rock.'[1]

When the Jazz Cabaret concert ended several of the performers were ushered over to the Radio City Music Hall to take part in a 'Midnight Jam Session' (which was attended by 6,000 people). For hour after hour, top jazz musicians improvised in informally assembled groups, and finally at around 4 a.m. an all-star unit took the stage, consisting of Louis Jordan (alto sax), Al Grey (trombone), Sonny Stitt (tenor sax), Tiny Grimes and Larry Coryell (guitars), Earl Hines (piano), Milt Hinton (bass), Oliver Jackson (drums) and Blue Mitchell (trumpet). Blue Mitchell had recently been working with the British blues singer John Mayall, who was the featured guest on this, the final segment of the event.

John Mayall, who was then thirty-nine, had long championed the work of American blues artists; his dedication and uncompromising performances had won him a big following both in Britain and in the USA and by July 1973 he was a big-selling attraction, who only a few months previously had starred in a successful concert at Carnegie Hall. At the time, John was usually billed as 'The Father of British Blues', but at Radio City Music Hall he was announced as 'The High Priest of the Blues' – this description stirred up Louis Jordan's competitive spirit, as he himself recalled:

> I didn't know he was supposed to be the greatest blues singer from England. I said to him, 'Let's do some choruses together.' And he turned green after I did the second one. I didn't say it – the papers said I washed him out. Now I am a black artist. He's come along and the whole world knows he's the greatest white blues singer in the world – because they have been told that in magazines, on the radio, on television. And where did he learn it from?[2]

George Wein observed the tremendous reactions that Louis generated at each of his New York appearances and promised he would contact him later about more bookings. Louis left for California, rested at home briefly, then began a weekend booking at Ruthie's Inn, in Berkeley. For this engagement Louis led a revamped version of his recent Tympany Five line-up; Irv Cox was still on tenor sax and Archie Taylor on drums, but Chris Hollis was temporarily following her solo career, and her place was taken by the New Orleans pianist Alexander 'Duke' Burrell (it was this line-up that Louis took to Honolulu for a brief booking). Octavio Bailly had studio commitments, and this brought bassist Dave Dyson into the group for a short time.

Louis's repertoire for the Berkeley booking was typical of his shows from this period. He played versions of his big sellers and some evergreens, but also included newish songs such as 'Help Me Make It Through the Night', 'Hey Jude' and 'Ain't no Woman Like the One I Got'. The linking announcements were brewed to an old formula, but when Louis felt good he added fresh ingredients on whim. His dictum was, 'I always try to say something funny to corral their thoughts.' He maintained his old technique of dishing out jocular advice to the audience: 'Hey lady, I'm talking to you, yes *you* honey,' he'd shout.

'Have some vodka and do what you ought not to.' When the crowd roared their appreciation, as they always did, he'd follow up with another burst: 'And this is for that lucky man beside you – have some tequila and feel her.' The audience never griped at the simplicity of these couplets – their critical faculties had been melted away by Jordan's charm, enthusiasm and perfectly timed delivery. When Louis shouted out an enquiring 'Everybody enjoying themselves?' there was always an affirming answer, then he would follow that question by climaxing the show with a rocking blues. When journalist Michael Lydon interviewed him after the Berkeley gig, Louis said: 'The blues, that's me, but not the mournful blues, the crying blues, but blues for feeling good. There's so many songs to sing and play, but I've always done best with ones that had something in it to make you laugh. Sometimes when I want to try something different my fans hardly let me, they like my humorous things so much.'[3]

That summer, Louis played several weekend residencies at clubs and hotels around the Los Angeles area, so he got plenty of time to relax. Fishing became a twice-a-week ritual, and he and his friends would either take a half-day boat, or set out at midnight from Pierrepoint landing, Long Beach for an all-night session afloat. Louis was a competent fisherman who took everything he caught home to eat. A local real-estate executive, George Whiteside, often played friendly poker with Louis:

> Louis wasn't a heavy gambler; he told me that he had learnt his lesson in Las Vegas. He liked to watch the baseball. He wasn't an avid fan but leaned towards the Dodgers. He told me he'd played short stop in his younger days. He never played golf and I couldn't get him interested in trying it. He was only a moderate drinker. I think the thing he liked to do best of all was converse; he was genuinely interested in conversation and in learning facts from what other people had to say.[4]

Martha agreed with this summary:

> Yes, Louis always loved to talk – once he'd got going. I can remember not long after we were married we sat in Louis's den all

night and talked. My mother, who was staying with us, came down around 9 a.m. and said, 'You're up early', but we hadn't been to bed – besides being man and wife we were also great friends. Louis became mellower as he grew older; he'd sit with a glass of whisky and take a philosophical look at the world. He could still be moody, but I got used to that, it was an inborn thing with him, it didn't need anything to set it off. I'd talk to him and he'd be miles away, and wouldn't answer, and then I'd say, 'Oh Wall! Oh Door! What do you think?' and he'd snap out of it. Or I'd ask him to shake his head if he agreed. He used to say, 'My voice is tired out, I'll be all right when I've had a rest.'

Louis was a magazine buff. He didn't read many books, but he loved to buy a pile of magazines covering lots of subjects and he'd sit there reading absolutely everything in them, including the mail-order advertisements. Through one of these ads he sent away to England for copper bands to put around his ankles and wrists and he swore they alleviated his arthritis – he wore them every day. He remained disillusioned with the record companies, but never let this disappointment get to him. He did a tour with the Pointer Sisters and he got standing ovations every night; the show went to Washington, DC, Philadelphia and New York, but when it came to Los Angeles they'd replaced Louis with a ventriloquist. Louis just smiled at this and said, 'If that's what they want, that's what they want.' By this time I was working for the schools system and Louis came on Careers' Day and gave a fascinating talk about making a career of music.[5]

Impresario George Wein kept his word and offered Louis a chance to take the Tympany Five to the Berlin Jazz Festival in early November 1973, with the prospect of other bookings in Europe. Louis readied a group consisting of Irvin Cox on tenor sax, Duke Burrell on piano, Archie Taylor on drums and Louis Kabok on double bass. Unfortunately, Louis Kabok (who had been working regularly with Louis's band in the preceding months) broke his arm in a cycling accident just before the band were due to leave for Europe, and Jordan had to find a replacement on the other side of the Atlantic. Luckily, the expatriate American bassist John Duke was on hand to fill the vacancy. In Berlin, Louis Jordan joined other big names such as Duke Ellington, Miles Davis and Keith Jarrett on the four-day festival and registered a big success.

The rest of Louis's tour was not as well co-ordinated as the Berlin Festival, however, and dates were fixed so hurriedly that local promoters had little time to advertise the band's appearances. The result was that many of Louis's fans in Sweden, Denmark and France were aware of the Tympany Five's visit only after the group had flown back to the USA. For a time it looked as though the ill luck that dogged Louis during his previous (1962) trip to Europe was going to be repeated. In Sweden he overslept and was almost late for his gig in Malmö on 30 October (an almost unheard-of lapse); he then had to borrow an alto sax because his own had been damaged. Despite these setbacks, Louis's gig at the Swing Inn was a success.[6] Also successful were his bookings in Denmark at the Montmartre, Copenhagen, and at Taksaeget in Aarhus (where he enjoyed a reunion with the American trombonist, Gene 'Mighty Flea' Connors).

During the latter part of the tour, Louis and the band arrived in France and played a club date in Paris on 5 November. Next day, the Black and Blue recording company had the foresight to record the group. If Louis's recordings in the late 1960s and early 1970s had given the faint impression that time was catching up with him, then the Paris date marks an amazing rejuvenation. On several numbers Louis takes chorus after chorus of inspired alto sax playing and his vocals are projected with all the old clarity, skill and panache.

The band sounds well integrated as it performs old favourites such as 'Saturday Night Fish Fry' and 'I'm Gonna Move . . .' and on material that Louis had not recorded before, 'I Believe in Music' and 'Every Knock is a Boost'. No effort was made to tailor the material down to a three-minute 'single' duration and this allowed Louis to project his songs relaxedly in much the same way as he performed them on his club dates. The version of 'I'm Gonna Move . . .' is over six minutes long and crammed with inspiration; 'Caldonia' incorporates part of Louis's cabaret dialogue to good effect; and 'Is You is . . .' contains a thirty-two-bar alto sax chorus from Louis that is one of the finest he ever recorded. Louis and Irv Cox indulge in a four-bar chase on 'Every Knock . . .' but the tenor saxist comes into his own by blowing four good choruses on the instrumental 'Red Top' (which also has some splendidly hard-hitting piano from Duke Burrell).

Burrell's comping on piano is excellent throughout, sparse but definite, and his chorus on 'Hard Head' is a gem.

Drummer Archie Taylor gets his chance on the instrumental version of 'Take the "A" Train', and fashions a series of crisp four-bar breaks, but elsewhere the recording is not kind to his cymbal work. Louis and Irv Cox phrase well together on the arrangements, the only bleak moments occurring when they overwork a gimmicky ending idea by tagging it on to six of the selections. The session remains a high point in Louis's latterday career, and the issue of a compact disc brought forth some additional blues instrumentals from Louis, on which he jams with Louis Myers on electric guitar, Dave Myers on electric bass and Fred Below on drums.

Martha, who did not accompany Louis on that tour, commented:

> Louis enjoyed a lot of that trip to Europe, and I know he was pleased by the receptions, particularly the Berlin dates, but he was also happy to visit Paris, where he met up with old friends from America, including blues singer Memphis Slim. He would have liked to have played more dates while he was over there, considering the long journey involved, but he enjoyed the sights and visiting the cathedrals. Louis had a Baptist upbringing, but I am a Catholic, and in his later years Louis came to Mass regularly with me. The fans in Europe made a fuss of Louis, and when he got back home there was a definite growth of interest in his career; various people started conceiving ideas to do films and television programmes about him. Actually Bill Cosby was the very first one to express an interest in filming the life story of Louis Jordan, but this was before he became a superstar and he just couldn't raise the money.[7]

Louis's next stay away from home was a long one. In the spring of 1974, he began a four-month booking in New Orleans, playing in the Marriott Hotel as a single, backed by local musicians. On-stage Louis still wore exceedingly flamboyant clothes, often sporting a leopard-skin jacket which he called his 'Hollywood coat', but off-stage his quiet, bespectacled appearance allowed him to wander the streets unrecognized as he took in the music that drifted out from the various bars on Bourbon Street. Louis made little effort to get involved in the local jazz scene, but enjoyed attending the New Orleans Jazz Festival. As soon as Martha began her summer vacation from the school board she flew to New Orleans to join Louis in the late stages of what had seemed a long residency.

Trumpeter Wallace Davenport, who was then running his own My Jazz label, asked Louis if he'd be interested in recording for it as an instrumentalist within Davenport's band. Louis jumped at the idea of being a sideman again, and contributed some superb solos to a batch of jazz standards recorded in New Orleans during May 1974. The enthusiasm with which Louis approached the session is epitomized by the way he opens his solo on 'Sweet Georgia Brown'. His commencing phrase bursts out of the saxophone with a vitality that instantly unites a lumpen rhythm section into a swinging unit. Louis goes on to weave a pattern of jumping phrases (including a humorous quote from 'Rose of the Rio Grande') in this intriguing solo. His work on 'Jersey Bounce' is even more spectacular; here the solo begins in the low register and gradually ascends by way of a series of balanced phrases which are both rhythmically and melodically strong. It is formidable jazz by any yardstick.

Louis remains in fine form throughout, sounding lucid and spontaneous, particularly on 'Melancholy Blues' and 'Ain't Misbehavin'', but less so on 'Indiana' which he had probably played once too often. Besides the merits of his solos, Louis also demonstrates his impressive concept of ensemble playing within a traditional framework, his work sounding just as authentic as that recorded elsewhere by the great Louisiana alto saxist Captain John Handy.

Louis's recordings with Wallace Davenport also involved him in accompanying the gospel singer, Sister Aline White. On 'I Shall not be Moved', Jordan sings the responses vociferously, claps with abandon and contributes an emotionally charged solo. Louis's creative approach to gospel music caused Wallace Davenport to use him in a different line-up (with organ and choir) on a further session with Sister Aline White in August 1974. Here Louis creates expressive, rocking solos on 'Going to Shout All Over God's Heaven', 'Lord, Lord, Lord', 'Down by the Riverside' and 'When the Saints Go Marching In'. These were the last recordings that Louis Jordan ever made. There were two ironic twists about the session: the gospel material had taken Louis right back to his childhood musical experiences in Arkansas; and the recordings, like his very first, were under the direction of a New Orleans musician. In retrospect it seems a tragedy that no one else had the foresight to record Louis purely as a jazz instrumentalist.

Louis returned to his home in Los Angeles in need of a good rest. Martha recalled:

I suppose I should have started to get a bit alarmed about Louis's health in 1974. Somehow we had let his insurance lapse, and this meant he had to go for a fresh medical. He did so, but when the letter arrived from the insurance company it said that acceptance was negative. Louis took this news relaxedly, saying, 'Well, I guess it's my age', and we left it at that. Louis seemed well enough and there didn't appear to be any cause for worry.[8]

After returning from a vacation in Jamaica with Martha, Louis made no effort to curtail his schedule and continued working as usual. In an article that *Ebony* magazine published (entitled 'Whatever Happened to Louis Jordan?) Louis cited his ambition: 'To keep on singing and playing until the Big Man calls me.' Late in 1974, he took a Tympany Five group consisting of Chris Hollis (piano), Julius Brooks (tenor sax), Archie Taylor (drums) and Billy Hadnott (double bass), to the Golden Nugget Casino in Sparks, Nevada. Three days into this engagement, Louis suffered a severe heart attack and was rushed to St Mary's Hospital in Reno. Chris Hollis telephoned Martha Jordan, who hastened to Nevada to be with Louis. After a few days of crisis, Louis gradually began to recover and after three weeks he was allowed to return home to Los Angeles, with strict instructions not to do anything too strenuous. Martha Jordan recalled:

The doctors told me that Louis was not to play the saxophone, he just had to take it easy. This was hard for Louis, who had played all his life, and who liked to be mobile, but he knew he had to listen to the doctors, and his Selmer sax stayed in its case. When Louis was taken sick I talked things over with his agent, Harold Jovien, and we decided not to publicize any news about Louis having a heart attack, because the public (and all the people in the entertainment world) so thought of him as being a super-energetic figure, it would virtually have meant the end of his career. When Louis got home he tried to keep cheerful, then one day he was standing looking out of the window and tears welled up in his eyes and he said, 'I guess everyone has forgotten me.' I realized then that we had made a big mistake in not releasing the news of Louis's illness. It's something I deeply regret to this day, because Louis was so saddened that he hadn't received any messages from all the many people he'd worked with over the years. He'd seen somewhere on TV, that Count Basie had received lots of 'get well' cards when he'd been taken ill, and this stayed in Louis's mind. I explained that we had thought it best to keep quiet, and so it was our fault that no one knew about it. Louis, bless him, instantly accepted the situation and gave out a broad smile, but I've never forgotten how upset he was.

The irony was that by this time Louis was back again in demand. George Wein had already booked him to appear in Europe at the Nice Jazz Festival in July, and offers of work were coming in regularly. One booker wanted Louis to work in Kansas City, even if he only sang, but even this would have been too much for Louis. But he gradually got stronger, and used to go out for a walk, and he was always talking about cooking up a mess of food, but really Louis wasn't a great chef; the best thing he fixed was oxtail soup. One day in February 1975, Louis had been out with me to make enquiries about my plans to take a night-school degree, so that our future would be a little more secure. We got back home at around 3 p.m. and Louis said, 'I think I'll take a rest', but just as he was standing by the side of the bed he keeled over. I became frantic as I tried to revive him, then I called the paramedics and they arrived as quickly as they could. But I knew it was all over, and this was confirmed when I heard one of the men talking over the telephone to a doctor. Louis had died instantly from a heart attack. It transpired that he'd had hardening of the arteries for quite a while. The funny thing was, that very morning he'd said to me, 'I feel better than I've felt in a long time.' That should have set alarm bells ringing for me, because that was exactly what my mother said before she died in 1966.[9]

Recalling the sad day, agent Harold Jovien said: 'During the last year of Louis's life people were becoming more interested in booking him, and I had just got an offer for him to go into Disneyland when a neighbour of his called to say that Martha had asked her to phone me with the news that Louis was dead.[10]

Louis died on 5 February 1975, and three days later his funeral service was held at the Spalding La Brea Chapel in Los Angeles. Among those who attended the service was Louis's long-time manager Berle Adams (then chief executive of the Universal–MCA conglomerate). Arthur Prysock sang 'My Buddy' and Lou Rawls 'Just a Closer Walk with Thee'; a poignant reminder of Louis's own music was provided by Irv Cox on tenor sax and Perry Lee on organ, performing 'Is You is or is You ain't My Baby?' After the service Louis's body was flown to the Oak Lawn Cemetery in St Louis, Missouri so that he could be interred alongside Martha's mother and father.

Louis was not rich when he died, so there was no question of Martha not having to go out to work. She sold the house in Los Angeles and moved to Las Vegas, where she was employed for a long time by the sheriff's office; later she worked as a travel agent. The issue of memorial albums brought some royalties to her, but earnings from several of the big former successes went to Fleecie Moore, who spent the last years of her life living comfortably in Delaware, until her death in 1989. She had outlived her successor Florence (Vicky) by many years. Ida, Louis's earlier wife, died in New York in May 1990.

Gradually there was a rebirth of interest in Louis's work. The British singer and pianist, Georgie Fame, who had long been a fan, often featured Jordan's songs, and so too did Joe Jackson, who formed a group based on the Tympany Five. The sound of Louis Jordan's music began to pep up various movie soundtracks, including the cult film *The Blues Brothers*, and Louis's ideas percolated into new styles. As the great bluesman B.B. King pointed out:

Louis was remarkable, because I think he was so far ahead of his time; what he was doing became the origins of rap. He was rhyming things that nobody else was able to do. I idolized his talent and one day I hope to do a tribute album, just recording things that he did in the hope that I could do justice to a great performer.[11]

A reawakening of interest in Louis's work coincided with a general change in attitudes towards the extrovert performances of yester-year's African-American screen stars; the vitality of the unique black entertainment tradition was freshly assessed. It at last became obvious that because an actor or performer had adopted a minstrel role it did not automatically signify that he was kowtowing towards a white audience, but that he was in fact keeping alive a tradition that was to nurture future generations of black performers.

The rebirth of interest by African-Americans in their own show-business heritage made it seem as if the words of Dr Martin Luther King were finally being heeded: 'The Negro must always guard against the dangers of becoming ashamed of himself and his past. We must teach every Negro child that rejection of heritage means loss of cultural roots, and people who have no past have no future.'[12]

The great black comedian Redd Foxx (John Sanford) put it succinctly when he said, 'If there hadn't been a Stepin Fetchit there wouldn't be an Eddie Murphy'; a music-world equivalent could be, 'Without Louis Jordan there would not have been a Miles Davis'.

The change in attitudes spawned many shows that featured black performers re-enacting the lives and movements of early African-American stars, and several of them, such as *One Mo' Time, Eubie, Bubbling Brown Sugar* and *Ma Rainey's Black Bottom*, enjoyed considerable success. In the wake of these triumphs, the American actor Clarke Peters, a devoted fan of Louis Jordan's work, decided to devise a musical that featured a cast performing a choice selection of Louis Jordan's recordings; the result was *Five Guys Named Moe*.

After a late-night try-out at the Cottesloe theatre, the show was staged at London's Theatre Royal, Stratford East – a venue noted for its enterprise. In 1990 the theatre won the Prudential Award and with part of the money commissioned *Five Guys Named Moe*. Critics and audiences loved the production, and so too did one of the world's leading impresarios, Cameron Mackintosh, who later that year brought the show to London's West End, for a long and highly successful run at the Lyric Theatre.

The zestful delivery of the two dozen songs in the show and the cleverly devised links delighted all who saw *Five Guys Named Moe* and in April 1991 it received the *Evening Standard's* Laurence Olivier Award for being the best musical of the year. Martha Jordan flew over to London for the award ceremony, overjoyed to see that Louis Jordan's music was once again filling people with happiness and admiration. *Five Guys Named Moe* subsequently opened on Broadway, so once again the American public were able to focus attention and affection on the works of a great innovator, performer and musician, Louis Jordan.

# References

Chapter 1: *Somewhere Deep in the Heart of the South* (pp.5–17)
1 Broonzy: *Big Bill Blues*, p.3.
2 Davis: *Miles: The Autobiography*, p.19.
3 Louis Jordan interviewed by Scott Ellsworth, Radio, KFI, 26 April 1971.
4 Author's conversation with the Gettis family, June 1991.
5 Ibid.
6 Ibid.
7 *Ramparts*, January 1974.
8 Conversation with the author, June 1991.
9 *Bandleaders*, March 1944.
10 *Record Research*, Issue 67.
11 Conversation with the author, 29 October 1991.
12 *Ramparts*, January 1974.
13 Bühmann Møller: *You Just Fight for Your Life*, p.15.
14 *Cadence*, December 1986.
15 Conversation taped by Carl Arnold and John Byrd, 1988.

Chapter 2: *Small Town Boy* (pp.19–34)
1 *Chicago Defender*, 16 November 1929.
2 Conversation with the author, 2 July 1991.
3 Louis Jordan interviewed by Scott Ellsworth, Radio KFI, 26 April 1971.
4 Conversation with the author, June 1991.
5 Conversation with the author, June 1991.
6 Conversation taped by Carl Arnold and John Byrd, 1989.

7 Ibid.

8 Ibid.

9 Conversation taped by Carl Arnold and John Byrd, 1988.

10 Louis Jordan interviewed by Steve Allen, 1973.

11 Conversation taped by Carl Arnold and John Byrd, 1989.

12 Ibid.

13 *Storyville*, Issue 68.

14 *Jazzfinder*, December 1948.

15 Ibid.

16 Ibid.

17 *Down Beat*, October 1936.

Chapter 3: *Helping Hand* (pp.35–49)

1 Conversation with the author, 3 March 1991.

2 *Storyville*, Issue 68.

3 Conversation taped by Carl Arnold and John Byrd, 1989.

4 Louis Jordan interviewed by Scott Ellsworth, Radio KFI, 26 April 1971.

5 Bernhardt: *I Remember*, p.138.

6 *Jazz Monthly*, November 1958.

7 *Storyville*, Issue 68.

8 *Jazz Monthly*, April 1969.

9 *Storyville*, Issue 101.

10 *Jazz Monthly*, April 1969.

11 *Down Beat*, 29 May 1969.

12 Conversation taped by Carl Arnold and John Byrd, 1989.

13 Ibid.

14 Conversation with the author, 9 August 1991.

15 *Melody Maker*, 8 August 1936.

16 Louis Jordan interviewed by Scott Ellsworth, Radio KFI, 26 April 1971.

17 *New York Age*, 24 November 1928.

18 Radio Free Jazz, June 1976.

19 *Down Beat*, 20 March 1969.

20 *Rhythm*, September 1936.

21 Conversation taped by Carl Arnold and John Byrd, 1988.

22 Conversation with the author, 16 April 1991.

23 Ibid.

24 *Metronome*, July 1941.
25 Conversation with the author, 16 April 1991.
26 Louis Jordan interviewed by Scott Ellsworth, Radio KFI, 26 April 1971.
27 *Metronome*, August 1939.
28 *Storyville*, Issue 135.

Chapter 4: *Trouble Then Satisfaction* (pp.51–61).
1 *Melody Maker*, 25 September 1937.
2 Ibid.
3 *Down Beat*, 4 April 1968.
4 *Down Beat*, September 1937.
5 *Down Beat*, 29 May 1969.
6 *Melody Maker*, 20 June 1936.
7 *Melody Maker*, 5 February 1938.
8 *Down Beat*, 4 April 1968.
9 Conversation with the author, 15 April 1991.
10 *Tempo*, March 1938.
11 *Tempo*, June 1938.
12 Conversation taped by Carl Arnold and John Byrd, 1989.
13 Conversation taped by Carl Arnold and John Byrd, 1989.
14 Conversation with the author, 15 April 1991.
15 Louis Jordan interviewed by Scott Ellsworth, Radio KFI, 26 April 1971.
16 Conversation taped by Carl Arnold and John Byrd, 1989.
17 Ibid.
18 *New York Amsterdam News*, 4 August 1938.

Chapter 5: *Keep A-Knockin'* (pp. 63–75).
1 Conversation with the author, 26 February 1991.
2 *Ramparts*, January 1974.
3 Conversation with the author, 26 February 1991.
4 Bastin: *Never Sell a Copyright*, p.91.
5 *Melody Maker*, 2 December 1940.
6 *New York Amsterdam News*, 30 December 1939.
7 Rutgers Institute of Jazz Studios (interview by Frank Driggs).
8 *Ramparts*, January 1974.

9 Library of Congress recordings, 1938.

10 Taylor: *Alberta Hunter*, p.65.

11 *78 Quarterly*, Vol. 1, No. 4.

12 Bernhardt: *I Remember*, p. 147.

13 Conversation taped by Carl Arnold and John Byrd, 1989.

Chapter 6: *Five Guys Named Moe* (pp. 77–88).

1 *Jazz Monthly*, October 1956.

2 Conversation with the author, 26 February 1991.

3 Album notes by Rudi Blesh, Circle S-3.

4 *Down Beat*, 15 December 1940.

5 Shaw: *Honkers and Shouters*, p.77.

6 Ibid., p.67.

7 Ibid., p.67.

8 Conversation taped by Carl Arnold and John Byrd, 1989.

9 Ibid.

10 Conversation with the author, 12 March 1991.

11 Ibid.

12 Shaw, op. cit., p.78.

13 Louis Jordan interviewed by Scott Ellsworth, Radio KFI, 26 April 1971.

Chapter 7: *I Found a New Baby* (pp. 89–103).

1 Shaw: *Honkers and Shouters*, p.67.

2 Ibid., p.67.

3 Ibid., p.78.

4 Ibid., p.78.

5 *Music & Rhythm*, July 1942.

6 *Down Beat*, 1 July 1942.

7 Shaw, op. cit., p.62.

8 Ibid., p.74.

9 Ibid., p.68.

10 Conversation with the author, 12 March 1991.

11 *Down Beat*, 1 September 1942.

12 Conversation taped by Carl Arnold and John Byrd, 1989.

13 *Down Beat*, 1 January 1943.

14 Conversation with the author, 1991.

15 *Down Beat*, 15 May 1943.

16 *Metronome*, August 1943.
17 *Down Beat*, 15 September 1943.
18 *Billboard Year Book*, 1945–6.
19 *Down Beat*, 1 December 1943.
20 *Chicago Defender*, 26 August 1944.

Chapter 8: *Caldonia* (pp. 105–20)
1 Conversation with the author, March 1991.
2 *Metronome*, June 1944.
3 Louis Jordan interviewed by Scott Ellsworth, Radio KFI, 26 April 1971.
4 Matrix 3478, according to discographer Ralph Harding.
5 *Down Beat*, 1 September 1944.
6 *Down Beat*, 1 August 1944.
7 Liner notes by Dave Dexter, MCA CD 4079.
8 Shaw: *Honkers and Shouters*, p.71.
9 Conversation with the author, 5 September 1991.
10 *Ramparts*, January 1974.
11 *Billboard*, 8 June 1946.
12 Shaw, op. cit., p.80.
13 Ibid., p.69.
14 Conversation with the author, 19 March 1991.
15 Louis Jordan interviewed by Scott Ellsworth, Radio KFI, 26 April 1971.
16 *Down Beat*, 1 July 1945.
17 Bernhardt: *I Remember*, p.177.
18 Conversation with the author, 14 March 1991.
19 Conversation with the author, 5 March 1991.
20 *Down Beat*, 1 August 1945.
21 *Ibid.*
22 Conversation with the author, 19 March 1991.
23 *Metronome*, July 1946.
24 Conversation with the author, 12 March 1991.
25 Conversation taped by Carl Arnold and John Byrd, 1989.
26 *Metronome*, November 1945.
27 Conversation with the author, 12 March 1991.
28 *Bandleaders*, March 1946.
29 Ibid.

Chapter 9: *Look Out!* (pp. 121–34).
  1 Hammond: *John Hammond on Record*, p.256.
  2 *Down Beat*, 30 July 1952.
  3 *Ramparts*, January 1974.
  4 *Down Beat*, 6 October 1950.
  5 *Blues Unlimited*, February–March 1974.
  6 Shaw: *Honkers and Shouters*, p.64.
  7 Conversation with the author, 30 April 1991.
  8 Conversation with the author, 23 April 1991.
  9 Crow: *Jazz Anecdotes*, p.128.
  10 *Metronome*, July 1946.
  11 Conversation with the author, 30 April 1991.
  12 Shaw, op. cit., p.68.
  13 Ibid., p.69.
  14 Ibid.
  15 LWT, 'South Bank Show', 12 January 1992.
  16 Conversation with the author, 3 March 1991.
  17 Conversation with the author, 5 September 1991.
  18 *Down Beat*, 15 July 1946.
  19 Conversation with the author, 30 April 1991.
  20 Conversation with the author, 12 March 1991.
  21 Louis Jordan interviewed by Scott Ellsworth, Radio KFI, 26 April 1971.
  22 Conversation with the author, 23 April 1991.
  23 Conversation with the author, 22 April 1991.
  24 *Blues & Rhythm*, Issue 59.
  25 *Metronome*, March 1947.
  26 *Down Beat*, 12 February 1947.
  27 Ibid.
  28 *Down Beat*, 12 March 1947.
  29 Conversation with the author, 12 March 1991.
  30 Conversation with the author, 30 April 1991.

Chapter 10: *It's a Lowdown Dirty Shame* (pp. 135–52).
  1 Conversation with the author, 3 July 1991.
  2 Travis: *Autobiography of Black Jazz*, p.419.
  3 Conversation with the author, 24 July 1991.
  4 Pepper: *Straight Life*, p.373.

5 *The Musician*, May 1988.

6 Conversation with the author, 28 Feburary 1991.

7 Phil Schaap, Bill Doggett interviewed by Radio WKCR, 27 October 1991.

8 *Metronome*, September 1958.

9 *Metronome*, February 1948.

10 *Down Beat*, 11 March 1949.

11 *Down Beat*, 24 March 1948.

12 *Down Beat*, 10 March 1948.

13 *Cadence*, April 1976.

14 Bill Hadnott interviewed by Peter Vacher, 18 October 1979.

15 *Down Beat*, 10 September 1952.

16 Conversation with the author, July 1991.

17 Letter to the author, 20 July 1991.

18 *Down Beat*, 24 February 1950.

19 *Jazz Journal*, January 1962.

20 Conversation with the author, 28 February 1991.

21 Bill Doggett interviewed by Phil Schaap, Radio WKCR, 27 October 1991.

22 *Australian Jazz Notes*, Issue 76.

23 Conversation with the author, 30 April 1991.

24 *Melody Maker*, 22 February 1975.

Chapter 11: *Work, Baby, Work* (pp. 153–70).

1 Conversation with the author, 30 April 1991.

2 Conversation with the author, 7 September 1991.

3 Louis Jordan interviewed by Steve Allen, 1973.

4 Bill Doggett interviewed by Phil Schaap, Radio WKCR, 27 October 1991.

5 *Metronome*, January 1951.

6 Conversation with the author, 14 March 1991.

7 Conversation with the author, 28 March 1991.

8 Shaw: *Honkers and Shouters*, p.84.

9 *Ebony*, January 1949.

10 Conversation with the author, 12 March 1991.

11 *Music Dial*, April 1944.

12 *Ramparts*, January 1974.

13 Conversation with the author, March 1991.
14 Conversation with the author, 5 June 1991.
15 Conversation with the author, 3 April 1991.
16 Conversation with the author, 5 June 1991.
17 *New York Amsterdam News*, 6 October 1951.
18 Conversation with the author, 5 June 1991.
19 Ibid.
20 *Down Beat*, 28 December 1951.

Chapter 12: *Slow Down* (pp. 171–85).
   1 *Down Beat*, 8 February 1952.
   2 *New York Daily News*, 7 August 1991.
   3 Conversation with the author, 12 June 1991.
   4 Conversation with the author, 9 October 1991.
   5 Shaw: *Honkers and Shouters*, p.82.
   6 *Trinidad Guardian*, 6 September 1951.
   7 *Melody Maker*, 17 January 1959.
   8 *Down Beat*, 2 July 1952.
   9 Louis Jordan interviewed by Scott Ellsworth, Radio KFI, 26
     April 1971.
10 *New York Amsterdam News*, 30 August 1952.
11 Conversation with the author, 21 October 1991.
12 Ibid.
13 Ibid.
14 Conversation with the author, 12 June 1991.
15 Conversation with the author, 20 August 1991.
16 Conversation with the author, 2 July 1991.
17 Conversation with the author, 24 July 1991.
18 Conversation with the author, 12 June 1991.
19 Conversation with the author, 20 August 1991.
20 *Down Beat*, 8 October 1952.
21 Conversation with the author, 20 August 1991.
22 *Down Beat*, 20 May 1953.
23 *Down Beat*, 3 June 1953.
24 *Cadence*, January 1983.
25 *Down Beat*, 2 December 1953.
26 *Ramparts*, January 1974.

Chapter 13: *Time Marches On* (pp. 187–200).
  1 Conversation with the author, 24 July 1991.
  2 Conversation with the author, 20 August 1991.
  3 Chester Lane interviewed by Peter Vacher, 23 August 1990.
  4 Chicago Defender, 13 November 1954.
  5 Conversation with the author, 12 June 1991.
  6 Conversation with the author, 24 July 1991.
  7 Conversation with the author, 2 July 1991.
  8 Conversation with the author, 21 October 1991.
  9 *Blues Unlimited*, February/March 1974.
10 *Melody Maker*, 17 August 1957.
11 *Down Beat*, 4 May 1955.
12 Conversation with the author, 12 March 1991.
13 Shaw: *Honkers and Shouters*, p.73.
14 Conversation with the author, 12 June 1991.
15 Conversation with the author, 3 July 1991.
16 *Down Beat*, 30 May 1956.

Chapter 14: *It's Better to Wait for Love* (pp. 201–15).
  1 Shaw: *Honkers and Shouters*, p.71.
  2 Conversation with the author, July 1991.
  3 Porter: *There and Back*, p.96.
  4 Conversation with the author, 29 October 1991.
  5 Porter, op. cit., p.97.
  6 *Jazz Hot*, April 1958.
  7 *Storyville*, Issue 79.
  8 Conversation with the author, 21 October 1991.
  9 *Coda*, July 1960.
10 *Down Beat*, 4 February 1960.
11 *Metronome*, August 1959.
12 Soundtrack of Sounds Great 8003 (Ford 'Startime' telecast, 8 March 1960).
13 *Down Beat*, 29 May 1969.
14 *Ramparts*, January 1974.
15 *Down Beat*, 12 October 1961.
16 *Down Beat*, 29 May 1969.
17 Liner notes for JukeBox Lil JB-605.

18 Conversation with the author, 31 March 1991.
19 Ibid.
20 Ibid.
21 Ibid.
22 Ibid.
23 *Melody Maker*, 29 December 1962.

Chapter 15: *Every Knock is a Boost* (pp. 217–31).
  1 *Ramparts*, January 1974.
  2 *Down Beat*, 29 May 1969.
  3 Conversation with the author, September 1991.
  4 Ibid.
  5 Ibid.
  6 *Down Beat*, 29 May 1969.
  7 Ibid.
  8 Conversation with the author, 27 October 1991.
  9 *Down Beat*, 29 May 1969.
  10 Louis Jordan interviewed by Scott Ellsworth, Radio KFI, 26 April 1971.
  11 Conversation with the author, 5 June 1991.
  12 *Down Beat*, 29 May 1969.
  13 *Melody Maker*, 22 February 1975.
  14 Conversation with the author, September 1991.
  15 Ibid.
  16 Ibid.
  17 Conversation with the author, September 1991.
  18 *Down Beat*, 12 September 1974.
  19 Conversation with the author, 12 July 1991.
  20 Conversation with the author, September 1991.

Chapter 16: *I've Found My Peace of Mind* (pp. 233–45).
  1 *Melody Maker*, 14 July 1973.
  2 Shaw: *Honkers and Shouters*, p.74.
  3 *Ramparts*, January 1974.
  4 Conversation with the author, 2 June 1991.
  5 Conversation with the author, September 1991.
  6 *Orkester Journalen*, December 1973.
  7 Conversation with the author, September 1991.

8 Ibid.
9 Ibid.
10 Conversation with the author, 12 July 1991.
11 Conversation with the author, 29 October 1991.
12 *Ebony*, January 1958.

# Bibliography

**Bastin, Bruce**: *Never Sell a Copyright* (Chigwell, England: Storyville, 1990)

**Bates, Daisy**: *The Long Shadow of Little Rock* (Fayetteville: University of Arkansas Press, 1987)

**Bernhardt, Clyde and Harris, Sheldon**: *I Remember* (Philadelphia: University of Pennsylvania Press, 1986)

**Berry, Chuck**: *The Autobiography*, (New York: Harmony, 1987)

**Broonzy, Big Bill** (as told to Yannick Bruynoghe): *Big Bill Blues* (London: Cassell, 1955)

**Büchmann-Møller, F.**: *You Just Fight for Your Life* (New York: Praeger, 1990)

**Bushell, Garvin** (as told to Mark Tucker): *Jazz from the Beginning* (Ann Arbor: University of Michigan Press, 1988)

**Charters, Ann**: *Nobody – The Story of Bert Williams* (New York: Macmillan, 1970)

**Cooper, Ralph**: *Amateur Night at the Apollo* (New York: Harper Collins, 1990)

**Dance, Stanley**: *The World of Duke Ellington* (New York: Scribner's, 1970)

— *The World of Swing* (New York: Scribner's, 1974)

— *The World of Earl Hines* (New York: Scribner's, 1977)

— *The World of Count Basie* (London: Sidgwick & Jackson, 1980)

**Davis, Miles** (with Quincy Troupe): *Miles – The Autobiography* (London: Macmillan, 1990, Picador, 1990)

**Feather, Leonard**: *The Jazz Years* (London: Quartet Books, 1986)

**Fox, Ted**: *Showtime at the Apollo* (New York: Holt, Rinehart & Winston, 1983; London: Quartet Books, 1985)

**Friedwald, Will**: *Jazz Singing* (London: Quartet Books, 1990)

**Governar, Alan**: *Meeting the Blues* (Dallas: Taylor, 1988)

**Haley, John W. and John von Hoelle**: *Sound and Fury (The Incredible Story of Bill Haley)* (Delaware: Dyne-American, 1990)

**Hammond, John**: *John Hammond on Record* (New York: Summit Press, 1977; London: Penguin, 1981)

**Harris, Sheldon**: *Blues Who's Who* (New York: Arlington House, 1979)

**Haskins, Jim**: *Ella Fitzgerald* (London: New English Library, 1991)

**Korall, Burt**: *Drummin' Men* (New York: Schirmer, 1990)

**Lieb, Sandra**: *Mother of the Blues – A Study of Ma Rainey* (University of Massachusetts, 1981)

**Lubin, Jacques and Danny Garçon**: *Louis Jordan Discographie* (Levallois-Perret, France: CLARB, 1987)

**Meeker, David**: *Jazz in the Movies* (London: Talisman Books, 1981)

**Miller, Paul E.** : *Miller's Yearbook of Popular Music* (Chicago: PEM Publication, 1943)

**Nizer, Louis**: *My Life in Court* (London: Heinemann, 1962)

**Nown, Graham**: *The English Godfather, Owney Madden* (London: Ward Lock, 1987)

**Oliver, Paul**: *The Story of the Blues* (London: Barrie & Jenkins, 1970)

**Oliver, Paul**, ed. : *The Blackwell Guide to Blues Records* (Oxford: Blackwell, 1989)

**Otis, Johnny**: *Listen to the Lambs* (New York, W.W. Norton, 1968)

**Porter, Roy**: *There and Back* (Oxford: Bayou Press, 1991)

**Sayger, Bill**: *Brasfield Remembered* (Corpus Christi, Texas: Sayger, 1982)

**Schiffman, Jack**: *Uptown, the Story of Harlem's Apollo Theatre* (New York: Cowles, 1971)

— *Harlem Heyday* (Buffalo, NY: Prometheus, 1984)

**Shaw, Arnold**: *Honkers and Shouters* (New York: Collier, 1978)

**Simon, George T.** : *The Best of the Music Makers* (New York: Doubleday, 1979)

**Stearns, Marshall and Jean**: *Jazz Dance* (New York: Macmillan, 1968)

**Taylor, Frank C.** (with Gerald Cook): *Alberta Hunter* (New York: McGraw-Hill, 1987)

**Taylor, Orville W.** : *Negro Slavery in Arkansas* (Durham: Duke University, 1958)

**Tosches, Nick**: *Unsung Heroes of Rock'n'Roll* (New York, Scribner, 1984)

**Travis, Dempsey J.** : *An Autobiography of Black Jazz* (Chicago: Urban Research Institute, 1983)

The following newspapers and magazines were consulted:

Great Britain: *Band Wagon, Blues & Rhythm, Blues Unlimited, Collectors Items, Footnote, Hot News, Jazz Journal, Jazz Monthly, Jazz News, Melody Maker, New Musical Express, Record Mirror, Rhythm, Storyville, Wire.*

Australia: *Australian Jazz Quarterly, Jazz Notes*

Canada: *Coda*

France: *Bulletin du HCF, Jazz Hot, Jazz, Jazz Magazine*

Jamaica: *Daily Gleaner*

Sweden: *Orkester Journalen*

Trinidad: *Trinidad Guardian*

USA: *Arizona Informant, Arkansas State Press, Arkansas Survey, Bandleaders, Billboard, Black Music Research Journal, Brinkley Argus, Cadence, Cashbox, Chicago Defender, Citizen (Brinkley), Clef, Detroit Tribune, Down Beat, Ebony, Hollywood News, HRS Rag, International Musician, In the Groove, Jazz Information, Jazz Quarterly, Jazz Record, Jazz Spotlite News, Jazz Times, Living Blues, Metronome, Mississippi Rag, Music & Rhythm, Music Dial, New York Age, New York Amsterdam News, New York Daily News, New York Evening Journal, New York Times, Orchestra World, Philadelphia Tribune, Pittsburgh Courier, Radio Free Jazz, Ramparts, Record Changer, Record Research, Sentinel-Record (Hot Springs), 78 Quarterly, Southern Mediator (Little Rock), Swing, Variety, Whiskey, Women and . . .*

# Select Discography

**1934**  *CLARENCE WILLIAMS and His Washboard Band* Swaggie 813   LP
I Can't Dance, I Got Ants in My Pants

**1937**  *CHICK WEBB and His Orchestra*                Classics 517   CD
There's Frost on the Moon
Gee But You're Swell
Rusty Hinge
Wake Up and Live
Clap Hands! Here Comes Charley
Harlem Congo

**1937–8**  *ELLA FITZGERALD*              Classics 500/506/518   CD
Chronological output

**1938–54** *LOUIS JORDAN* – Let The Good Times Roll
Nine CD's covering Jordan's
DECCA recordings.   Bear Family (Boxed Set) BCD IH 15557

**1938–9**  *LOUIS JORDAN* – At the Swing Cat's Ball   JSP 330   CD
Toodle-oo on Down
So Good
Away from You
Honey in the Bee Ball
Barnacle Bill the Sailor
Flat Face
Keep a-Knockin'

Sam Jones Done Snagged His Britches
Swingin' in a Cocoanut Tree
Doug the Jitterbug
At the Swing Cat's Ball
Jake, What a Snake
Honeysuckle Rose
'Fore Day Blues
But I'll be Back
You ain't Nowhere
You're My Meat

**1940**    *LOUIS JORDAN* – In Memoriam      MCA 6.22175   LP
June Teenth Jamboree
You Run Your Mouth and I'll Run My Business

**1940**    *LOUIS JORDAN and His Tympany Five* – GI Jive
1940–47                    Jukebox Lil JB602   LP
I'm Alabama Bound
T-Bone Blues
Pompton Turnpike

**1940**    *LOUIS JORDAN* – Hoodoo Man      Swingtime 1011 LP
Hard Lovin' Blues
You've Got to Go when the Wagon Comes
Lovie Joe
Somebody Done Hoodooed the Hoodoo Man
Bounce the Ball
Penthouse in the Basement
After School Swing Session
Oh Boy, I'm in the Groove
Never Let Your Left Hand Know what Your
Right Hand's Doin'
Don't Come Crying on My Shoulder
Waitin' for the Robert E. Lee

**1940–3**  *LOUIS JORDAN* 1940–1942 – Knock Me Out   Swingtime 1012
A Chicken ain't Nothing but a Bird
Do You Call that a Buddy?
I Know You, I Know What You Wanna Do

The Two Little Squirrels
Pan-Pan
St Vitus Dance
Brotherly Love
How 'bout That
Mama Mama Blues
The Green Grass Grows All Around
Small Town Boy
I'm Gonna Move to the Outskirts of Town
The Chicks I Pick are Slender, Tender and Tall
That'll Just 'bout Knock Me Out
It's a Low-down Dirty Shame
Ration Blues

**1942–4** *LOUIS JORDAN* – The Headliners (other tracks
by Fats Waller and Louis Armstrong)  Storyville 6001 LP
Down, Down, Down
Fuzzy Wuzzy
Honey Chile
Five Guys Named Moe
Caldonia
Jumpin' at the Jubilee

**1943–5** *LOUIS JORDAN* – The V-Discs  Official 6061 LP
Is You is or is You ain't My Baby?
Knock Me a Kiss
I'm Gonna Move to the Outskirts of Town
I've Found a New Baby
Five Guys Named Moe
Jumpin' at the Jubilee
You Can't Get that No More
The End of My Worry
How High am I?
Hey Now, Let's Live
Deacon Jones
I Like 'em Fat Like That
Bahama Joe
Nobody but Me

**1944**   *BING CROSY* (two tracks with Louis Jordan)

|  | Queen Disc Q 058 | LP |
| --- | --- | --- |
| My Baby Said Yes | (MCA) GRP 16032 | CD |
| Your Sox Don't Match |  |  |

**1945**
**and**
**1947**   *ELLA FITZGERALD* (with Louis Jordan)

| Stone Cold Dead in the Market | MCA MCL 1705 | LP |
| --- | --- | --- |
| Baby It's Cold Outside |  |  |
| Petootie Pie | MCA-Coral |  |
|  | 6.22178 | LP |
| Don't Cry, Cry Baby |  |  |

**1941–7**   *LOUIS JORDAN* – Greatest Hits          MCA – 1337   LP

Buzz Me
Somebody Done Changed
Salt Pork, West Virginia
Texas and Pacific
Jack You're Dead
Reet Petite and Gone
Open the Door Richard
Boogie Woogie Blue Plate
Early in the Mornin'
Is You is or is You ain't My Baby
Rusty Dusty Blues
What's The Use of Gettin' Sober
I Like 'em Fat Like That
Five Guys Named Moe

**1940–7**   *LOUIS JORDAN and His Tympany Five* – GI Jive Jukebox Lil

|  | JB–602 | LP |
| --- | --- | --- |

GI Jive
Deacon Jones
Mop! Mop!
You Can't Get that no More
If It's Love You Want Baby
Friendship

I Know what You're Puttin' Down
Every Man to His Own Profession
Have You Got the Gumption
We Can't Agree
Chicky-mo, Craney-crow
Roamin' Blues
You're Much Too Fat

**1939–54** *LOUIS JORDAN and His Tympany Five* – Out of
Print                                                          Official 6025      LP
Don't Worry 'bout that Mule
It's So Easy
Inflation Blues
Why'd You Do It Baby
It's a Great, Great Pleasure
Teardrops from My Eyes
Garmoochie
The Soon-a-Baby
You Didn't Want Me Baby
A Man's Best Friend is a Bed
Hog Wash
You Know It Too
Lollypop

**1947–52** *LOUIS JORDAN and His Tympany Five* – Cole
Slaw                                                          Jukebox Lil
                                                              JB–605             LP

Pettin' and Pokin'
I Know what I've Got
Don't Burn the Candle at Both Ends
Cole Slaw
Push Ka Pee Shee Pie
Baby's Gonna Go Bye Bye
Heed My Warning
Hungry Man
You Will Always Have a Friend
Weak-Minded Blues
Is My Pop in There?

Time Marches on
Oil Well, Texas
Azure-Té
Junco Partner
Jordan for President

**1945–50** *LOUIS JORDAN and His Tympany Five* – Let the
Good Times Roll            Coral CP 59     LP
Let the Good Times Roll
Choo Choo Ch'Boogie
Beware
Saturday Night Fish Fry
Beans and Corn Bread
School Days
Buzz Me
Caldonia
Blue Light Boogie
Ain't Nobody Here but Us Chickens

**1944–8** *LOUIS JORDAN* – Look Out Sister (unissued
film soundtracks)          Krazy Kat KK 7415    LP
Jack You're Dead
Caldonia
My New Ten Gallon Hat
Don't Burn the Candle at Both Ends
Chicky Mo
We Can't Agree
Boogie in the Barnyard
You're Much Too Fat
Roamin' Blues
Early in the Morning
Look Out Sister
Jumpin' at the Jubilee
Please Don't Cry and Say No
Down, Down, Down
Five Guys Named Moe

**1945–7**  *LOUIS JORDAN* – Reet Petite and Gone
(unissued film soundtracks)  Krazy Kat KK 7414  LP
Texas and Pacific
All for the Love of Lil
Wham Sam
I Know what You're Putting Down
Let the Good Times Roll
Reet Petite and Gone
That Chick's Too Young to Fry
Ain't that Just Like a Woman
If It's Love You Want
Caldonia
Honey Chile
Tillie
Buzz Me

**1945–9**  *LOUIS JORDAN* – Collates  Swing House
SWH9/CTP 48 Cass.

Broadcasts including:
Infantry Blues
How High the Moon
Mean and Evil Blues, etc

**1945**  *LOUIS JORDAN* (other tracks by Hot Lips
Page/Don Byas)  Rarities No. 46 LP
Jubilee broadcasts including:
Jumping at the Jubilee
She's My Honey Child
I've Found a New Baby
Back Home Again in Indiana, etc

**1948–9**  *LOUIS JORDAN* and the Tympany Five. Five
Guys Named Moe  Bandstand
BCD 1531  CD

Let the Good Times Roll
Knock Me a Kiss
Five Guys Named Moe
Buzz Me

Daddy-o
On the Sunnyside of the Street
All for the Love of Lil
Safe, Sane and Single
Don't Let the Sun Catch You Crying
Broke but Happy
How Long Must I Wait for You?
I Like 'em Fat Like That
Sometimes I'm Happy
Texas and Pacific
That's Why We Can't Agree
The Drippy Drippers

**1939–51** *LOUIS JORDAN* – Jivin' with Jordan          Charly
                                                          CDX 7 Double LP

    Includes:
    No Sale
    Barnyard Boogie
    Early in the Morning
    Daddy-o
    Onions
    Psycho Loco
    Lemonade
    Chartreuse

**1950**    *LOUIS ARMSTRONG* (and LOUIS JORDAN) MCA(F)
                                                          510.176     LP

    Life is So Peculiar
    You Rascal You

**1951**    *LOUIS JORDAN and His Orchestra*    MCA Coral
                                                          6.22418 AK    LP

    (Three 1951 Big-band sessions)
    Please Don't Leave Me
    Bone Dry
    I Love that Kinda Carryin' On
    Three Handed Woman
    Fat Sam from Birmingham

Cock-a-doodle-doo
There Must be a Way
Come and Get It
Stop Makin' Music
Slow Down
Work Baby Work
Never Trust a Woman
All of Me
There Goes My Heart
Lay Something on the Bar

| | | | |
|---|---|---|---|
| **1953** | *LOUIS JORDAN* (with Nelson Riddle's Orchestra) | MCA MCL 1807 | LP |

I Didn't Know what Time it was
It's Better to Wait for Love
Only Yesterday
Just Like a Butterfly

| | | | |
|---|---|---|---|
| **1939–53** | *LOUIS JORDAN* – Look Out . . . It's Louis Jordan | Charly CRB 1048 | LP |

Includes:
House Party
I Want You to be By Baby

| | | | |
|---|---|---|---|
| **1953–4** | *LOUIS JORDAN and His Tympany Five* | EMI CDP 7965672 | CD |

(The complete Aladdin sessions)
Yeah Yeah Baby
Louis's Blues
I Seen What'cha Done
Fat Back and Corn Likker
Put Some Money in the Pot
Gotta Go
The Dipper
Time's a Passin'
Whiskey Do Your Stuff

Gal You Need a Whippin'
It's Hard to be Good
A Dollar Down
Dad Gum Ya Hide, Boy
Till We Two are One
Ooo Wee
Private Property
For You
Messy Bessy
I'll Die Happy
If I had Any Sense I'd Go Back Home
Hurry Home

**1955–6** *LOUIS JORDAN* – Rock 'n' Roll     Bear Family
Call     BFX 15257     LP
Rock'n'Roll Call
A Man ain't a Man
Texas Stew
Hard Head
Where Can I Go
Baby You're Just Too Much
Baby Let's Do It Up
Chicken Back
It's Been Said
Slo', Smooth and Easy
Bananas
Whatever Lola Wants

**1956–7** *LOUIS JORDAN* – Rockin' and     Bear Family
Jivin' Vol. 1.     BFX 15201     LP
(Mercury recordings)
Big Bess
Ain't Nobody Here but Us Chickens
Choo Choo Ch'Boogie
Knock Me a Kiss
Caldonia
Let The Good Times Roll
Is You is or is You ain't My Baby?

272

Beware Brother Beware
Don't Let the Sun Catch You Crying
I'm Gonna Move to the Outskirts of Town
Salt Pork West Virginia
Run Joe
Early in the Morning
Cat Scratchin'
Morning Light
Fire
Rock Doc
Ella Mae
I Want to Know
I've Found My Peace of Mind
Fire

**1956–8** *LOUIS JORDAN* – Rockin' and      Bear Family
Jivin' Vol. 2.      BFX 15207    LP
(Mercury recordings)
The Jamf
Saturday Night Fish Fry
I Never Had a Chance
Got My Mo-jo Working
Sunday
Sweet Lorraine
The Slop
I Hadn't Anyone Till You
The Nearness of You
Because of You
A Man ain't a Man
I've Found My Peace of Mind
Sweet Hunk of Junk
I Love You So
Wish I Could Make Some Money
That's What True Love Can Do
I Don't Want to Set the World on Fire
A Day Away from You
Route 66
I Cried for You

**1962–4** *LOUIS JORDAN* – Hallelujah (Tangerine
recordings)                           HMV CLP 1809LP
Saturday Night Fish Fry
The Troubadour
Honey Bee
My Friends
Hard Head
What'd I Say
Cole Slaw
Time is Running Out
You're My Mule
Don't Send Me Flowers
El Camino Real
Hop, Skip and Jump

**1962**     *LOUIS JORDAN* with the Chris Barber Band    Black Lion BLCD
760156        CD

Fifty Cents
A Man ain't a Man
No Chance Blues
I'm Gonna Move to the Outskirts of Town
Don't Worry 'bout the Mule
Choo Choo Ch'Boogie
I Wish I Could Shimmy Like My Sister Kate
Is You is or is You ain't My Baby?
Back Home Again in Indiana

**1968–9** *LOUIS JORDAN*                       Pzazz LP 321     LP
I'll Get Along Somehow
Watch the World
The Amen Corner
Monkey See, Monkey Do
Wild is the Night
One Sided Love
Sakatumi
New Orleans and a Rusty Old Horn
Bullitt

What's on Your Mind?
You Gotta Go

**1972**  *LOUIS JORDAN* – Great Rhythm &        Bulldog
Blues Vol. 1                                    BDL 1000        LP
Choo Choo Ch'Boogie
Caldonia
Let the Good Times Roll
I Got the Walkin' Blues
Saturday Night Fish Fry
Ain't Nobody Here but us Chickens
Beans and Cornbread
I'm Gonna Move to the Outskirts of Town
Helping Hand
I'm A Good Thing

**1973**  *LOUIS JORDAN*                         Black and Blue
                                                59.059 2        CD

It's a Lowdown Dirty Shame
Three Handed Woman
Hard Head
I Believe in Music
Saturday Night Fish Fry
I'm Gonna Move to the Outskirts of Town
Red Top
Take the 'A' Train
Every Knock is a Boost
Is You is or is You ain't My Baby?
Caldonia
Groovin' in Paris (I and II)
Something for Fred
Something for Louis

**1973**  *LOUIS JORDAN* – Jump 'n' Jive         JSP Records
                                                1069            LP

Let the Good Times Roll
Ain't Nobody Here but Us Chickens

Hard Head
Take the Ribbon from Her Hair
I Believe in Music
St Louis Blues Boogie

| | | | |
|---|---|---|---|
| **1974** | *WALLACE DAVENPORT* – Sweet Georgia Brown | My Jazz 135 | LP |

Sweet Georgia Brown
Sugar Babe
Indiana
Melancholy, Blues
Tuxedo Junction
Jersey Bounce
Ain't Misbehavin'
I Shall not be Moved

| | | | |
|---|---|---|---|
| **1974** | *ALINE WHITE* – I Shall Not be Moved | Pontchartrain P. 140 | LP |

I Shall not be Moved
Going to Shout All Over God's Heaven
Lord, Lord, Lord
Down by the Riverside
When the Saints Go Marching in

**Comp-ilation**    *LOUIS JORDAN* – The Best of . . .     MCA CD 4079CD

Choo Choo Ch'Boogie
Let the Good Times Roll
Ain't Nobody Here but us Chickens
Saturday Night Fish Fry
Beware
Caldonia
Knock Me a Kiss
Run Joe
School Days
Blue Light Boogie
Five Guys Named Moe
What's the Use of Getting Sober

Buzz Me Blues
Beans and Corn Bread
Don't Let the Sun Catch You Crying
Somebody Done Changed the Lock
Barnyard Boogie
Early in the Mornin'
I Want You to be My Baby
Nobody Knows You when You're Down
and Out

**Comp-
ilation** *LOUIS JORDAN* – Five Guys        MCA
        Named Moe                     DMCL 1718    CD
        Five Guys Named Moe
        Choo Choo Ch'Boogie
        Ain't Nobody Here but Us Chickens
        Beware Brother Beware
        Early in the Mornin'
        Saturday Night Fish Fry
        Let the Good Times Roll
        Push Ka Pi Shee Pie
        Is You is or is You ain't My Baby?
        Reet Petite and Gone
        Schooldays
        Jack You're Dead
        Pettin' and Pokin'
        I Know what I've Got
        What's the Use of Getting Sober
        Caldonia

# Index

Adams, Berle, 82, 83, 84–6, 90, 91, 94–5, 97, 99, 100, 105, 109–11, 113, 116–17, 118–19, 124, 127, 131, 133, 148, 149, 158, 159–60, 162, 164, 170, 173, 243
Adams, Joe, 209–10
Aladdin Records, 187, 188–9, 193, 199
Alexander, Bob, 20
Alexander, Van, 54
Ali, Bardu, 46, 52–3, 54, 56
Allen, Dave, 225
Allen, Hortense, 161, 202
Allen, Steve (UK), 156
Allen, Steve (USA), 198
Ambrose, Bert, 47
American Federation of Musicians, 30, 36, 94
American Forces' Network, 128
American Society of Composers, Authors and Publishers (ASCAP), 82
Anderson, Herbert, 225
Anderson, Ivie, 202
Andrews, Kenny, 219
Andrews Sisters, 107
Apollo Theatre, New York, 121–2, 125–6, 130, 145, 175, 183, 190, 207
Arkansas Baptist College, 17, 204
*Arkansas Survey*, 12
Armstrong, Lillian Hardin, 71–2
Armstrong, Louis, 31, 72, 82, 95, 131, 155–7, 205, 218, 234
Associated Booking Corporation (ABC), 206–7, 209, 210, 211, 218, 230
Astor Productions, 110–11, 127, 131, 142–3
Austin, Billy, 101, 102, 139, 169
Austin, William 'Bill', 108

Bailey, Ann, 154–5, 175
Bailey, Bill, 99
Bailly, Octavio, 229, 235
Baird, Judge William, 103

Baker, Gene, 39
Baker, Mickey, 199
Barber, Chris, 210–14
Barnet, Charlie, 79
Barone, John, 61, 64–6, 68, 77–8, 79, 202
Bartley, Dallas, 85, 87, 91, 93, 113, 137, 142, 225
Basie, Count, 55, 132, 162, 177, 180, 242
Bassey, Shirley, 217
Baxter, Danny, 109
BBC, 213
Beachcomber, Omaha, 94
Beatles, 136, 213–14, 221
Bechet, Sidney, 13, 36, 92
Below, Fred, 239
Belvedere Orchestra, 27
Bennett, Buster, 19–20, 21
Bennett, Max, 224
Berg, Billy, 101, 102, 131, 133, 139, 140, 142
Berle, Milton, 198
Berlin, Irving, 127
Berlin Jazz Festival, 237–8
Bernhardt, Clyde, 36–7, 73, 113
Berry, Chuck, 123
Berton, Vic, 47
'Beware', 120, 124, 126, 138, 199
*Beware* (film), 126–7
Bigby, Bill, 180
*Billboard*, 106, 110–11, 174
Birch, Maceo, 177, 181
Bishop, Walter, 74–5, 82
Black, Valerie, 126
Black and Blue recording company, 238
Blackmon, Teddy, 40
Blake, Ellsworth, 30
Blakey, Art, 15, 42
Blanchard, Harold, 40
Blevins, Leo, 225
Block, Martin, 68
'Blue Ribbon Salute', 99–100

*The Blues Brothers*, 243
Blues Spectrum label, 229
Boling, Arnold 'Scrippy', 56-7
Booker, Bobby, 39
Boone, Chester, 60, 64-5
Bostic, Earl, 138, 176
Boswell, Connee, 117
Bradford, Perry, 68
Bradshaw, Tiny, 187, 217
Brasfield, Wilbur, 134, 136, 143, 149
Brenston, Jackie, 194
Bresler, Jerome, 93
Briggs, Lillian, 184
Brigham, Eunice, 24
Bright, Ronnell, 224
Brinkley, Arkansas, 5-7, 37, 204
Brinkley Brass Band, 5-6, 8, 10-11
*Brinkley Citizen*, 134, 142, 204
Broadcast Music Incorporated (BMI), 110
Brooks, Dr J.E., 7
Brooks, Julius, 225, 241
Brooks, Randy, 129
Broonzy, Big Bill, 7
Brown, Charles, 229
Brown, Irving 'Skinny', 163
Brown, James, 125-6
Brown, Oscar 'O.B.', 24
Brown, Pete, 45, 67, 81, 99
Brown, Vernon, 89
Brubeck, Dave, 187
Bryant, Bobby, 223-4
Bryant, Clora, 203
Bryant, James 'Brady', 17
Bryant, Willie, 41
Buchanan, Charlie, 43
Bunn, Teddy, 206, 211
Burgess, Bob, 162, 163-4, 165-6, 167, 168, 169, 225
Burley, Dan, 63-4, 80-1, 178
Burrell, Alexander 'Duke', 235, 237, 238-9
Burton, John, 143
Bushell, Garvin, 58
Bushkin, Joe, 156-7
Bushnell, Bob, 146, 153, 155, 162, 172-3
Busse, Henry, 32
Byrd, Eddie, 95, 113, 129

'Caldonia', 109-12, 116, 131, 138, 199, 204, 238
'Caldonia' film, 110-11, 124-5
Calloway, Cab, 31, 229, 234
Calvin, Dolores, 135
Campbell, Floyd, 95, 98
Cannon, Jim, 112
Capitol Lounge, Chicago, 82-6, 90, 95, 156

Capitol Records, 109, 150
Capone, Al, 21, 25, 26
Capone, Ralph, 21
Caribbean, 161
Carpenter, Thelma, 126
Carter, Benny, 45, 67, 81-2, 96, 173
Carter hotel chain, 160, 169
*Cashbox*, 189
CBS, 192
Cedar Rapids, Iowa, 89-90, 96
Chaplin, Charlie, 132
Chappelle, Pat 'Fats', 12, 14
Charles, Ray, 209, 218
Cheatham, Doc, 234
'Chesterfield Music Shop' radio show, 116
*Chicago Defender*, 135, 190
'Choo-Choo Ch'Boogie', 128, 136, 138, 207, 212, 214, 218, 221
Cleveland, Jimmy, 198
Club Belvedere, Hot Springs, 23-4, 25, 27
Cobb, Rev. Clarence, 190
Cobbs, Alfred, 'Al', 162, 163, 165, 168-9
Coco, Steve and Eddy, 161
Cole, Cozy, 42-3, 234
Cole, Eddie, 172
Cole, Nat 'King', 122-3, 150, 152, 165-6, 170, 192, 217, 221
Coles, Honi, 234
Collins, Mickey, 143
Columbia Records, 111
Columbus, Chris (Joe Morris), 123, 129-30, 147, 155, 162, 171
Comegys, Leon, 162, 163
'Command Performance' radio shows, 106
Como, Perry, 198
Connors, Gene 'Mighty Flea', 238
Consolidated White River Academy (CWRA), 5-6, 9
Costanzo, Jack, 166
Contreras, Manuel, 39
Cooke, Sam, 217
Coon, Carleton, 23, 47
Cooper, Ralph, 35-6, 40, 61, 99-100, 126
Coryell, Larry, 234
Cosby, Bill, 239
Courtney, Cress, 119
Cox, Ida, 12
Cox, Irv, 228, 229, 230, 235, 237, 238-9, 243
Crawford, Bixie, 142
Crosby, Bing, 98, 106-7, 224
Crosby, Bob, 106
Crosby, Dixie Lee, 106
Crouch, William Forest 'Bill', 110, 131
Cushenbury, Mother, 33

Damone, Vic, 190
Dance, Stanley, 53, 144
Dandridge, Putney, 69
Darling, Denver, 128
Davenport, Wallace, 240
David, Mack, 80
Davis, Jackson 'Jackie', 175, 202, 204, 205, 219
Davis, Martha, 142
Davis, Maxwell, 179, 184
Davis, Miles, 7, 238, 244
Davis, Sammy Jr, 147, 148, 191
Davis, William 'Wild Bill', 114–15, 117, 120, 128, 137, 139, 146, 149, 157–8, 162, 171, 173
Davison, Harold, 211
De Paris, Wilbur, 37, 38
Decca, 45, 64, 66–8, 71, 72, 73, 78–9, 86–7, 91–3, 98, 102. 106, 107, 111–12, 116, 117, 128, 131, 132, 136, 142, 147–8, 149, 150, 158, 160, 162, 168–9, 179, 183, 185, 187, 193, 194, 224
Deen, John, 204
Delta Rhythm Boys, 151
Desmond, Paul, 45
Dexter, Dave, 109
Dill, Callie, 24–5
Dixie Melody Syncopators, 16
Dodds, Johnny, 213
Doggett, Bill, 139, 140–1, 142, 146, 149–50, 156, 157–8, 161–2, 171
Dorsey, Jimmy, 68, 138
Dorsey, Tommy, 98
*Down Beat*, 34, 54, 95, 98, 107–8, 116, 122, 127, 138, 141, 159, 171, 174–5, 183, 185, 187, 230
Drayton, Charlie, 64, 72, 75, 78, 79
Drew, Allen, 63
Duffy, George, 39
Duke, John, 237
Duncan, Al, 206
Duncan, Al, 206
Dupree, Reese, 39
Durante, Jimmy, 198
Durham, Eddie, 80
Dyson, Dave, 235

*Ebony* magazine, 241
Eckstine, Billy, 99, 163, 179
Edwards, Teddy, 15, 233–4
Eisenhower, Dwight, D., 205
El Dorado, Arkansas, 17, 19–21, 22
Eldridge, Roy, 82, 234
Elks Rendezvous, New York, 61, 63–6, 68, 77–8, 79, 137

Ellington, Duke, 32, 52, 55–6, 81, 98, 118–20, 129, 136, 168, 180, 221, 228, 238
Ellington, Mercer, 168
Erbe, Carle, 118–19
Essex Records, 185, 194
Evans, Ernest, 25
*Evening Standard*'s Laurence Olivier Award, 244–5
Ewing, John 'Streamline', 224

Fame, Georgie, 243
Faubus, Orval Eugene, 205
Feather, Leonard, 81, 156, 169–70, 176, 208–9, 218, 222–3, 226
Federation of Commercial Broadcasting, 150
Feldman, Al, 54
Feyne, Buddy, 75
Fields, Ernie, 115
Fields, Ida *see* Jordan, Ida
Fields, W.C., 13
Filmcraft Studios, New York, 126
Finney, James, 20
First Church of Deliverance, 190
Fitzgerald, Ella, 43–4, 45–6, 54–8, 77, 117–18, 128, 137, 147–8, 155, 179, 181–2, 189, 217, 221, 234
*Five Guys Named Moe*, 244–5
Flanagan, Tommy, 208n.
Flax, Marty, 162, 163
Fletcher, Clinton 'Dusty', 132, 179
Flintall, Herman, 79
Flynn, Errol, 102
*Follow the Boys*, 101
Ford, Valli, 168, 169
Ford Motor Corporation, 207
400 Restaurant, New York, 129
Fox Head Tavern, Cedar Rapids, 89–90, 96
Frazier, George, 57
Freeman, Bud, 93
Freeman, Ernie, 219

Gabler, Milton, 92–3, 111–12, 117, 128, 183, 185, 194–5
Gaillard, Slim, 39, 61
Gaines, Charlie, 29–34, 35–6, 37, 38, 39, 40, 130
Gaines, Charlie Junior, 32
Gaines, Stanley, 32, 38, 146, 197
Gale, Moe, 43, 49, 52, 56, 57
Gale, Tim, 57
Gale Agency, 179
Galloway, Sigmund, 203
Garner, Erroll, 155

Gayten, Paul, 222–3, 224
General Amusement (Artists) Corporation
  (GAC), 82, 83, 86, 90–1, 96–7, 105, 163,
  174, 206, 230
Gettis, Joackim Pelege, 5–6
Gettis, Naomi, 9
Gettis, Virgil, 10, 11
Gillespie, Dizzy, 36, 99, 143, 174, 234
Glaser, Joe, 82, 156, 206, 211, 218, 230
Gomez, Vincente, 192
Gonsalves, Paul 221
Goodman, Benny, 48, 55, 117–18
Goodman, Harry, 70
Goodman, Saul, 59
Gordon, John E., 127
Graham, Leonard (Idrees Sulieman), 108
Grant, Coot, 64
Gray, Jerry, 159
Gray, Wardell, 144
Gray, Wilhelmina, 139
Green, Silas, 12, 16
Green Gables Club, Hot Springs, 23, 24–5
Greenfield, Al, 82–3
Greenfield, Jack, 16
Grey, Al, 234
Griffith, Bea, 131
Grimes, Tiny, 234

Hadnott, Bill, 142, 145, 146, 148, 153, 241
Hailey, Theodore (Teddy Hale), 161
Halcox, Pat, 212–13
Hale, Teddy, 161
Haley, Bill, 185, 193–5, 200
*Hallelujah, Louis Jordan is Back*, 218
Hammond, John, 34, 54, 121
Hampton, Gladys, 140
Hampton, Lionel, 140, 141
Handy, Captain John, 240
Handy, W.C., 11
Harlem Renaissance, 72
Harmony Kings, 20, 22
Harper, Geechie, 38, 39
Harris, Wynonie, 233
Hartman, Johnny, 161
Hastings, Lowell 'Count', 187
Hawkins, Coleman, 90, 93
Hawkins, Erskine, 111, 234
Hayes, Debby, 208–9, 210
Hayes, Edgar, 61
Hayes, Florence (Vicky) *see* Jordan, Vicky
Hendricks, Frederick Wilmoth, 117n.
Hendricks, Jon, 184, 189
Henry, Danny, 63
Hentoff, Nat, 184

*Here Comes Mr Jordan*, 102
Herman, Woody, 98, 111–12, 141, 179, 182
Herz, Frank, 52
Heywood, Eddie, 122
Hickman, Leo, 137
Hill, Abram, 80
Hill, Benny, 30
Hill, Teddy, 56, 143
Hilliard, Jodie, 13–14
Hines, Al, 228
Hines, Earl, 99, 100, 234
Hinton, Milt, 234
Hite, Les, 80
Hoffman, Robert, 72
Hogan, Carl, 114, 123, 142
Hollis, Chris, 227–9, 231, 235, 241
Hollon, Kenneth, 73–4
Holtkamp, L.K., 12
Hooper, Jean, 155
Horne, Lena, 79, 192
Horton, Vaughan, 128
*Hot Chocolates*, 38, 40
Hot Springs, Arkansas, 21–8, 101–2
Houdini, Wilmouth, 117
Houston, Clarence, 225, 227
Houston, John, 225, 227
Houston, Leonard, 227
Howard, Bob, 69
Howard, Joe, 118–19
Hudson, George, 108, 123, 136, 139
Hunter, Alberta, 73
Hunter, Ivory Joe, 148
Huntington, F.G., 12
Huntington Memorial Hospital, 133

Imperial Serenaders, 19–20
Ink Spots, 229
Internal Revenue Service, 187–8, 220
'Is You is or is You ain't My Baby?', 101–2,
  212, 214, 243
Izenhall, Aaron, 115–16, 120, 121, 123, 124,
  127, 134, 145, 147, 151, 154, 155, 161, 162,
  168, 171

Jackson, Joe, 243
Jackson, Josh, 113, 127, 146, 148–9, 155, 162,
  171
Jackson, Mike, 87
Jackson, Olivier, 234
Jackson, Roosevelt James 'Ham', 142, 153
Jackson, Willis, 175–6
Jacquet, Illinois, 93
Jamaica, 161
James, Harry, 98

Jarrett, Keith, 238
Jay, Thurber, 179–80, 182, 187, 188, 197
*Jazz Hot*, 44, 234
Jefferson, Hilton, 41, 59
Jennings, Bill, 153, 155, 162, 171
Jeter-Pillars Orchestra, 17, 123
Jo, Damita, 230
Johnson, Budd, 199
Johnson, Clarence, 60, 64–5, 74, 79
Johnson, Eddie, 136, 139, 141, 142
Johnson, Harold 'Money', 163
Johnson, James P., 80
Johnson, Johnny, 178
Johnson, Lem, 66–7, 69
Johnson, Pete, 126
Johnson, 'Stovepipe', 87
Johnson, Walter, 37
Jones, Jo, 208n.
Jones, Jonah, 69
Jones, Quincy, 199
Jones, Wilmore 'Slick', 105, 108
Jordan, Adell (LJ's mother), 5
Jordan, Fleecie (*née* Moore, LJ's third wife),
    96, 109–10, 116, 118, 120, 132–4, 135, 142,
    143, 153–4, 168, 201, 243
Jordan, Ida (*née* Fields, LJ's second wife),
    27–9, 30, 32–3, 39, 40, 47, 57, 59, 65, 78,
    84, 96, 103, 141, 243
Jordan, James Aaron (LJ's father), 5, 7–13,
    14, 142, 178, 204, 210
Jordan, Julie (LJ's first wife), 17, 22, 28, 30,
    141
Jordan, Louis: early life, 5, 6–17; plays in
    Brinkley Brass Band, 8, 10–11; works
    with minstrel troupes, 12–16; persistent
    hernia, 14, 100; first marriage, 17; in El
    Dorado, 19–21; in Hot Springs, 22–8;
    joins Dr Sells's Travelling Medicine
    Show, 28–9; in Philadelphia, 29–34;
    marriage to Ida Fields, 30, 32–3, 84; goes
    to New York, 35–7; joins LeRoy Smith,
    37–40; with Chick Webb's orchestra, 41–
    9, 51–9; friendship with Ella Fitzgerald,
    44, 54–5, 57; love of Arkansas, 51; forms
    first band, 57–61; forms Tympany Four,
    61, 63–5; first records, 66–9, 71–5;
    Tympany Five formed, 67; music
    appeals to both black and white
    audiences, 94–5; and Fleecie Moore, 96;
    drafted for military service, 97; entertains
    servicemen, 99–100, 196–7, 221–2;
    exempted from military service, 100; in
    films, 101–3, 106; Ida divorces, 103;
    marries Fleecie, 109; films, 110–11, 117,
    124–5, 126–7, 131, 142–3; reorganizes
    Tympany Five, 113–16; tonsilectomy, 113;
    and Vicky Hayes, 120, 132–3; 154;
    influence on other musicians, 123;
    'Caldonia' lawsuit, 131; Fleecie stabs,
    133–4, 135, 167; plays Caribbean music,
    137; arthritis, 141, 154, 171, 205, 208, 237;
    financial problems, 141–2, 150; lays off
    Tympany Five, 141, 142; plastic surgery,
    142; reconciliation with Fleecie, 142;
    gambling, 151, 236; Berle Adams leaves,
    159–60; forms big band, 160–70; marries
    Vicky, 168, 207–8, 210; forms new edition
    of Tympany Five, 171–3; ill-health, 171;
    loses all his band parts, 179; Decca fails to
    renew his recording contract, 185, 187;
    tax problems, 187–8, 220; influence of,
    194–5; and Martha Weaver, 201–2, 209–
    10; dissolves band, 205, 208; marriage to
    Martha, 217, 236–7; suffers heart attack,
    241–2; death, 242–3; rebirth of interest in,
    243–5
Jordan, Maggie (LJ's grandmother), 5, 7–8,
    9
Jordan, Martha (*née* Weaver, LJ's fifth
    wife), 201–2, 209–10, 217, 218–22, 224,
    226–7, 229, 236–7, 239, 240, 241–3, 244–5
Jordan, Patty, 17
Jordan, Taft, 41, 43–4, 46, 56, 57, 58, 65
Jordan, Vicky (*née* Hayes, LJ's fourth wife),
    120, 132–4, 154, 168, 201, 207–8, 210, 243
Jordanettes, 154, 161
Jovien, Harold, 230, 241, 243

Kabok, Louis, 237
Kansas City, 164
Kapp, Dave, 86, 162, 185
Kapp, Jack, 67, 162, 185
Keaton, Dr W.T., 17
Keel, Howard, 203
Kelly, George, 184
Kelly, Mayor, 95
Kelly, Tom, 16
Kenton, Stan, 116, 141, 163, 192
Kenyon, Rod, 89–90, 94
Killebrew, Preston, 19, 21
King, B.B., 203, 226, 243
King, Dr Martin Luther, 244
Kirby, John, 66–7, 68, 69–70, 177
Kirkby, George, 191
Kirkwood, Johnny, 180–1, 187, 188, 191,
    197
Krupa, Gene, 42, 48, 234
Ku Klux Klan, 22, 166

Laine, Frankie, 179, 182
Lane, Chester, 20–1, 180, 181, 185, 187, 189, 191, 202
Lang, Leroy, 206
Larkin, Milton, 225
Las Vegas, 150–2, 190–1, 193, 203–4
Lee, Canada, 126
Lee, Mabel, 131
Lee, Perry, 243
Leeds Music, 109, 131
Leslie, Bill, 205
'Let the Good Times Roll', 128–9, 218
Levaggi, Joe, 56–7, 58
Levin, Mike, 91
Levy, Lou, 101, 109–10, 116
Levy, Norman, 126
Lewis, Johnny, 39
Lewis, Ted, 101
Liggins, Joe, 229
Lincoln, Abraham, 71
Linton, Charlie, 41, 43–4, 45, 46, 54
Little Rock, Arkansas, 205
Lombardo, Guy, 56
London, Julie, 221
*Look Out Sister*, 142–3
Lucas, Al, 208n.
Lunceford, Jimmie, 71, 81, 87, 90, 172
Lutcher, Nellie, 196, 234
Lydon, Michael, 236

Mabley, Moms, 218
MacDonald, Jeanette, 101
McGinty, Artiebelle, 12–13
McIntyre, Hal, 98
McKibbon, Hal, 224
Mackintosh, Cameron, 244
McKnight, Dr Edward, 14
McLaughlin, Leo Patrick, 21
McRae, Teddy, 44
McVea, Jack, 132
Madden, Owney, 21
Madison, Walter, 28
Malachi, John, 163, 164
Marion Anderson School, 9
Marshall, Joe 'Kaiser', 37, 126
Martin, Walter, 59, 60, 64–5, 72, 77, 80, 95
Mastin, Will, 147, 148, 191
Mayall, John, 234–5
Mayfair Casino, Cleveland, 39
*Meet Miss Bobby Sox*, 106
*Melody Maker*, 214, 234
Melrose, Lester, 88
Melrose, Walter, 88
Mercer, Johnny, 106

Mercury Records, 159, 198–200, 205
Merrick, Dr Walter, 137, 146
Mesner, Ed, 187
*Metronome*, 125, 128, 155
MGM, 101, 194
Mighty Minstrel Show, 12, 13
Miller, Glenn, 90
Miller, Henry, 150–1
Mills, Billy, 225
Mills Brothers, 83
Mitchell, Alex 'Razz', 108
Mitchell, Blue, 234
Mitchell, Bob, 147, 162, 171–2, 187, 202, 230
Mitchell, Harold 'Hal', 147
Mobley, Jimmy, 205, 206
Modernaires, 129
Monestier, Jean-Marie, 226
Monogram, 117
Montgomery, Robert, 102
Moody, James, 185
Moore, Bill, 225
Moore, Fleecie *see* Jordan, Fleecie
Moore, Numa 'Pee Wee', 163
Morehouse, Chauncey, 47
Moreland, Mantan, 13, 118
Morgan, Al, 105
Morgan, Loumell, 142
Morgenstern, Dan, 42
Morris, Buddy, 116
Morris (Edwin H.) Music, 131
Morris, Jessie, 155
Morris, Joe *see* Columbus, Chris
Morton, Jelly Roll, 72
Mosley, Leo 'Snub', 70–1
Muhammed, Elijah, 208
Murphy, Eddie, 244
*Music & Rhythm*, 88
Music Corporation of America, 159
Musicians' Union, 42, 99, 142, 205
My Jazz label, 240–1
Myers, Dave, 239
Myers, Louis, 239

NBC, 45, 122, 192, 198
Nelson, Oliver, 162, 164
New Capitol Cabaret, New York, 68
New Orleans Jazz Festival, 240
*New York Amsterdam News*, 64, 81, 175
Newman, Joe, 208n.
Newton, Frankie, 66, 68
Nice Jazz Festival, 242
Nicholas Brothers, 126
'1951 Revue', 161
Noone, Jimmie, 90

Number One Rhythm Club, 68

Oakley, Helen, 44
Old Kentucky Minstrel Show, 12
Oliver, Dr J.A., 204
Oliver, King, 157
Oliver, Marvin, 206
*On Striver's Row*, 80
'Open the Door Richard', 132
Osborne, Will, 117
Otis, Johnny, 52, 130–1, 142, 192, 229
Otis, Shuggie, 230

Pabst Blue Ribbon Beer Company, 99, 100
Page, Hot Lips, 80, 111–12, 122, 144
Page, Patti, 198
Palmer, Earl, 224
Palmer, Gladys, 38
Pantages theatre circuit, 12
Paramount Records, 73
Paramount Theatre, New York, 135–6
Parker, Charlie, 92, 99, 100, 138, 145, 146,
   187, 214
Parker, Frank, 197
Parker, George, 220
Parker, Leonard, 19, 20–1
Pasadena Justice Court, 135
Patterson, Ottilie, 211, 212
Patterson and Jackson, 99
Payne, Bert, 172–3, 179, 181, 182, 187, 190,
   196–7
Peer, Beverly, 57, 58–9
Pepper, Art, 138
Perry, Ermett, 162
Perry, Lincoln, 52
Peters, Clarke, 244
Peterson, Jimmy, 162, 163, 172–3, 177, 179
Philadelphia, 29–34
Philip, Prince, 227
Philips, Flip, 45
Phillips, Esther, 234
Phillips, Leonard, 15
Phillips, Lloyd, 37
Phillips, Reuben, 162
Phoenix, Arizona, 153–4, 201, 207–8
Pillars, Hayes, 17
Pointer Sisters, 237
Pollard, Bud, 127
Porter, Joe, 37
Porter, Ralph, 26, 135–6, 197
Porter, Roy, 202–4
Powell, Austin, 202, 204, 205
Prather, Henry, 79
Presley, Elvis, 136, 195

Preview Music, 111, 116, 131
Price, Sammy, 71, 73, 226, 234
Prichard, Emma, 24
Procope, Russell, 67
Providence Masonic Lodge, 26–7
Pryor, Jimmy, 19–20
Prysock, Arthur, 243
Pzazz label, 222–4

Quinichette, Paul, 142, 144–5, 146

Rabbit Foot Minstrels, 14–15, 16
Radcliffe and Rodgers, 38
Raft, George, 101–2
Rainey, Ma, 12, 14
Rains, Claude, 102
Rambert, Richard, 19–20
Randolph, Amanda, 80
Rawls, Lou, 221, 243
Ray, Floyd, 95
Razaf, Andy, 87
RCA Victor, 111, 193, 195, 199
Reagan, Ronald, 207
Redd Foxx, 244
Redman, Don, 69
Reese, Della, 227
*Reet, Petite and Gone*, 131
Reid, Lizzie (LJ's aunt), 5, 9, 142
Reid, Mack, 9, 142
Reno, 178–9
Reynolds, Howard, 206
Reynolds, Marie, 112
Rice, Charlie, 172–3, 205
Richmond, June, 131
Riddle, Nelson, 183, 185, 198
Riverdale Children's Association,
   127
RKO, 147
Roach, Max, 181
Roane, Edward Francis 'Eddie', 80, 87, 91,
   106, 107, 108, 115
Robin, Sid, 146
Robinson, Bill 'Bojangles', 151, 155
Robinson, Elaine, 155, 175
Robinson, Mabel, 74
Robinson, Wesley, 30
Rocco, Maurice, 83, 84, 221–2
Rockwell, Tommy, 82, 83
Rogers, Timmie, 134
Rolling Stones, 136
Rollins, Sonny, 138
Ross, Irving, 128
Rouse, Charlie, 145
Royal, Ernie, 198, 199

Salt and Pepper Shakers, 17
Sampson, Edgar, 41, 46
Sanders, Joe, 23
Sanford, John, 244
Saunders, Red, 83
Savini, Robert M., 110, 127
Savitt, Jan, 32
Savoy Ballroom, New York, 43, 48–9, 55–6
Schiffman, Frank, 125
Schiffman, Jack, 125
Schifrin, Lalo, 223
Schilinger, Sol, 163
'School Days', 148
Schwarz, Milton, 82–3
Scott, Jack, 224
Scott, Raymond, 175
Sells, Dr, 28, 29
Shaw, Arnold, 83, 109–10
*Sheffield Star*, 211–12
Shepard, Ollie, 93
Sherman, Joe, 97, 98
Simon, Freddie, 108–9
Simon, George T., 43, 117–18, 124
Simon, Stafford 'Pazuza', 68–9, 71
Simpkins, Jesse 'Po', 99, 105, 113–14
Simpson, Jack, 47
Sinatra, Frank, 127
Sissle, Noble, 36
Skinner, Carroll, 223
Slack, Freddie, 101
Slim, Memphis, 239
Smalls, Cliff, 234
Smith, Bessie, 12, 31
Smith, Dorothy 'Dottie', 177, 178, 179, 191, 195, 197, 201, 202, 204, 206
Smith, Eddie, 213
Smith, LeRoy, 33, 37–40, 44, 45
Smith, Lloyd, 168
Smith, 'Stuff', 69, 83
Smith, Tab, 138, 176
Smith, Willie 'The Lion', 126
Smythe, Vanita, 131
Snaer, Albert, 37
*Somebody Up There Digs Me*, 199
Soundies Disbribution Corporation of America, 103
Spanier, Muggsy, 69
Spencer, O'Neil, 70
Spirits of Rhythm, 112
Spivak, Charlie, 101
Stacy, Frank, 116
'Startime' television show, 207
Steele, Jesse, 19
Stewart, Slam, 61

Stitt, Sonny, 210–11, 234
Stone, Jesse, 80
Sturgis, Rodney, 63, 64, 66, 67
Sullivan, Ed, 198
Sullivan, Maxine, 126
Supreme Court, 131, 204–5
*Swing Parade of 1946*, 117
Symphony Sid (Sidney Torin), 75

Tangerine label, 209, 215, 217–19
Taylor, Archie, 228, 231, 235, 237, 239, 241
Taylor, Sam 'The Man', 199
Taylor, Yack, 72
Tennyson, William, 117
Terry, Clark, 108
Theard, Sam 'Spoo-De-O-Dee', 129, 157
Theatre Owners' Bookers Association (TOBA), 12
Thomas, Arnold 'Tommy', 74, 80, 82, 84, 106, 108
Thomas, George, 112
Thomas, Matthew B., 179–80
Thomas, Peggy Hart, 106, 137, 145, 146, 155, 161
Thompson, Sonny, 113
Three Miller Brothers, 38
Thunderbird Hotel, Las Vegas, 150–2
Times Square Music, 138
Tolbert, Skeets, 69
Torin, Sidney, 75
Tosches, Nick, 194
Tracy, Jack, 183
Trammell, Lee, 108
Trautman, Morty, 163
Travelling Medicine Show, 28–9
Trent, Alphonso, 24, 71
Trinder, Tommy, 154
Trinidad, 175
*Trinidad Guardian*, 175
Trueheart, John, 42
Trumbauer, Frank, 44
Tucker, Lorenzo, 131
Tucker, Sophie, 185
Turner, Henry, 80, 85
Turner, Joe, 194, 229, 233
Turrentine, Tommy, 108
Twentieth-Century Fox, 101

Ulanov, Barry, 45, 100
United Services Organization (USO), 90, 99, 101
Universal Studios, 101

V Disc sessions, 121

Vacher, Peter, 145, 202
Vaughan, Sarah, 99, 139, 140
Vocalion, 34, 73

Walker, T-Bone, 80, 96
Wallace, Sippie, 112
Waller, Ben C., 178, 199–200
Waller, Fats, 30, 31, 65, 69, 72, 95, 202
Walsh, Ellis, 149
Waring, Fred, 32
Warwick label, 209
Washington, Booker, T., 13
Washington, Dinah, 137, 188, 207
Watson, Paula, 147
Weaver, Martha *see* Jordan, Martha
Webb, Chick, 41–9, 51–9, 65, 70, 71, 143,
   144, 160, 177, 185, 233
Webb, Sally, 54
Webster, Ben, 93
Webster, Freddie, 80
Wein, George, 233–4, 235, 237, 242
Weldon, Bill, 87–8, 92, 93, 109
Wettling, George, 42
Wexler, Jerry, 174
WGN Chicago, 23
White, Sister Aline, 240
White, Joe, 15
White, Josh, 95
Whiteman, Paul, 32, 54
Whiteside, George, 236
Wilburn, Collis, 143

Wilkins, Ernie, 108, 199
Williams, Bert, 13, 38, 60–1
Williams, Clarence, 33–4, 41
Williams, Courtney, 64–5, 69, 71, 79
Williams, J. Mayo, 64, 66, 67, 72–3, 74, 81,
   82, 86–8, 92
Williams, Richard, 234
Williams, Ruby, 23–5, 27
Williams, Sandy, 53
Williams, Selmer 'Tuna Boy', 23, 24,
   27
Willoughby, Joe, 137, 146, 173
Wilson, Charles E., 205
Wilson, Lucius, 22–3
Wilson, Rosiere 'Shadow', 99, 105
Wilson, Wesley 'Sox', 64, 92
Winchell, Walter, 133
Winchester, Daisy, 74
Winters, Jim, 30, 33
WNEW, 68, 75
Wolcott, F.S., 12
Woods, Milton, 131
World Transcription Service, 106
World War II, 90–1, 97, 99–100
Wright, James, 136
Wynn, Larry, 93

Young, Lester, 15–16, 74, 81, 177
Young, Trummy, 87

Zanzibar Club, New York, 118–20, 121